A WILD Call

Martyn Murray

FERNHURST
BOOKS

Published in 2017 by Fernhurst Books Limited

62 Brandon Parade, Holly Walk, Leamington Spa, Warwickshire, CV32 4JE, UK

Tel: +44 (0) 1926 337488 | www.fernhurstbooks.com

A catalogue record for this book is available from the British Library

ISBN 978-1-912177-02-8

Front cover photograph: Birds flying above the ocean in St Kilda, UNESCO Heritage Site, Scotland © Michele D'Amico supersky77
Back cover photograph: Martyn Murray's yacht, *Molio*, moored at St Kilda © Martyn Murray

Designed & typeset by Rachel Atkins

Printed in Bulgaria by Alliance Print Ltd.

For my parents
Greer and Wendy
With love and gratitude

For what avail the plough or sail,
Or land or life, if freedom fail?

Boston

RALPH WALDO EMERSON

Contents

Preface

In Scotland, whisky is a sacred drink. Amber as the life oozing from an old Caledonian pine, acrid as the smoke drifting down a ghost-filled glen, subtle as the twilight on a Hebridean shore. One swallow warms your heart like the first kiss on a long winter's night; two swallows still the raging torrents of your mind as mountain waters in the slow deeps of a highland pool where gravid salmon lie; three swallows awaken your imprisoned soul and a longing for the old way, the merry way, and the chance to live free. Raising your glass is a custom older than the nation. It summons a bygone glory, seals a lifelong pact and etches forever a shared moment on the long journey home. The last thing my father said to me was: "Come on over Martyn…we'll have a dram together."

I packed my bags and drove over the next morning, but Dad had gone on ahead of me. So I raised my glass alone that night and as I took the third swallow a conversation began. Sailing was our shared passion, our common language. It was what we yearned for when trapped in a dull meeting or stuck in frustrated traffic. Our family boat, *Primrose*, bore no resemblance to the designer craft that pack marinas today; she was a working Cornish vessel from the 1890s, a wooden-planked, heavy-beamed, deep-keeled, gaff-rigged cutter with a tree trunk for a mast. She carried a press of tanned canvas in a stiff breeze, leaning sedately with the weight of wind yet lifting to the surge of sea, bowsprit thrust forward over the waves. In my imagination her character matched those of my father and mother: like my father, load-bearing and warm hearted, dependable as Scottish oak; and like my mother, brave as the first English primrose and sunny as the spring itself. My

9

brothers and I relished the daily fare of maritime adventure, one day exploring islands or anchorages, the next hunting for lobsters and shell-fish, and the next inhaling the curiosity of seaside shops with their racks of comics and trays of sweets. It introduced a wild but disciplined freedom to our urban lives which I didn't stop to think about at the time.

Glass in hand I walked over to the bookcase in the hall. One of the shelves was packed with my father's favourite sailing books. I chose half a dozen and took them up to bed. The margins were filled with hand-written notes in his familiar tight longhand that few could read, save my mother and the pharmacist who had received countless scrawled prescriptions from his surgery. I stayed up late that night engrossed by the world of sailing in a bygone age. Time passed in a quiet routine: by day I went for long walks and chatted to Mum, in the evenings I went to bed early and read about sailing. On one of those evenings, I began to realise that something in those books was speaking to me. Dissatisfaction with my life had whispered in my ear for years and recently had grown to a shout. I'd taken time off to push out in different directions, looking for new sources of inspiration, but it hadn't helped. In fact the more I tried to deal with it, the worse it had become. I felt trapped in my adult skin. Somewhere I had taken a wrong turn.

I kept coming back to one book, *Dream Ships* by Maurice Griffiths. It had a blue woven cover and well-thumbed pages filled with descriptions of the author's favourite small craft illustrated by sketches of their construction, deck layouts and accommodation. I marvelled at their swept lines and cosy cabins, imagined myself hauling up the sails, making voyages to distant lands and tying up at the quay in a foreign harbour. An idea began to form, strengthening as each day went by, of finding my own dream boat, bringing her home to Scotland and preparing her for a voyage to St Kilda, that tight cluster of rocky isles lying far out in the Atlantic Ocean beyond the sheltering wall of the Hebrides, where the roar of surf mingles with the seabirds' cry, the sea mist rises to the falling smirr, and what lies beyond enters freely within. Even then at the first inkling I sensed that a passage to St Kilda would have the power to change my life. I stayed for three weeks and by the time I left, I knew exactly what I wanted. It was the sweetest dram I've ever had.

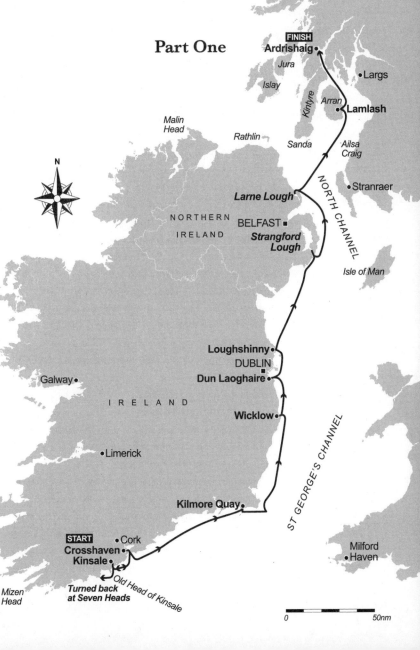

Part One

FINISH
Ardrishaig •

Mull

Jura

Islay

Kintyre

• Largs

Arran

Lamlash

Malin
Head

Rathlin

Sanda

Ailsa
Craig

Larne Lough

NORTH CHANNEL

• Stranraer

NORTHERN

BELFAST ■

IRELAND

*Strangford
Lough*

Isle of Man

N

Loughshinny •

DUBLIN

Galway •

Dun Laoghaire •

IRELAND

Wicklow •

ST GEORGE'S CHANNEL

Limerick •

Kilmore Quay •

START

• Cork

Crosshaven •
Kinsale •

Milford
• Haven

Old Head of Kinsale

*Turned back
at Seven Heads*

Mizen
Head

0   50nm

Chapter 1

Wild Boat Chase

"She's pissing out water like an old boot," said a voice from a neighbouring boat on the pontoon causing me to look up in alarm.

"What?" I yelped hoping he was just a novice, perhaps noticing pools of rainwater collecting in the folded tarp and cascading off the algae-stained deck whenever the boat rocked.

A pair of blue eyes appraised me from the cockpit of an ocean-going yacht, taking in my office shoes and mental disarray. The easy confidence of the long distance sailor oozed from every one of his salty pores. "The bilge pump is on night and day; ergo, she's leaking from somewhere." He spoke with an imperious Oxford drawl.

Could this abandoned lady have a fatal flaw? I eyed her over again. Teak decks swept back from a high business-like bow, dividing to pass either side of the central cabin with its eight ship's portholes followed by a roomy cockpit where I now stood in dripping jersey, before merging again at the aft deck, which ended in a counter stern with long overhang. Rigging descended on all sides from the tops of the main and mizzen masts to the outer fastenings of the wooden hull. Her classic lines, penned a lifetime ago by Fred Shepherd the doyen of pre-war designers, must have captured many an owner's heart. Masts and spars were painted white not so much to match the topsides, I thought, as to protect against the tropical sun. She was a nomad all right, with her sheets, fairleads, winches and cleats ready for action on any of the seven seas, and every bit as sturdy as those on my neighbour's boat. But she was a ragged Nomad, in truth more of a stricken refugee. It would be madness to take her on. Yet I needed her every bit as much as she needed a new owner. She could turn the tide in my life. I'd felt it the moment I set eyes on her. That tide was fast ebbing away and as my creative freedom choked off, so my spirit died. All my efforts to wrest back control and take command of my life again had come to nothing. It was as if I was caught in my dreams by a faery's spell, and unable to wake up. If there was a way to break that spell then this boat rocking back and forth at my feet could help me find it. I felt certain of it. The wild confidence that had brought me to that small bustling harbour on the edge of a great storm-filled ocean took hold again. "I can bring her back to life."

He looked across the gap of oily estuarine water between us and behind the grey beard with its crown of white, like Hemingway's in his later years, there could have been a smile. "Shame to see a boat like that left to rot."

I eyed the green algae and dirty deck sensing the hours of work and endless expense. The sky seemed to darken again. And there was something else nagging away. "She may not be so popular back home."

He looked over once more, one eyebrow ever so slightly raised. I felt the challenge but wasn't ready to meet it. Instead I busied myself with checking deck gear and making notes. I tried to forget Papa Hemingway. But you couldn't face that penetrating gaze and pretend you hadn't noticed. Looking back, I see myself standing at a gateway: in one direction business as usual, in the other a threshold to be crossed and the beginning of a journey. Not just any journey but a rite of passage that was long overdue. It was something I had missed as a teenager and again in my twenties, and again and again thereafter. There it was, right in front of me one more time. I clambered down the rickety ladder to continue my inspection in the main saloon. I inhaled the familiar damp smell of wooden boat. Rot, I thought, I bloody hope not.

Dim light pushed its way through opaque plastic fillers that blocked the original glass portholes. Their bronze surrounds were matted with verdigris. I switched on my torch. Mahogany furnishings glowed golden red under the beam, interspersed with cream panelling on the bulkheads. The arch of the coachroof above matched the curve of the bunks on either side. Immediately to my left was the galley with twin sinks next to a gas cooker; to the right a chart table with some ageing navigation equipment. Above it was a lovely brass clock and next to that a chromed barometer, cheap and rusting, which didn't seem to fit. A photograph was taped to the foot of the starboard bunk showing her racing in the Caribbean off Antigua, sails taut, decks scrubbed, crew grinning. Beyond was a locker stuffed full of bulging sail bags; the heads opposite gave just enough room for a Baby Blake toilet and a small sink. Further forward was a double fo'c'sle bunk narrowing to the forepeak, now jammed with extra sails and surplus gear. It was like stepping into the 1930s. Spartan, sturdy yet intimate. An exception to the period was a collection of music cassettes in two long racks above the bunks comprising mostly jazz and blues albums.

Tattered? Yes. Tired? Obviously. Unloved? I didn't think so. She was deserted now but someone had loved this boat. He'd left his clothes in a seaman's bag, his letters under the navigation table and some tinned food in a locker by the galley. One day he had walked away from his life aboard and apparently vanished. I began to inspect each part of the boat systematically. Much of the visible damage was superficial – stained cushions, rusted cooker, mildewed paintwork, broken hinges, missing catches and corroded electrics. What I needed to know was whether the dishevelled gear and unknown years of neglect concealed anything more sinister. Had the owner come across an insurmountable defect and given up, or had life simply intervened to separate man and boat? I piled cushions to one side and opened up the hatches under the port bunk. As I did there was a click and gurgle from below, followed by the splash of water streaming into Cork Harbour.

Under the bunks were plastic boxes with tools, engine spares, shackles, screws, reels of electrical wire, fillers, paint and all kinds of other chandlery. I pulled them out one by one. The contents were in an awful state – rusted, discoloured, damp and broken – but the planking underneath looked fine. I spotted a smudged brown line running along the topmost plank. It took a few moments for the penny to drop: it was a waterline, an inner, rusty waterline. The boat must have been half full of water. I touched the line with my finger: it smudged. Half full of sea water and not so long ago; that would explain the state of her gear. Out of curiosity I checked the seacock next to the double sink. It was jammed open. If she'd filled just a little more, seawater would have flowed back along the drain outlet, welled up inside the sink and over-flowed into the cabin taking the boat under in a few hours. It explained the only new things on the boat: an orange extension lead looping into the cabin from the pontoon connected to a powerful battery charger, now humming away on the pilot berth, hooked up to a lorry battery that connected to the bilge pump. I unscrewed the plastic caps of the battery to check the electrolyte level: the cells were dry. It must have been left to charge continuously. I emerged from below with a frown. At the far end of the pontoon, four little penguins frowned back. I was so preoccupied I almost overlooked them. They should have been off the coast of Chile; I'd no idea what they were doing here. As I looked, they huddled together like naughty school boys playing truant. The cloud of worry dispersed and I began chuckling.

Papa Hemingway was up the mainmast working on the VHF aerial from the safety of a crow's nest. I walked over to take a look at his boat. She was built for the deep ocean with a heavy fibreglass hull. An eye of Horus was painted on the bows, its white pupil surrounded by a thick black iris as if the eye of some giant deity was staring across the ocean keeping a lookout for reefs and shoals. The teak deck was covered in heavy-duty cruising gear. A pair of massive anchors sat on wooden blocks that jutted out from the prow like railway sleepers; their chains snaked aft wrapped in old sailcloth and disappeared into deck boxes. A red lifeboat was secured in-between, with a spring release mechanism for emergency deployment. Behind that were a deep working cockpit with tiller steering and an aft deck with wind turbine and self-steering vane. A massive rudder hung on the transom.

I waited as Papa climbed down the mast steps and made his way to the cockpit. "Some boat you have here," I remarked. "She looks as if she could go anywhere."

He scrutinised me again, slow and easy, like an African hunter gaug-ing his quarry lying wounded in a thicket.

"We've been around."

I was unsure if he meant round the world but before I could find out, a spark came to his eye, "How about that wooden ketch? She needs someone to look after her."

I looked back at the boat. There was a stream of water gushing from an outlet on the side. "She's run down but the basics look good. I'll need an expert's opinion on that leak."

"I'm on my way tomorrow or I'd give you a hand. I've been hanging about for a month working on this girl's gearbox," he patted the cabin roof. "It packed up in Horta. The mechanic here helped rebuild it. He's a good handyman. That's his boat." He indicated a large steel ketch further along the pontoon.

"Where are you heading?" I asked.

"Next port is Porto Santo. I'm joining up with friends, then we sail in convoy to Volos."

"Is that home?"

He shook his head. "The sea and my boat are home." In another person it might have sounded grandiose. "Every long-distance sailor is my friend. If you join in," he tilted his head back and observed me closely, bearded jaw thrust forward, eyes glinting under almost closed lids, as if daring me into some lethal schoolboy challenge, "you'll be part of the closest community in the world. It's like nothing else. It's the essence of freedom."

He stepped on to the pontoon, called a gruff "good luck" and walked off towards the marina. I watched him climb the gangway and make his way to the road. He had found freedom, but only by dedicating his life to the seven seas. I looked again at the wooden ketch rocking gently by the pontoon, still attached to land by its orange power line, the umbilical cord that kept her afloat. She was the boat of my dreams. But I didn't plan on taking her to Tahiti, at least not yet. First I wanted to find freedom at home.

In the late 60s and early 70s, dreams abounded. It was not unknown for an office clerk to walk into a city boutique, gear up with kaftan, beads and a 'This is the first day of the rest of your life' badge, dump his suit in a dustbin and join a bunch of like-minded drop-outs in a commune. There was eagerness in the post-war generation to explore new ways of living and enough slack in society to let it happen. People were less ambitious and the state was more relaxed. Traffic control was perfunctory, crowds didn't alarm the authorities, mass surveillance was non-existent, marijuana and psychedelic drugs were tolerated, there was less intrusion all round. It gave people an opportunity to express themselves in their own way; as a result there was room to dream and Great Britain was a creative powerhouse. My first dream came along whilst I was studying zoology at Edinburgh University, commuting from a derelict cottage in a roofless sports car. It struck home like a vision of St John the Divine. I would study the lives of individual elephants in Africa. Back then if you had a good idea, universities could provide funding for a personal PhD study.

Pretty soon I was immersed in the life of an African field biologist, not with elephants as it happened, but impala with their female gang society controlled by mob-boss males. Walking through the woods on foot brought me into close contact with the wild animals which buzzed with spiritual presence. As the days and months went by, the hidden rhythms of the bush revealed themselves bringing their own questions. Why did trees flush green at the driest time of the year? What drives the long-distance migration of wildebeest? Why did the moon trigger the rutting of impala males? As I walked quietly along the animal paths my mind sought for answers, flicking back and forth over the mental terrain just as my eyes looked for wildlife, darting back and forth over my surroundings. It was like living in an enchanted forest but one inhabited by Africa's megafauna where new discoveries in Darwin's theory of natural selection took the place of an infallible magic mirror.

I didn't pay much attention to the changes going on in Britain, just took care to avoid jobs that might box me in. I moved to conservation, my next dream, choosing to operate as a freelance consultant. It meant hanging on to a thin thread of work but it took me to remote places, introduced me to rural communities with their unfailing dignity, generosity and ingenuity, and gave me back part of the year to follow my own interests. When I did finally stop to look around in the early 2000s, I didn't like what I saw. Surveillance cameras were popping up like mushrooms on a moist day in autumn; crowd control was paramilitary; robotic answering systems turned enquiries by phone into an ordeal; companies snared personal information on the web; the work place was permeated by systems-thinking; students were saddled with loans by an older generation that had enjoyed free education; and even the universities, once temples of free-thinking, had been subverted by the need for corporate funding, or so it seemed to me. I noticed that those starting out in life had less opportunity to express their real selves, to hang out with like-minded pals and dream the good dreams – the ones that could be hammered into life, the ones that set you free. But then I had to admit, I was out of touch.

There was something else I had to admit. I wasn't fired up by my own work anymore. Hunting down solutions to the declining wildlife of Africa and Asia had been an amazing adventure that had stretched my creativity. But it had begun to take on the stale feel of the morning after party. We planned in boxes, made assessments on spreadsheets and reported in frameworks. Rote answers to prefabricated questions held sway over creative solutions and wider knowledge. I looked across at the wildlife organisations. Once proud and principled, they too had acquiesced to commercial ideals and ready-made solutions. Few of my work colleagues understood my passion for the wild which, if I were rash enough to show it, was usually met with embarrassed silence or outright suspicion.

Everywhere I looked there was a chasm between people and nature. I knew it was the fundamental problem even as I did my best to ignore it. Back it would come time and again to taunt me, like some will-o'-the-wisp luring unwary travellers into the bottomless marshes. It was for that reason more than any other that I detested the corporate take-over of my profession. It had severed the vital connection with wildlife just where it should have been strongest. It was an impasse.

If I was stuck at work, it was no better at home. Being single and with my children at university, I was freer than at any time since my early twenties. Yet nothing happened on the romantic front; I just didn't seem to connect to anybody. Instead of a new chapter opening up in my life, I was left on the side lines like an extra watching teammates play the all-important game. Flat, numb and puzzled, I was adrift in the mid-fifties doldrums. Until that is the sea began to call me.

The first boat I'd looked at was a Holman 28, big enough for two or three adults yet easily sailed singlehandedly. The Essex Marina was asking £7,500, making it by far the cheapest boat on offer. There was nobody in the small office so I walked down to the forest of masts which filled an inland pond surrounded by reed beds. It was connected to the open sea by a muddy east-coast creek that wound its way through the flat wetlands. As I stood wondering where to look first, the lively song of a reed warbler announced the arrival of spring. I set off along the first pontoon and soon found the Holman: she was tethered forlornly to a metal cleat, listing to one side, looking as worn out as the day itself. The price might have been low but it was hopelessly optimistic. The varnish on the coachroof wasn't flaking, it had disappeared altogether. The coaming was broken, sails dirty, halyards frayed, deck paint cracked and the metal mast looked as though it had been scoured with Brillo pads. Even the 'For Sale' sign was bleached from months of sunlight and curled at the edges. I shook my head. It was a tired dream at best. Was this all that remained of my youthful hopes?

The owner of the marina walked across, reading my face before I'd even spoken. "Lovely boat the Holman but perhaps not what you're after?"

"What I'm after is a boat with a soul," I replied. He had the grace to smile. In the vague hope that he might know of a hidden classic looking for an owner, I filled him in on the details. "A wooden yacht, maybe something from the 1930s or earlier, a touch bigger than this one," I nodded at the Holman, "with curved lines that mirror her own wave as she surges through the sea, one that I might just fall in love with." I looked him in the eye wondering if he understood.

"I know what you want," the owner gazed over the crowd of shining white hulls, "but I've nothing like that at the moment. If you give me a phone number I'll let you know when something comes along." He led the way back to his office. It seemed a waste to return home without seeing other boats, so I pressed him harder. "I'm down from Scotland.

Are there any wooden boats in Essex that I could look at while I'm here?"

He shook his head, but as I was getting into my car he had a change of heart. "If you drive down to the Container Port in London Docks, there's an old yacht lying in a siding. She might do you." I checked my watch. There was just time.

She took a bit of finding, but just before dark I spotted a tall mast and pulled up alongside a decrepit wharf. A stack of containers was rusting on the far pier, some nondescript tubs lay in the oily water below and an old motor boat lay semi-submerged along one of the side walls. *Iwonda* was moored on the nearside, varnished coamings and canary yellow hull brightening up her surroundings like a spring flower in a bombsite. I climbed down a ladder and stepped on board. She barely stirred. In front of me was a wide cockpit half covered by a faded tent. I peered underneath. Two wooden doors led into the main cabin, one to port and the other to starboard. I chose the one to starboard and crawled under the tent to grasp the bronze handle. It turned and the door opened easily. Inside was a sumptuous saloon with dark red divans and acres of polished wood. A steel centreboard was artfully integrated with the central mahogany table, its wings folded down. A solid fuel stove stood at one end. She rocked gently as I moved causing water in the bilges to slosh about and spread a putrid whiff of the dock. Did her opulent clothing mask a diseased bowel?

Back on the wharf I met up with some sea scouts who were living on a Brixham Trawler moored in the adjacent dock. "Any idea who the owner of *Iwonda* might be?" I asked. There were some shrugs and head shakes.

One young sailor from north of the border was staring at me intently. He glanced down at the boat and then back at me. "She's like a greyhound in a kennel. Ken what I'm saying?" He spoke in a high-pitched voice on the edge of panic and I recognised the anguish of a fellow exile. He came forward a few more steps until his face was only inches from my own. "Someone's got to free her." His breath smelt as sour as the harbour but he held my eye in an unforgiving stare for some seconds, daring me to deny it, before turning abruptly to follow the others.

Iwonda has made a conquest there, I thought. The light was going so I took a few more photos from the pier before setting off for home. There was plenty of time to mull over possibilities on the long drive north. That trawler lad might have taken a cheap shot to try and get me hooked but there was nothing phony about his feelings for the beautiful craft lying bound to iron rings in a dirty wharf. Surrounded by walls, she was hidden from sight even by the sharp-eyed river-craft folk. She should have been out in the east-coast estuaries amongst the wildfowl, reed beds and tidal banks. She needed an owner to love her, to wash her decks and light her oil lamps in the twilight. But there she was, alone in her cell, dirty, uncared for, slowly dying. Her fate hung in the balance.

Might I take a risk and free her? I could get her out of that sewer for a start, clean her up and make a proper assessment. There would be much to take on. The deck was rough looking and might be rotten. She was leaking below the waterline. I thought about the options as the miles rolled by. Somewhere near Scotch Corner I saw that the real question was whether *Iwonda* would be a safe boat at sea. I mentioned the boat to my brother and he put the word round the local yacht club. A friend of the previous owner rang me out of the blue.

"Did you know that *Iwonda* was kept in the harbour at Dunbar?" he asked.

"What here on the Forth?"

"Aye, right on your doorstep. What a bonnie boat. We'd sail her to Bass Rock and back on an evening. She was fast. Never took us more than three or four hours. It could be a bit wet mind you. Her bows are that low, she'd take the seas on the foredeck. Nothing to worry about, they just washed o'er the side." He paused a moment. "Mind you," and he paused again, briefly but long enough to get my full attention, "she capsized once in a squall off the Bass. Came up all right but it was a bad moment."

I wondered no more. With her flat bottom and centreboard, she was a boat for the east coast creeks and inlets of England. I hoped the right person would come along and loose her from the iron rings, but she was not built for the deep waters and gusting winds of the west of Scotland. I started searching again. The next boat I went to see was the antithesis of *Iwonda* – an immaculate 43 foot Morgan Giles sloop with teak planks that were copper fastened to oak frames and a deep keel. Yet something didn't feel right. The boat lacked warmth.

So it went all summer, as I visited one boat after another. Either I feared some ghastly malady hiding beneath charming looks or else, though sound in deck and hull, the boat left me unmoved. It was a bit like speed dating I imagined. None of the candidates lived up to my dream. Eventually I grew tired of it. My success in the world of boating was proving no better than it was in the world of romance. Soon I was working overseas on a demanding consultancy. I could see that I didn't really need a boat. It would just be a worry when I was called away. My life was fine really. Midlife crisis be damned, it had just been a bit of a wobble.

"Have you found a mermaid to keep you warm at night?" asked Neil who had rung for some craic. He had been my neighbour at a research station in the heart of the African bush. We helped each other out from time to time but more often than not it was he who pulled me out the mud, and, invariably, with some Irish anecdote to lighten things up.

"Not one that hangs around," I replied.

"But she's out there waiting for you; that's for sure." I grunted in a non-committal kind of way. Neil switched tack, "You'll be having more luck with the boat hunting?"

"Hah!" I snorted. "No woman, no boat. The gods have abandoned me."

"Well there's a thing all right. Tell you what. Why not try over here? There are some rare beauties in the creek – just waiting for a Scotsman to come by. Sure they've only seagulls for company. Come over now and I'll show you."

Irish boats. It got me thinking. I'd searched in Scotland and England and even glanced at the ads for boats on the Continent. For some reason I hadn't looked in Ireland. But that was in the summer. It was November now and the triple combo of cold, wet and wind was enough to dissuade me from further boat hunting even if I had still been interested. On the other hand, southern Ireland sounded tropical compared to the east coast of Scotland. It would be good to have a break and there was no harm in idling around some of the marinas. Later that week I boarded the shuttle from Edinburgh to Cork. Neil was waiting for me in arrivals. Despite the years I recognised him immediately. Perhaps a bit balder on top but ramrod straight, head cocked to one side like an eager gundog, and with that same mischievous smile playing at the corners of his mouth which barely managed to quell the riot of Irish humour bubbling inside.

"How are you?" he greeted me.

"Ready to go," I replied.

"Good man yourself! Come on then, I'll show you the best places on our way back to my office. Tomorrow you can borrow the car and get stuck in." He drove me down to Carrigaline passing through woods that were holding on to the colours of autumn. We passed the road that I would take the next day to search for boats along the Owenabue River, which ran down to Crosshaven, the original home of Irish sailing. "It's packed full of yachts. I'll put the word out amongst some sailing friends." We turned north following a small road to the Cross River Ferry, which took us over to Carrigaloe. From there we drove along a country road to Fota Wildlife Park where Neil had his office and then on to his home.

Rosie greeted me at the front door with a hug. "Come in, come in. You'll not mind the chaos." I walked in feeling at once at home, just as I had back in Africa. Rosie had that enticing Irish mix, part mystic, part minx, leavened with a no-nonsense country charm and a talent for home-making. Later that evening, we went to their local. The music was grand and the lead singer, a wild redhead, reminded me of someone else, somebody I was trying to keep out of my thoughts. I felt her gaze for a moment as she looked in our direction.

Rosie leant over, "There you go Martyn, buy the girl a drink now."

I laughed, which is what Rosie had wanted of course. "I've just met someone, actually, at a party in Edinburgh."

"Well you're a dark horse all right. So who is this girl?"

"Kyla." I shook my head wondering how to describe her. "Tangled red hair like that one," I glanced at the singer who was now halfway into an Irish ballad about a young maid and an untrustworthy soldier, and was singing as if she'd been there. "Green eyes that seem to see right through you. But whenever I get close, she sends me packing." I shook my head again. "She's a puzzle all right."

"Neil, did you hear that? The boy is smitten."

"Leave him be Rosie, he's got more serious things on his mind than women."

Rosie gave him a friendly shove. "What would you know about it, you eejit."

Turning back to me she put her hand over my glass to stop me drinking, "Come on now Martyn, it's not like you to be scared off by a few words."

"I was driving down to England to see her. I was more than halfway, when she turned me back. Cut me dead."

"Women can be right hard," began Neil but stopped when he got a look from Rosie.

"Is that it?" asked Rosie. "I'll let you into a little secret boyo. A woman may seem harsh at times, even very harsh and for no reason. But we have our reasons. And what we admire in a man is someone who is not put off. So don't you be a sap now."

"Maybe," I nodded. "Maybe you're right."

"Rosie is usually right on these things," said Neil, "but Martyn aren't your forgetting something?"

"What's that?" I asked readying myself for a wisecrack.

"It's your round!"

Next morning Neil roused me at 06:30 with a mug of Irish tea and a bowl of porridge. I dropped him at the wildlife park, crossed the ferry and drove on to Carrigaline and the Owenabue River. I slowed to enjoy its tree-lined meanderings and eyed up the boats on their moorings. Part way along was a lagoon with a number of fine yachts. In 1589 Sir Francis Drake hid a squadron of five ships there to escape the Spanish fleet. He had been chased across the Celtic Sea and managed to enter the great natural harbour of Cork ahead of the Spaniards.

Once through the tight narrows, he'd turned hard to port and sailed up the Owenabue rounding two sharp doglegs to moor in the lagoon. The masts of his ships would have been shielded from view by the tall woods and Corribiny Hill but it was still a gamble. The Spanish ships did pursue, entering Cork harbour and sailing round its extensive shores but they never found the English ships. Looking at the hidden pool, speckled now with raindrops and fallen leaves, I thought of Drake concealed on the hilltop watching the Spanish ships as they hunted for him. What a shout he must have given when they finally gave up and sailed out of the narrows.

A jingle from my cell phone brought me back to the present. It was Neil. "Get along to Feste Marina, now – it's near the yacht club. Ask for Torstein. He's the Norwegian owner. My friends on Great Island say he had a wooden ketch for sale. It's a while back, mind you, but you never know." He hung up, in a hurry to deal with the next wildlife emergency – some escaped penguins.

A mile down the road I found the sign and turned into the boat-yard. A stack of yachts were out on the hard in preparation for winter, propped up on galvanised boat cradles. Behind them was a makeshift workshop. I walked over, catching glimpses of the water between the boats. The creek was three or four hundred yards wide at this point with a line of trees on the far bank. A number of yachts were tied alongside the pontoons out in front, taking advantage of the mild Irish autumn to enjoy some late sailing. Nobody was sailing today. There was a biting easterly wind bringing wintry showers. I knocked on the shed door and then shoved it open. Inside a man in overalls was busy welding; he broke off for a second to point me at a small office in the far corner. I walked over and went through the open door. A large man sat hunched over a metal desk, like a bear with a sore head, staring at some figures. He was wearing a heavy biker's jacket.

"Are you Torstein by any chance?" I asked, anticipating another dead end in my wild boat chase.

He looked up revealing a large drooping handlebar moustache beneath two smaller handlebars that served as eyebrows. "Who are you?" he growled in a thick Norwegian accent.

The thought of the warm café that Rosie had mentioned crossed my mind. It was a lot more inviting that talking to this terse Norseman in his freezing office. "My name's Martyn. I'm looking for a yacht. What I'm really after is a wooden boat."

The Viking's gaze had diverted back down to the page of accounts which seemed to hold a particular fascination for him. "So what do you want from me?"

The thought of coffee crossed my mind again. I pictured a window seat next to an open fire with a view of boats coming and going. "I'm staying with friends in Midleton," I replied. "Neil works at Fota Wildlife Park; one of his friends said you might have a wooden ketch for sale."

"Fota! So tell your friend we've got some of his penguins here." He stared at me again without blinking but I noticed the briefest twinkle in his eye. Then he fished about in a drawer and chucked over some keys. "He's on the first pontoon, on the left, red covers, you can't miss him." And with that he buried his head in the accounts again. Despite every effort, I felt my heartbeat quicken.

I strolled across the yard going deliberately slowly, reminding myself that I was just a tourist. Passing between the opulent rows of fibreglass boats I came to the marina gate; beyond were half a dozen pontoons with an assortment of yachts and motorboats lying alongside. I walked down the gangway to the nearest pontoon watching my feet as the wood was slippery in the rain. Glancing left I found her almost at my feet. Like a dream straight from Maurice Griffiths's book: thirty-six feet of ocean-going wooden yacht, two-masted with a powerful bowsprit, sweeping decks well raised above the sea, a graceful counter stern, deep cockpit and long cabin. She was weatherworn but to my eyes the epitome of sea magic. My curious smile widened quickly into a broad grin. The search was over.

Back in the office, I gleaned a few more facts from the Norseman. The owner's name was Barry. He'd sailed over from the Caribbean some time ago and left the ketch at a nearby yard. Then he'd departed for the Emirates. She'd sat on land for two years or perhaps more, seemingly abandoned and then been moved to the marina and put on sale. She'd been there for another two years. There was a cousin somewhere around who looked after things. I gave the Viking my card with an email address and asked him to pass it on. He pushed it to one side, grunted something, and went back to his accounts.

"Jeannie Mac! but you don't waste time," exclaimed Neil a few weeks later as I handed him a pint of Murphy's. "Mind now – she'll give you nothing but trouble." We had retired to Cronin's in Crosshaven and I was telling him about my negotiations with the boat's owner. Emails had been flying back and forth from Scotland to the Emirates. He'd wanted £42,000 for her. I pointed out that she had sunk at her mooring and looked semi-derelict. In the end, he'd dropped to £28,000 and agreed to a survey. I'd found the best wooden-boat specialist in England and asked him to meet me in Crosshaven. He'd been examining the boat all day, pricking each timber to test for rot, checking for signs of structural damage or bodged repair work, and assessing what life was left in the sails, rigging and electrics. His notebook was filling up with comments in a tight, spidery hand. "You must be mad now." Neil looked genuinely concerned.

"Ah, but she's a rare beauty. How can I pass her by?" My head was spinning with ideas about rescuing my dream boat and sailing her to Scotland. "I'll have to get the price down. The owner knows the score. Nobody is buying wooden yachts. And if the surveyor finds any more problems... there's bound to be more problems... he'll drop the price."

"I hear she was stood out the water for two years. The mast was lying on the fecking sod."

"Willie told me he'd cut the rot and scarfed in a new piece of Yellow Fir."

Neil nodded; he knew Willie's reputation for repairing wooden boats. "And what if there's more rot? What if you're fecking about in the ocean and the bottom drops off?"

The door swung open and the surveyor walked in with the quick-eyed movement of a ferret, a nautical ferret at that I thought, with a single gold earring and a loose kit bag over one shoulder. I shifted along the bench to give him some room while Neil fetched him a pint from the bar, placing it carefully on the polished wooden table. The surveyor took a deep swallow.

"You've had a long day," I declared.

He took another long pull which brought the level right down and wiped the foam from his beard. "What a lovely old girl," he said.

"Now he's looking just like the Cheshire Cat," said Neil, eyeing my broad grin over his glass.

"I've been over every inch that's accessible and as far as I can tell, she's sound," continued the surveyor. "The oak frames are strong and there's no sign of rot in the planking. The strakes are made from Pitch Pine which is full of resin. That's been protecting her. The teak deck is a bit worn but it should last another ten years. Mind you it will need some caulking. Structurally she's sound as a bell. The mast and spars are true and the engine is almost new." He took another draught of beer and paused briefly to flick through his notes. So far so good, I thought. "In other respects mind you, she's in a deplorable condition. The sails and rigging are at the end of their working life. The electrics are corroded. The main switchbox is pretty much shot. There's rust coming up from the keel bolts. There's a gap between the deck and the sheer strake on one side. The toilet pump is jammed; so are the seacocks. The navigation instruments are old and unreliable. The whale pump isn't working. The stove needs replacing and while you are at it, you should replace the gas piping. The soft furnishings are dilapidated. Pretty much everything is worn out.

"That sounds good but it doesn't sound good," I replied. It felt like I was on a roller coaster.

"There's a saying," the surveyor explained, "when it comes to valuation – one-third for the hull, one-third for the spars, sails and rigging, and one-third for the engine, instruments and other gear."

By that reckoning, I reckoned she was one-third sound, one-third worn, and one third a mixture of new and deplorable. I scratched my head in puzzlement.

"Now that's a marvellous equation, that is," said Neil, "the yoke is half good and half bad."

"If you can do some of the restoration work yourself," said the surveyor, "it won't be so bad."

29

"I could give it a go," I nodded "but where would I start?"

"Tell you what," said the surveyor. "I'll write out a programme for you with the things that need to be done right away and those that can be done over the next few years."

"Thanks, that would be useful." As I thought about it, the sun seemed to come out. "More than useful, that would be bloody marvellous," I signalled to the bar for another round.

"Wait a minute," said Neil. "How about the leaks? We don't want him fecking drowned just when you've got him to open his pockets."

"There's a leak from the rudder mounting," said the surveyor. "You can see the stains running down the hornbeam – it wants sorting but shouldn't be difficult. One of the garboards needs re-caulking. I can't see any big problems there. I would re-fasten all the planks just to be safe."

"You think she's up for long-distance cruising?" I asked.

"She's a strong boat. She'd take you anywhere once you've seen to her, but don't underestimate the work."

I took a big breath. "So how about the price? What do you think she's worth?"

The surveyor grimaced. "It's hard to put a price on a boat like this. It's as much about what someone is willing to pay as it is about the condition of the craft." He took a deep pull from his second pint. "She's got a great pedigree. She's sound enough. But she's rundown. The market for wooden boats is flat. I'd say anywhere between twenty and thirty thousand pounds."

"I'd need to get her at the bottom end to afford her." It felt as if I was looking over a cliff edge – a cliff made of tenners.

"I've got an old sailing barge," said the surveyor. "Keep her in a creek next to my house in Essex. Wonderful old girl. She takes a bit of looking after, just like this boat will." He smiled for the first time. "You'd have a lot of fun with her."

True to his word, the surveyor wrote a report as thick as an old telephone book with pages of notes on the boat's condition and a plan in each section for how to bring her back to cruising condition in affordable steps. I sent a copy to the owner with a note highlighting the more costly repair work needed. Barry sent it back unread with a covering note. "It's £28,000 or nothing. You have to understand that this boat was my home for 3 years in the Caribbean. I sailed her across the Atlantic twice. I know exactly what she's worth and I'm damned if I'll let her go for a penny less. I'd rather pay the marina charges and sort her out myself when I get back."

I went back over my savings again. They didn't come close. It would be reckless to ask the bank for a loan given the unpredictable nature of my work. It all pointed to no deal. The problem was she had a name now, *Molio*. It was the affectionate name given to St Molaise by the people of Arran when he arrived from Ireland at the end of the sixth century to live the life of a hermit. And with her name came connection. *Molio* was not just a boat anymore. She was my passage to freedom. For all his dire warnings, Neil understood. When a man is trapped in a complicated world of work and commitments, freedom comes at a price. But it is surely a price worth paying. I made an appointment with the bank manager in my home town.

A few months later, I met Barry on board *Molio* to make an inventory of gear. He was a friendly man, the type of sailor who would lend a hand if you were in a fix, or invite a party of guests on board for a meal in the evening. At the same time, he seemed restless with an eye on the next horizon. He'd brought over his new wife from the Emirates. It was perhaps the final act in exchanging one life for another. He didn't want anything from the boat. He hardly wanted to touch her. He nodded at a large duffel bag on the bunk. "You're about my size; hang onto the clothes if you like." Later I would send a parcel of personal letters and photos to the Emirates, receiving in return papers and photos of *Molio*'s previous life with a video of her racing in the Antigua Classics. But for now, he wanted out. We went quickly over the inventory and retired to Cronin's to sign the bill of sale. Neil and the Viking were already there as witnesses. We stopped business for a minute to share a glass. Then I wrote the cheque and handed it over. As I did, I noticed the look on the Viking's face. He was incredulous. How could a Scotsman part with so much cash for a decaying wreck? But then, he didn't know; this boat was the gift of a father to his son.

The Parts of a Ketch

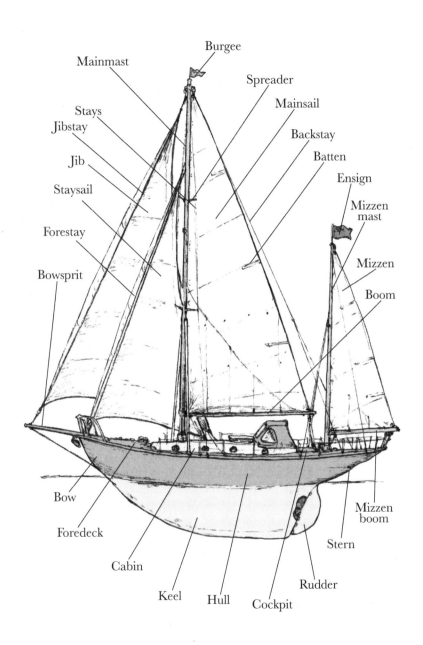

Burgee

Mainmast

Spreader

Stays

Mainsail

Jibstay

Backstay

Jib

Batten

Staysail

Ensign

Forestay

Mizzen mast

Bowsprit

Mizzen

Boom

Bow

Mizzen boom

Foredeck

Stern

Cabin

Rudder

Keel

Hull

Cockpit

Chapter 2

Dog Watch

Neil served up a large bowl of porridge overflowing with creamy milk while the rest of the house slept on. It had become part of the summer's pleasant routine. He took Dusty, the family's black Labrador, up the road to the field while I listened idly to the radio. The weather forecast promised a fine day with the possibility of thunder. Just three months from the purchase of *Molio*, I'd returned with a couple of months in hand to sort her out and sail back to Scotland. I looked again at the map of Ireland, my eyes tracing the south and west coasts. I was drawn to the romance of the Irish west coast, as I was to Scotland's. If I was going to choose that way home, I had to be confident of my boat. In a storm, the giant seas rolling in from the Atlantic would create a confusion of the safe channels in amongst the coastal rocks and shoals. If caught out the only option, especially in driving rain and poor visibility, would be to get clear of the land and wait it out. *Molio* would have to withstand hours of pounding without complaint. The worst scenario would be the boat taking in so much water in heavy seas that I was forced to try for shelter in amongst the reefs.

Stuffing a pint of milk in my pack, I chucked it in the back of the rented car and set off for Feste Marina. A few minutes later I was savouring a mug of coffee in *Molio*'s saloon surrounded by tools, boxes of gear, floorboards and half-finished repairs. I jotted down some notes for the day's work, wondering again how long it would take to ready *Molio* for the open sea.

My aim for the summer was simple enough: to restore boat and gear sufficiently for a trouble-free passage to Scotland while spending the minimum on her. But the following summer I had more ambitious plans. St Kilda was the furthest and most remote archipelago in the constellation of archipelagos that make up the Hebrides. For inshore sailors on the west of Scotland, it was the ultimate challenge. In a small way, it was their Everest. Sailing *Molio* to St Kilda single handed was my goal. The passage might have seemed trivial to Papa in his ocean-going yacht, protected by the all-seeing eye of Horus, but I was a long way from that level of competence. So it was a kind of initiation test, a way of proving myself. I knew my father would have approved; we had even talked about the possibility but never managed it.

As ship's surgeon my father saw active duty on the HUNT-Class Destroyer, *HMS Bleasdale*, and the Fleet Minesweeper, *HMS Plucky*, in the Atlantic, North Sea, Mediterranean and the Far East, taking part in the Dieppe Raid, Normandy Landings and many other episodes of war. Whilst attached to a flotilla of Motor Torpedo Boats based at Felixstowe he met my mother, who was serving as a nurse in the Voluntary Aid Detachment and so began a wonderful love affair that lasted beyond their diamond anniversary. Like many others who took part and survived, he didn't talk about the war, preferring instead to make the most of the peace that followed, a peace that he and a whole generation had fought for and bequeathed to us. He raised a family of boys with my mother and built a thriving GP practice in Ayrshire with his medical partners. A GP's life was hard in those days with many nights of broken sleep to attend urgent and not so urgent calls and with most weekends foreshortened by surgeries. He found a respite from it all in his passion for the sea. He was never happier than when sailing a small yacht off the west coast of Scotland, preferably with family or friends for crew, but quite content on his own. He taught my brothers and me by example about boat handling, navigation and the art of cruising, and, just as importantly, how to keep a boat happy and safe.

Memory of the great struggle which overtook my father's generation has receded with time, and in Britain we have become more or less passive recipients of that hard-won freedom. Yet I have a sense that the liberty they handed down is being eroded now by an enemy within.

My children and their friends don't appear to have as much freedom to choose their own style of living. Jobs are more tightly prescribed. Lifestyle options are fewer. The consequence of 'time out' is more frightening. And for those already in the swim, many share my unease over the increasing amount of intrusion into their lives. They protest at the 'system', yearn for escape from the pressure cooker, dream of being free as a bird. But despite well-fought rearguard actions against the worst excesses of regulation, incremental intrusions keep slipping past. Some time ago I began to suspect that freedom really was in retreat. I could see that the choices which defined life in the past – how to live, where to live and what to learn – were the very areas of life most likely to be prescribed today by economic pressure or government regulation. There might be a cloud of creative opportunity exploding on the web but I was by no means sure it would open the door to living free. Would tomorrow's teenagers climb the wild Scottish Mountains solo on a whim, or sail in the outer isles with no intrusive contact from the outside world?

In Old English, 'freedom' has the sense of belonging to a landed class with many privileges as opposed to living in the alternative state of bondage or slavery. This is the outer form of freedom in which liberty turns on the whim of your captor or owner. In Hindi and other Indian languages, the word for freedom translates as the 'state of being under one's own rule'. This is the inner or personal form of freedom. What exactly does personal freedom mean? That question intrigued me. If freedom is found wherever the spirit is free then how do we help make it so? Are we merely the docile recipients of freedom handed down to us by society or can we direct our lives towards greater personal freedom? What made me come alive? What makes any of us come alive for that matter? What makes us free? We may have the keys to personal freedom in our own keeping, but it seems that it can be just as hard to open the prison door.

It has been a struggle to fashion a fairer society in the west. Campaigners have fought for each legal right that now protects the vulnerable, such as the right to vote, the right to strike and the right to receive equal treatment in the workplace. Sometimes the rights are expressed as freedoms – freedom of speech, freedom of the press, freedom of worship and so on. In Britain we pride ourselves on our civil liberties and the long history of legal reform. But if such great progress has been made, why, I wonder, am I ill at ease? What if it were not just the vulnerable but all of society that was at risk? How could we protect against that kind of threat? It seemed to me that our thinking on freedom should be grounded in our own experiences, it should be more personal. We needed greater opportunity to find fulfilling work, more time to explore different careers, freedom to choose our preferred partners, and protective privacy to shield us from corporate tracking and security profiling.

My eyes went back to my notebook. I'd gone well above my ceiling to purchase *Molio*, so cosmetic repairs would have to wait. As it was, I had a dozen jobs on the go: re-mounting the fo'c'sle hatch; repairing a broken deck rail; overhauling the switch panel and navigation equipment; servicing the manual bilge pump; clearing the blocked heads; fitting a new battery and cables; freeing off seacocks; testing the engine... the list went on and on.

By mid-morning even *Molio*'s cool cabin was heating up. I stripped off my shirt and jeans, put on some shorts, and sat down at the chart table to look at the main switch panel. It was a handsome, custom-made unit with a black anodised face on which a host of toggle switches were mounted, each with its own red diode indicator and matching fuse and with its name etched in block letters on the right hand side. Four were for the various cabin lights, another four for navigation lights, one for the VHF radio, one for illuminating a compass in the cockpit, three for other navigation devices, and so on. A dial at the bottom permitted testing the charge of the ship's two batteries. The panel was set into a mahogany frame and mounted on the side of the boat above the chart table.

I loosened a couple of screws which allowed the whole thing to swing open on hinges. At the back was a rat's nest of wiring and junction boxes. The wires emerged from spade connectors that oozed brown fluid from their bases and green paste where they joined with copper wires. One six-way connector was hidden beneath a mound of white powder. For all its snazzy looks, the panel wasn't waterproof. I stared blankly at the corroded mess. I wasn't familiar with boat electrics. On my father's yacht we'd used oil lamps for lights, paper charts for navigation and a crank handle to start the engine. There wasn't any wiring. Did I need this stuff? I sat for a while just staring at it. I remembered the time when I'd opened the bonnet of my first car, an ex-army Austin Champ, the British equivalent of an American Jeep. I'd just left school and bought it unseen at an army auction for thirty-five pounds. When the keys were handed over I found that the engine wouldn't start. Lifting the bonnet I was confronted by a massive engine surrounded by a dozen or more hefty components housed in pale green waterproof casings from which pipes and braided cables ran in all directions. It was complex and beyond me. In the end I used the last of my cash to have a garage sort out the problem and sold the working champ to a friend.

That moment of exasperation with my ignorance niggled away. The first thing I did after enrolling at university was to sign up for a course in car mechanics. Every Wednesday evening I went to the physics department where a retired mechanic taught us the basics. He presented each system in turn – electrical, ignition, fuel, lubrication, cooling, air intake and exhaust – and explained carefully how it worked. It wasn't hands-on tuition but whenever possible he demonstrated components on the bench. It gave me a picture of how the different parts of a petrol engine were connected into a functioning whole. By the end of the course I no longer felt helpless. My next car was a 1956 MGA roadster, which cost seventy pounds. I spent a large part of my student life under the bonnet of this shapely beast and soon bumped into others who shared a common love for adventurous motoring. Although we never gave ourselves a name, it was essentially an owner's club for old sports cars and off-road vehicles. During the next three years there were few problems relating to wear, rust and misuse that we didn't encounter or learn to solve. I progressed from simple adjustment of the contact point gap to full restoration from the chassis up. I have sometimes wondered which education from this period was the more valuable, my bachelor's degree in zoology or our informal training in car mechanics.

Making the crossover in my mind from boats to cars changed everything. It dawned on me that *Molio*'s switch panel was less complex than the back of an MG dashboard and that opened up a host of ideas for renovation. I found some vinegar behind the stove, a toothbrush by the sink and a piece of fine emery paper in the toolbox, and got to work. After an hour, it was possible to see what was salvageable, what needed soldering and what required replacement. I squirted everything in WD40 and put the kettle on for coffee.

Sometimes you need an expert to make the repair but it's never as satisfying as doing the job yourself. The expertly repaired technology works. It does what you ask of it, but it is inert. If you keep buying in repairs, or replacing broken units with new ones, your space gets filled by strangers – stuff that doesn't speak to you. Inevitably you become more passive towards technology. I'm as guilty as anyone. By the time I finally pushed my work aside at the end of a day in the office, I was usually suffering from left brain fatigue. I didn't want to think: I wanted to escape from thinking. I unwound by taking a walk by the sea, chatting with friends in the pub, watching TV, messing with my PC or whatever. Learning new skills and fixing things in that frame of mind became a monumental hassle. As time went by, I knew I was becoming more passive. It felt like a trap. And that's why I was sitting in an old boat in a muddy creek: I was scouting about for a way round that trap.

I turned my attention to the switch for the VHF radio. There was no power. I replaced the fuse and tested the set again. It powered up showing the channel number on an orange backlit display. I left it on channel sixteen which is used all round the world for calling ships and coastguard stations. There was no traffic, but then there was no aerial to pick up a signal. I put on a floppy hat and went up on deck. The midday sun was burning down from overhead and heavy clouds were massing in the west. I paced along the teak deck in bare feet noticing how good the unvarnished wood felt. Between the planks were seams of black sealant that had cracked with age. I hoped they were still watertight. Up by the mast there were some coils of cable sealed in a plastic bag and lying on the deck. After repairing *Molio*'s mast, the yard had added new navigation lights and VHF aerial at the top but when the mast was stepped into place on the boat there had been no-one to connect up the wiring. My next job was to drill holes at the foot of the mast to take the cables and run them back below deck to the switch panel. As I worked, the clouds stacked up higher on the horizon and the smell of rain wafted over the marina. It reminded me of Africa in the wet season. I worked with a bit more urgency. By two o'clock, I had a base unit fitted to the deck with three large holes through to the cabin below. There was a crack of thunder and the first drops landed in the water beside the pontoon. Big heavy drops. In seconds the skies had opened. I put my hat over the holes and scampered back to the cockpit and down below. The rain drummed heavily on the coachroof. I sat at the chart table and watched the ceiling with interest.

Sure enough a glistening bead of moisture soon appeared between two deck planks above the galley bulging quickly into a plump drop that fell on to the hob next to the kettle. Others followed in rapid succession. I shoved a pan on the stove to collect the rainwater. The next drop hit the mattress on the starboard bunk and almost immediately another landed on the port side. More saucepans were deployed. They made a sort of music, something I remembered hearing on my father's old boat. As more drips appeared, I put out sponges to hold the moisture. Then I found a magic marker and began putting little crosses on the roof wherever the drips were forming. It would help me track down the source of the leaks later. I was rather pleased with my engineering approach to the problem, but as the minutes went by more and more drips appeared. Soon the pale cream roof was turning grey with the mass of tiny crosses. The mattresses were soaked and so was everything else. Nothing was spared, not even the switch panel, certainly not me. I put on a waterproof sailing jacket. *Molio* was a sieve.

The rain stopped as suddenly as it had begun. I'd had enough of my leaking home. I retrieved my pack from a protective bin bag, climbed onto the pontoon and set off for the shops. The heavy clouds dispersed and by the time I arrived the pavements were steaming in the sun. I bought a coffee and carried it over to my favourite bench. It was a great spot: in one direction I looked out at boats messing about on the water and in the other watched people milling about on the esplanade.

A Wild Call

My pet pastime was keeping tabs on the Crosshaven dogs. These characters walked about the town without a care in the world and with no sign of their owners, who doubtless would have been considered, should one have turned up inconveniently, a source of great embarrassment. This was their turf where they could hang out with their pals in their chosen gangs. Soon a likely cur came ambling down the hill from the houses above the shore. Tail held high, he walked across Lower Road as though he owned the place and left his mark on the rear tyre of a parked car. Adopting a jaunty gait he trotted across the green to check out a rubbish bin where he was joined by two others. He reminded me of our own Labrador Retriever, Ben, a big dog with thick golden fur and a pink nose. At home, he was the gentlest animal you could imagine. I remembered my young brother as a toddler crawling all over him, pulling at his hair and even pushing stubby fingers into his eyes. Ben didn't snap or growl or even bare his teeth. He only turned his head to one side and when it finally became too much, gently stood up, walked a few steps and sat down again. Outside of the home it was another matter. Ben defended our house like a castle keep under siege. He and the postie were mortal enemies and only the bulging sack prevented bloody engagements; the butcher's boy kept a fresh bone in the basket of his bike which he chucked to Ben in order to gain admittance to the driveway. Stray dogs were chased just as vigorously.

On home ground Ben was very much a people's dog, but out on the street he ignored the townsfolk and entered the world of dogs. He was the top dog in our part of town and even the big boxer next door deferred to him. I called him 'king of the esplanade' because he routinely had a retinue of half a dozen other dogs following him down the seafront. He would be out for most of the day, returning for his dinner at midday and the occasional walk with one of us boys in the afternoon. On one occasion I remember riding my bike up to the high street to visit Woolworth's. I parked it outside and wandered round the aisles eying up the sweets and toys. Going round the far end of the central counter I met Ben coming in the opposite direction. He wagged his tail and I patted his head and then we each carried on going round our own way. A couple of hours later, we met up again at home. It was a free life for dogs and boys.

The Crosshaven dogs knew each other very well. They also knew where they stood in the hierarchy so there was little friction. They must surely have enjoyed their casual life of daily explorations, chance meetings and stringing along with chums. There was time to scratch an ear, loiter and sleep in the sun. They exuded carefree confidence. I couldn't help but compare their lives with those of the less fortunate mutts in my hometown today. They spent much of their time on an extendable lead, attended by owners who doubled as dutiful, if reluctant, poop-scoopers. Being neither leashed-in or under effective control, yet being attached to their owners, they were confused and easily frightened by strangers. The big dogs felt they must defend their masters and mistresses, often barking and pulling at their leads without a clue as to what was appropriate. When off the lead the owners were fearful of these aggressive tendencies and tried to distract their charges with ball launchers, avoiding encounters that might go horribly wrong. The little gang of dogs disappeared amongst the shoppers leaving me with thoughts about freedom.

Some of my most carefree adventuring, such as overlanding across Africa, had depended on my acquiring a set of skills that built self-reliance. Such skills are a bit like the rigging wires which hold *Molio*'s masts: they open up new worlds through precise functioning. Skills are often associated with learning a trade but they can be thought about in a much larger sense, one which includes all the techniques and practises that we use in expressing ourselves, whether through music and dance, language and literature, digital and mobile media, arts and crafts, science and technology, business and industry, politics, sport, fashion, body adornment, and so on. All these forms of expression involve skill. Take sailing. The more I practised sailing as a boy, the more competent I became at tacking the boat, changing sails, helming, navigating and anchoring. When he saw I was ready, my father let me take his boat on my own. As a teenager, I sailed her up the west coast to Skye and beyond, voyaging in my own time and in my own way in the seas we both loved. By becoming more skilful in your chosen pursuit, you not only develop self-confidence but perhaps earn a little respect. That is why the mastery of a chosen skill is one of the keys to living free.

I could see that restoring *Molio* to sailing trim would be an education in itself. Already I was learning about her equipment, picking up new tips every day and improving my techniques. I could feel the craftsmanship tying me closer to the boat. In time, I would hopefully know how to fix something at sea without thinking. It is surely the skilled connection to an occupation that actually instils freedom into our lives.

Moreover, any new skill acquired opens a door on new experiences that were previously unavailable. Sailing literally opened up new horizons for me: undiscovered lands, seaways and island communities that abounded with opportunity. It is the same in any walk of life that embraces a practised use of judgement – climbing, farming, fishing, cooking, repairing, sewing, designing, building, computing, business management, financial planning, caring for others, organising social events, BMX free-styling or fixing old cars. If you became proficient at it, the door begins to open on your personal freedom. You need to check that it is the right door you are opening, one with your name on it. If you learn some new skill on behalf of another person, a parent perhaps or the office boss, and the activity happens to be of no personal interest, then you may become proficient but would feel little satisfaction and no joy. If on the other hand it is a pursuit you desire and you work away, perhaps in your own 'free time', then your journey can truly begin. Wherever you happen to be in that spectrum between the unwanted and wanted skills, it will be those you cherish the most that unlock your inner freedom.

I can imagine Neil butting in at this point. "That's all very well, Martyn, but there's more to life than skills. We are not just machines. Family and friends are at the heart of things." And of course he is right. Even Papa, sailing somewhere in the southern Pacific with the protection of his eye of Horus, is part of a sea tribe. It is perhaps the most scattered tribe on the planet, but ocean liveaboards are knitted together by strong social ties and long-distance communication. Most of us belong to more than one tribe: we dwell in many tribelets. When other members of your tribelet share your passion then far more can be done to further your dream. Through the sailing club, members can resist harbour development that would destroy a slipway used for boat launching. A ramblers' group can work to reopen a public right of way. Any individual that possesses a useful skill will be afforded greater status and granted more leeway in their group – whatever its nature. The sailor who can climb a mast to fix the rigging, or mend a sail, has always been in demand whether on an eighteenth century naval frigate or in today's yachting playgrounds. Skill and unity of purpose is how your tribelet prospers and how its members expand their personal freedoms.

Walking back to *Molio* my thoughts returned to her leaking decks. One option would be to sail her to Scotland just as she was. My sleeping bag would get wet and the electrics might conk out completely, but neither was terminal. It was tempting to go in the settled weather. On the other hand, I would be vulnerable to any fast-moving storms and here in Cork Harbour I had ready access to the chandler's and other shops. A bit of patience now would pay off. It would give me time to find a dinghy that could double as a life raft. Who knows, I might even persuade Kyla to come along. She probably wouldn't thank me for saying it, but she had the same carefree swagger as the cur that had ambled down the hill just now. That swagger had caught my attention the first time I set eyes on her.

I'd been invited to a friend's birthday party in a terraced house behind the Meadows in Edinburgh. Even in the flamboyant company present, she was hard to miss, if not for the tangle of flaming kelp cascading over a peasant-gypsy top, then for the easy, Bond-girl confidence. Hard to age, but I guessed mid to late thirties. She was surrounded by friends and I didn't know any of them. I stood awkwardly with a glass of red in hand, feeling the warmth that she radiated and wondering if I could pluck up enough courage to say hello. It was already getting late.

I considered myself objectively: nothing special to look at, unless her thing was unruly brown hair with a few silver strands, ginger beard and a kind of wayward look about the eye; questionable dress sense as certified by the strange Mongolian jacket covering a much-worn fisherman's jersey; passionate in a Scottish-Romantic kind of way; reserved without a drink in hand, but with one, in danger of being absurdly garrulous, especially on favourite topics of boats, travel, nature, raising kids and human behaviour; moderately fit at best; scraping by moneywise thanks to a precarious self-employed job; prone to hanging about at home and then disappearing unexpectedly to far flung corners of the Earth. Loser? Well hardly a catch. I knew it even if I chose to ignore it. Maybe I needed to remember it now. Maybe I didn't. In any case, redlocks would label me as just another older guy who wanted her. I hated being judged.

"Honestly now, why would she choose you?" I turned to find our host, Paul, at my side, spliff in hand and a mane of glossy black hair even longer than redlocks's.

"Because I'm not a sycophant," I retaliated.

"Peace brother," he simpered, offering up his joint. "Have you noticed her friends?"

We were in the hall, standing between doorways, one leading into an incense-filled living room and the other to a candle-lit bedroom, surrounded by larger than life people – hippies, healers, hopheads, pagans, spiritual activists, tree huggers and at least one Pleiadian that I'd met earlier. For all I knew, the mythical undead were amongst us. Certainly they were street savvy, mysterious and uninhibited; judging from what was going on in the bedroom, they didn't have many boundaries either. I was sure they had lots more interesting things to talk about than I did. "Not much chance for an aging traveller," I remarked, taking a drag.

"Those guys are just dogs," he smirked. "Well, we are all dogs but they are just mongrels. Come on, I'll introduce you." Seeing my reluctance, he grabbed my arm and began dragging me forward. "Don't worry, she doesn't bite."

Time to make a fool of myself, I thought, and followed Paul across the room. Close up I realised how tall she was; almost on a level with me. She was arguing some point with spirited animation. And there was something else I noticed. A kindness about the eyes which comes only with age, and then rarely.

"Kyla," said Paul, interrupting an intense rejoinder by a big fellow opposite, "meet Martyn, a fellow traveller on the road to nowhere." And with that vague aphorism he pushed me forward.

When her green eyes met mine, I almost panicked. Maybe she noticed for she looked down and touched the felt of my jacket. There was olive green paint under her fingernails. "That's so soft. Where's it from?"

"Mongolia," I stammered. "Taiga country, up north."

"Land of the shaman," she sighed, looking up again, "and those wonderful herds of reindeer. I'd love to go there."

"They are my favourite people," I began, and then noticed the big guy she'd been talking to glaring at me. "Look I'm sorry, I didn't mean to barge in." I finished abruptly, off balance, but not moving.

She glanced in his direction, "I can talk to Cormac anytime." She turned back to me. "He's just my flatmate. Tell me about Mongolia."

Her voice fluttered like a caged bird, not in my ear but somewhere above my stomach. It was disconcerting to have her fluttering about inside me like that. Just for a moment I let myself wonder whether my long exile in love's wilderness might be coming to an end. Only for a moment though. The gatekeeper to my heart stood firmly by, watching the euphoria with a dour expression. I'd learnt to be cautious with my heart.

"Those guys are the best," I replied. "They are team players and a bit like west coast Scots – you know tough and funny at the same time. After a few shots of vodka they are so soulful. They sing about their animals and their women. They love to sing. If you drink enough you end up singing with them."

"And what do these big soulful men say to their women?" Kyla asked. "That they remind them of glossy fat camels?" She looked up with a mischievous grin.

"They say that their women are like wild gazelles tripping down to the stream, tails flicking."

"Ohh, I would like to be someone's gazelle with long eyelashes and a frisky tail."

Just then Cormac came back. "We're leaving Kyla. Are you coming?"

I checked my watch. It was after midnight. Kyla raised a finger to indicate she would be along in a minute. Cormac gave me another glare. It was now or never, I thought.

"We don't have any reindeer in my home town, but we do have seabirds, lots and lots of them." She looked straight into my eyes, waiting for me to continue. "If you are interested," I continued wishing I didn't sound so awkward, "it's only half an hour by train. I could show you our seabird centre."

"Only if you show me a puffin as well," she replied, eyes laughing.

"Why do I like women who like puffins?" I kidded back.

"Why do you? Are you attracted by our bills?"

"I'll show you a puffin. That's a guarantee."

She went to say goodbye to Paul but not before giving me her mobile number.

We met at the Seabird Centre the next weekend. I walked into the café wondering if she would show up and there was the tangle of fiery locks that I'd not really expected to see again. She was sitting at a small table by the big window with a view straight across the sea to Bass Rock which was creamy white from nesting gannets. There was a kind of dreamy look in her eyes.

"There are one hundred and fifty thousand birds on the Bass."

She turned to face me smiling, "So many? It is a wonder they can find each other."

"They squawk a lot. I'm sure that helps," I replied, sitting down beside her.

"Maybe I will need to squawk louder." Seeing my puzzled look, she put her hand on mine. "I'm leaving here. I mean I'm leaving Edinburgh – in two weeks' time. I wanted to tell you before we got to know each other. I've finished my final painting at the art school. I must get away now. I'm going to Wales. I've been asked for a job interview. It's in the west, near where my parents live. My sister is there too."

As Kyla talked, I began to make a mental note of all her likes and dislikes. Soon I had a rough grasp of her preferred landscape. She liked large families, hippie communes, painting and sketching, teaching at primary school, men on motorbikes, horse riding, camping, Scottish mountains, Welsh coastline, wildflowers, all kinds of animal, and cooking with home-grown herbs. She also liked dinghy sailing, but was unsure about small yachts out on big seas. Nor did she like choral music, TV, cruelty to animals, aggressive men, prisons, walls, fast travel, ready meals or champagne. She was a nature woman and seemed to live at an intuitive level.

"Look," I said suddenly. "The sun is out. Let's go hunting for puffins."

"First one to spot a puffin gets a wish', she replied zipping up a biker's jacket and tying back her hair. We walked down the steps to the tiny harbour where a score of small boats danced to their moorings, the wind thrumming in their rigging. We traversed the flagstones on one side and followed a narrow path along the rocks to a small lighthouse. The sea was driving past from the east, waves running six foot high. A few hundred yards further out, the surf was breaking on the Craig.

"That's where the puffins nest," I yelled above the wind pointing to the island.

"Let's go to the end," Kyla replied and, without looking back, set off for the far rocks.

I caught up with her at the point. Out there we were surrounded by sea. Gulls swooped below the crests as a score of white horses galloped towards the shore. A fat black and white eider drake held his position in the waves next to our rock. I took out my binoculars and scanned the water. Not finding any puffins, I shifted attention to the grassy slopes of the Craig. There were seagulls there standing on the rabbit lawn. I searched systematically amongst them hoping to catch sight of a puffin leaving its nesting burrow but the wind was buffeting the binoculars making it hard to be sure what was puffin and what was gull.

"Oh there you are; you clever wee muffin."

I looked at Kyla and then followed her gaze down to a sheltered rocky inlet at our feet just in time to catch the plop of a diving puffin.

"You can see it underwater," cried Kyla. Sure enough I caught the white blur as it darted down to the seabed some twelve feet below, transformed from a chubby clown into a sleek and fast predator. It hunted along the bottom taking advantage of the sheltered water, then darted back to the surface. We watched it fishing for a few minutes before it gave up and swam out into the waves to try its luck elsewhere.

"How do they keep one fish in the mouth and then catch another without letting go of the first?" Kyla asked. It was a good question, especially when you sometimes see puffins with six or more sand eels hanging from its bill.

"I'll show you," I smiled in anticipation. "What you have to do is put a finger in my mouth like this. Then put another finger close."

She put the index finger of her right hand between my teeth and then raised the index finger of her left hand to just in front of my mouth. I opened my mouth very quickly and snatched the second one.

"Oooh," she laughed. "That was fast."

As we walked back to the lighthouse, Kyla linked her arm in mine. She had made her wish but wouldn't tell me what it was. We bought some Italian ice cream from the van, and then all too soon she asked me to walk her back to the train station. She didn't stop talking but, as with the slowing melody of a caged bird, I sensed she was tiring. We found a train waiting at the platform. Before she boarded I asked if she was sure about going south.

"It will be good to get back to teaching." She frowned as if considering her next words. "I need to be on my own to work a few things out."

"Fair enough," I nodded.

"I enjoyed today. Can I call you?" The impish grin was back in place.

"Next time it's seals."

"I love seals."

As the train pulled away I smiled and shook my head. It had been lots of fun but I still didn't expect to see her again.

She'd found a small cottage in Pembrokeshire and started work in a primary school, covering for one of the teachers on maternity leave. She also helped run the school's nature club. Our phone conversations were warm and easy. I'd thought they were intimate. On a wild impulse, I decided to surprise her. I set off one Friday to drive four hundred miles to her cottage in my old VW estate. On the back seat was a cool bag with two good sized trout, wild caught, and lying in a bed of ice. Beside them was a shallow cardboard box with rosemary and parsley picked from my garden, cloves of garlic, sea salt, lemons, fresh spinach picked from my sister-in-law's garden and new potatoes. A bottle of Chablis lay in its own bed of ice. I knew not to take her by complete surprise. So I stopped at a service station halfway to ring. Far from being delighted, she'd turned cold as a stone.

I'd thought idly of carrying on anyway, wondering if she wouldn't feel differently about it when I arrived. But there was something in her voice that held me back. Behind the snarl was a cornered animal. It was as if she feared something. Probably I was just another man shoving his way into her private life, ready once he got there to start pushing her around. I'd got it all wrong. I mulled over the conversation for a few more minutes and then remembered the advert for a small yacht in Classic Boat that I'd circled in pencil. My disappointment seemed to vanish. The marina was only three or four hours away. I turned back onto the highway and looked for signposts that would take me east, aware of a sudden surge of excitement.

Frowning still at these memories, my heart warmed at the sight of *Molio* rocking gently alongside the pontoon. But I needed to sort that leaking deck. I climbed aboard, noticing the hand-smoothed time-worn coaming that surrounded the cockpit and enjoying the sensation of being on my own boat. Easing open the heavy teak hatch above the companionway, I climbed down the polished mahogany ladder to the cool well of the cabin where I put the kettle on for more coffee. My mobile was charging on a ledge above the chart table. I took it down and tracked back to the last text she'd sent.

I know you meant well. Can we talk about this?

No suggestion of an apology. I remembered throwing the phone down determined not to have anything more to do with her. Looking at the text now I could see it was a clear attempt to work things out. Perhaps I'd been a bit small in taking her rejection so heavily? I'd ignored a couple of calls. Then she'd stopped ringing. Maybe Rosie was right. It was time to forgive and forget. I wondered how she would feel about my ringing now after all this time. I tapped in the number.

After a couple of rings, Kyla picked up.

"Hello Kyla it's Martyn." There was silence at the other end. "You remember – the guy you turned down." I heard the sound of a door closing and then her voice again.

"I didn't turn you down."

"Oh yeah? Well I know some sea scouts who were happy about it."

There was another silence. "Happy about what?"

"I gave them the two wild trout."

"Just as well you didn't come down then."

"Why?" I asked eventually.

"I don't like trout. Too strong for me. If you want to cook me fish, it has to be sea bass." There was a note of laughter in her voice.

Even though I was heaving with suppressed laughter myself I wasn't going to let her off the hook that easily. "So was that a one-off then; turning me back?"

"Did it never cross your mind, my dear bearded man, to ask before setting off to see me?"

That was fair enough. It was something I could deal with. And she wasn't angry at my silence. She kind of wanted me to cook fish for supper, not that I was in any hurry to repeat that fiasco. Perhaps she was as sorry as I about the whole thing.

"So now I'm asking."

There was a pause, "What are you asking?"

"Will you sail from Ireland to Scotland with me?"

This time the pause extended into a silence, so I filled in. "I found my boat. She's a lovely wooden ketch. I've been working on her at the marina here in Cork Harbour for most of the summer. She'll sleep four, five if needs be, except she's full of spare sails and things at the moment. Still there's plenty of room."

"What's her name?" she asked.

"She's called *Molio*."

"Moll-lee-oh," she repeated the name slowly.

"She's pre-war. Built in Exmouth. You'll love her."

"What does Molio mean?" she asked.

"He was a monk, a hermit. He lived on the Holy Isle, the one next to Arran. That was around the time of St Columba, about 600 AD. It's a bit of a long story. I am thinking of going round the west of Ireland, then crossing the Irish Sea to the Mull of Kintyre and making landfall on the Holy Isle." Even as I said it, I realised it was way over the top. The prospect of a long sea passage might easily scare her off. But then I didn't really expect her to come at all.

"When are you leaving?" she asked sounding unsure.

"In two weeks' time."

There was another pause. "I don't need being swept off my feet Martyn. I just need steady and reliable."

I could feel the distance between us. "I'm sorry for not being in touch, Kyla. After what happened, well I thought you didn't want me in your life. Lots of guys must chase you. I know they do. It must be a nuisance. I didn't want to be just one more problem that needed to be got rid of. Maybe I was overly sensitive about it. But to be honest, I was hurt." I trailed off at that point. There wasn't much more I could say. She either liked me or she didn't. She either forgave me now, as I'd forgiven her, or she never would.

"It's not your fault," she said. "Sometimes with guys..." She was silent for a few seconds and I thought maybe she wouldn't go any further, but then she added in a quiet voice, "I feel trapped. I can't stop myself."

"When you get to know me better, if you get to know me better, I think you will find I can never be trusted."

"Very funny Martyn."

"Here and now, I would love to have you come with me on *Molio* for however long you can manage."

"What you need more than me is a lucky mascot," she said.

"I haven't just thought this up, you know." That was technically true, I'd been thinking about the trip for months. But whether *Molio* and I were truly prepared for it... well that was another matter. "There are plenty of sheltered harbours and we'd take it day by day, only travelling if the weather permitted. You'd be my mascot. Come for a couple of days. I could use another pair of hands."

I waited while she thought it over. Finally she said in a stronger voice, "I can come for a week but I shall demand extra sleeping time. It's been nonstop here."

I exhaled slowly. "They'll be plenty of time for sleeping. If you can take the helm while I'm picking up a mooring that would be great."

"No promises then. And Martyn..."

"Yes?"

"Thanks for ringing."

I replaced the mobile on a little ledge above the chart table. "Yes!" I yelled in delight. But even as my fist punched the air, I knew it was up to me to make this go right. There were some rolled-up Admiralty charts in a plastic bin bag above the port bunk. I pulled them down from the shelf and took out one showing the South Coast of Ireland. I laid it out on the saloon table and began to study the various anchorages along the coast and their accessibility according to the state of the tide and the wind direction. Not for the first time, I wondered if I had the necessary seamanship. When I'd learnt to sail there were no training schools or courses. You picked it up by crewing for others. Nowadays there are courses of all kinds. The Royal Yachting Association offers training in theory and hands-on sailing and friends who had taken navigation and seamanship rated it highly. They were full of expertise in weather systems, dead reckoning, collision regulations, safety drills and the latest chart plotter software.

I'd learnt sailing and cruising skills from my father. That had been a long time ago and I hadn't skippered a yacht for over twenty-five years. On the face of it, setting off for Scotland on my maiden voyage in *Molio* wasn't the greatest idea. But sailing was part of me now, almost instinctive. I'd had a long apprenticeship. Looking round the cabin at the gear being overhauled, I felt happy and content. I knew what I could and couldn't do, what was safe and unsafe. I was comfortable in a small boat out in a big sea. What's more, there was an even greater risk in not making the attempt. If I withdrew from this challenge, I was sure my life would contract. The passive side would get a firmer grip. That couldn't be tolerated. My decision was made but did I have the right to take Kyla out into the Atlantic on a seventy-year-old boat that was, in the words of the surveyor, in deplorable condition? I finished my coffee and drove into Cork to pick up some deck sealant. I spotted a pair of rubber kneepads and bought those too.

Over the next fortnight, whenever it was dry, I was on my knees sealing up the seams between planks. When it rained I went below and worked through other items on the list. It was tedious work but after a while I didn't seem to notice. I've always liked fixing things, and afterwards it gave me pleasure each time I used them. Finally I was ready to go.

A torrent of gingery curls in amongst the passengers arriving at Cork Airport was the first clue, and then I spied her impish face peeping out between the tresses like an otter peaking from its bracken-covered holt. The only thing missing was a big swishy tail. I strode forward to lift her high off her feet with a passionate hug.

"Put me down," she gasped. "You'll break my bones." As I let go, she straightened her outdoor jacket with a smile. "You can make yourself useful by carrying this." She handed me a light daypack.

"Is that all you have?" I asked, wondering about the heavy clothing needed for sailing off Ireland.

"I'm not staying long, Martyn."

"Come on," I called, undeterred. "I'll show you *Molio*."

At the marina, *Molio* was tied alongside the outer pontoon facing downstream ready to head down the main channel. Her foresail – a flying yankee – was furled on the outer forestay, and the covers had been removed from the main and mizzen sails. The shrouds were tensioned and the rigging screws secured with mousing, the deck was scrubbed and her gear stored below. A new Avon inflatable bobbed on a double painter astern and a red ensign fluttered from atop the mizzenmast. My plan was to take *Molio* westwards round the notorious Mizen Head and then head north along the exposed Atlantic coast. I had Admiralty charts and the Irish Cruising Club's Sailing Directions to help us find shelter from the gales. Rosie had washed the cushion covers to provide a more homely welcome and helped me stock up with tins and dried food. We'd put perishables in a coolbag with two frozen ice packs and I'd bought some South African Pinotage for the first anchorage we reached.

"Oh, she's beautiful," cried Kyla, quite taken aback for a second. "Mmm. I don't think she's a white boat. She should be green. Devon green. Isn't that where she comes from?"

"Maybe you're right," I agreed, stepping on board and taking her bag below.

She joined me in the cabin and looked around, touching the mahogany furnishing. "It's like my old Gypsy caravan." Taking down the oil lamp which was sitting in gimbals above the ship's bell, she removed the glass chimney to examine the wick, satisfied she put it back. "You'll need to rub these brasses." On the other side, the tarnished Sestrel clock ticked steadily next to the rusty barometer. *Molio* stirred gently. "Ooh, I can feel her moving already."

The sound of heavy feet on the pontoon announced a visitor. Neil's voice boomed out, "Ahoy there *Molio*." His head appeared at the top of the companionway ladder. "Will you be sitting there all day now?"

"I've been waiting to crack this open," I grinned, pulling a bottle of Laphroaig out of a locker.

"In the absence of a decent Irish whiskey, I suppose it'll do," said Neil.

"This," I said, pouring out 3 snorts, "will put hairs on your chest."

"Ooh eeh," said Kyla, "don't get plastered now."

"Remember, Martyn, the west coast is not to be trifled with. The sea can come in like rolling mountains. Even in summer. Sure Rosie and I are down there every year. I've seen it with my own eyes."

I could see the concern etched on his brow. "Don't go scaring the lassie now Neil. *Molio* is built for these waters and I'll be taking it slow."

I glanced at the clock. Twelve-thirty. The tide would be ebbing. It would take us out the harbour into the ocean, far from the protection of the marina and friends like Neil. Was *Molio* seaworthy enough for the Atlantic? Was I ready? I downed my glass. For better or for worse, it was time to go.

A turn of the key and the engine rumbled into life, settling down to a deep-throated growl. It was a 48 HP Lombardini marine diesel which supplied more power than *Molio* needed. As her former owner, Barry, had pointed out, "When you're motoring into a crowded marina, it can stop her dead in her tracks. With all that expensive hardware about, and not much rudder control, that can be mighty useful."

Neil cast off the warps and shouted, "Any trouble Martyn, and you come right back; that goes for you too Kyla. We've bags of room." I gunned the engine and *Molio* thrust her bows into the ebbing stream.

Chapter 3

Did We Mean To Go To Sea?

The tide drew us through the narrow entrance of Cork Harbour under the massive ramparts of Camden and Carlisle Forts and out into the vast expanse of Atlantic Ocean. Grey waves swollen in the long journey from South America rolled under us. *Molio* had stamped her beefy presence on the rows of factory-made boats at the marina, but out here on the untamed ocean she was no more than a toy. It was intimidating. I wondered again if we were ready for the west of Ireland with its wild rock strewn coastline. Kyla felt it too, not saying a word as I handed her the helm. Forward at the mast, the tan mainsail was soft to the touch from years of wear: it ran up the bronze track without a hitch. I looked up at the thin sail, patched all over like well-loved jeans. It wouldn't last much longer. The mizzen went up next with its matching tan patchwork, and then the number two jib with just a single patch. Finally I went back to the cockpit to let loose the yankee but no matter how much I tugged at the sheets it wouldn't unfurl. Going forward again I saw that several loops of line had come off the drum and were jammed at the bottom of the sail. The only way to free it off would be to get out along the bowsprit.

The sea had grown lumpier as we moved offshore. *Molio* lurched about as if a seahorse plagued by biting minnows, one minute rolling and the next plunging her bowsprit into steep waves in the effort to shake free. I decided to leave the yankee for the moment. Back in the cockpit, I asked Kyla to head WSW keeping about two miles offshore. Lacking the large foresail, we made poor progress. We pitched and plunged and soon Kyla's rosy cheeks took on a greenish tinge. I started the engine and, with its thrust added to the sails, we surged through the waves. It wouldn't be the last time that I was grateful for the powerful engine. A couple of hours later we reached Kinsale Harbour and motored round the protective promontory to anchor off James Fort next to *La Mouette*, a French yacht with classic lines. Down below there was a slight smell of diesel. I switched off the engine; the ignition light failed to come on. I frowned, another job to add to the list.

Knowing that Kyla would hate even the slightest tang of fuel I opened the fo'c'sle hatch to blow in fresh air and volunteered to cook supper. She sat in the sheltered cockpit viewing the boats coming and going in the beautiful estuary. Chopping carrots, green beans and sweet peppers into a wok, I began humming an old tune from bygone days.

> *Now, I've a song to sing boys*
> *Yo de Oh de Oh*
> *Here's a health to Primrose*
> *Yo de Oh de Oh*
> *Once aboard the Primrose*
> *Golly how the food goes*
> *One and all for Primrose*
> *Yo de Oh de Oh*

Kyla smiled down from the cockpit and joined in; substituting for *Golly how the food goes* whatever came to mind – *Lookout for the buffaloes*, *Skipper prone to overdose*, *Kyla jumps out of her clothes*...

She came down into the cabin and poured us both a tumbler of white wine, then turned to face me, her back against the companionway ladder and began softly to sing one of Robert Burns's most beautiful love songs 'Ae Fond Kiss' in a warm earthy voice that seemed to enfold us. As the last words ended, she turned away to break the spell and began washing the dishes.

I climbed up the little ladder to the cockpit for a last look round. There was just enough light to check my bearings using some trees and houses on the shore. I satisfied myself that we hadn't moved and then went up to the bow to make sure the anchor cable was sitting snugly on the stemhead roller. It rubbed occasionally against the smaller chain of the bobstay but the breeze was light and there was no sea at all in the sheltered harbour. It would be fine until morning.

Down below Kyla was already curled up in a sleeping bag on the starboard bunk. I turned down the oil lamp before blowing it out, kicked off my shoes and an outer layer of clothing and got into my sleeping bag on the port bunk which was wide enough for two. Mentally I shrugged. Teething problems were inevitable in life, as on boats. Overall it had been a good start.

During the night the wind began gusting, causing *Molio* to swing restlessly as she came under the alternating influence of wind and tide. In the small hours I climbed back on deck to look around again. Under the moonlight I could see we were holding our position. The French boat was turning in step with *Molio*; the lighter craft scudded about almost at random. Dark clouds were massing on the horizon. I went below for a few hours more sleep. By morning there was a full sou'westerly gale with rain lashing down. There was no point in going to sea under those conditions so I put the kettle on for tea and adjusted the position of sponges and pans to catch the drips. Two weeks of applying sealant had reduced the number of deck leaks considerably. I pulled on a heavy sweater, jeans and sea boots and sat down at the chart table to study the Sailing Directions one more time. The idea was to make our way westward in easy steps to Crookhaven. Then we could assess the boat's performance and the weather forecast before committing to Mizen Head and the exposed west coast. The sound of a singing kettle called me to attention and I prepared a strong brew. Kyla was still curled up in her bunk and dead to the world. I nudged her and put a steaming mug of Irish tea within arm's reach.

The frontal system passed during the morning and as rain gave way to shine, I went up to the cockpit to enjoy the view. Kyla was tempted out of her cocoon by my running commentary on harbour life. She took one look at the sunny bay and decided on a swim. I hung a boarding ladder over the side and went below to do battle with the ship's toilet. Rolling up my sleeves I removed one end of the discharge pump with an adjustable wrench. Baby Blake seemed to revel in this attention, gurgling with delight as I tried to extricate the plunger. In the end it had me beaten. I told it icily that we would make do with buckets. I made a mug of coffee and went back up to the cockpit. In the gusts a thousand wavelets sparkled with sunshine. Kyla was swimming about the boat enjoying the wind and sun, going hard to keep up with the current. "It's beautiful, come on in," she called. If selkies could have dancing legs instead of fish's tails I thought, then surely she was one. The tide was running fast across the wind, twisting *Molio* unpredictably, first one way then the other making me uneasy. "I've some things to do on board," I shouted back.

A line of bubbles approached and a scuba diver surfaced alongside, attracted no doubt by our mermaid. I asked him to check the anchor. Obligingly he dived below and I watched the bubbles as they tracked away from the boat. Meanwhile the mermaid pulled herself onto the rubber dinghy to sunbathe. A few minutes later the diver reappeared, holding on to the dinghy and ogling the selkie within. "How was it?" I yelled down.

He looked up reluctantly, "The yoke is dug in all right, but the sand is that soft – just shells."

"Thanks," I replied. Seeing my preoccupation, the diver took his leave, working his fins hard against the current. I went aft to service the outboard engine which was slung on the stern pushpit. Ten minutes later I heard Kyla shouting from the dinghy, "Martyn, quick! Something's wrong."

Looking up from the engine, I saw the French yacht closing in on us. For a moment I thought they were setting out to sea and not paying attention. Then with a leap of alarm I realised it was we who were moving. *Molio* was lying sideways to the wind and drifting westwards. Her anchor must have dislodged from the shell sand and was now being dragged across the seabed at three knots. Eleven tons of *Molio* would cause serious damage to whatever got in her way, especially if it were struck by her bowsprit, poised like a battering ram at the front end. I glanced west; there were plenty of moored boats in the way. I bounced below with the agility of a frightened gibbon and turned the ignition key on the engine. No click, no power, nothing. I leapt back to the cockpit. The skipper of *La Mouette* was on the deck shouting to someone below. I noticed his Antigua Classics t-shirt. The guy looked like a pro.

"No engine!" I yelled at him as we slid past within two feet. He dived below and reappeared with a coil of rope. The divide between us was opening rapidly. I ran to the bow, dodging between sheets and shrouds. The Frenchman saw my plan and hurled the rope. He was a fit, lean man. The rope landed on the galvanised pulpit jutting over the bowsprit. In a trice I had the end and flung it round the Samson Post in a figure of eight. The Frenchman had already fastened his end to a deck cleat. The line came taut. There was a creaking of strained rope and metal fittings. *Molio* slowed her reckless pace, paused and reluctantly swung to heel. I stared at a line of trees near James Fort to check our movement. They steadied and then held their relative position to one-another. The Frenchman's anchor was holding us both, but for how long?

"Should we call the coastguard?" shouted Kyla from the dinghy.

I looked around weighing up our options. I could try to sort the engine. I could rig a second anchor. Both would take time. How long would *La Mouette*'s anchor hold twenty tons of boat surging and jibbing in the swirling tide? Then I spotted a yellow buoy dancing in the waves off our port bow. "There's a mooring buoy about fifty metres over there," I called to Kyla. I ran to the bow and gesticulated to the Frenchman. He nodded, and immediately began pulling in an inflatable rib that was riding astern of his boat. He brought it alongside and jumped in, started the outboard engine with a button and powered over to the buoy. This guy was slick, I thought, slicker and more organised than me. Whilst he inspected the buoy I helped Kyla get back on board. A minute later the Frenchman pulled alongside *Molio*. He had that quizzical Gallic look, long nose, one eyebrow slightly raised, lines of debate on the forehead and of laughter round the mouth. Unlike me, he looked calm and in control. "Alors, I take a look. It has a thick mooring rope, about 3 cm diameter," he held up his finger and thumb so there could be no mistake in understanding. "It will hold you I think."

"Thanks, we'll go for it," I didn't try my French on him; it was just good enough to cause confusion. "Can you take a rope to the buoy?"

"But of course," his eyes sparkled with delight. "Marius is at your service."

I laughed. "Thanks Marius. My name is Martyn and the mermaid in the cockpit is Kyla."

He smiled in acknowledgement, "Mon dieu qu'elle est belle."

I nodded in agreement. Too beautiful I thought to myself. Not that she flaunted her looks; it was my growing enchantment that concerned me. After tying *Molio*'s three longest ropes together, I attached one end to the Samson post in the bow and passed the coils under the pulpit "Here Marius, I hope it's long enough."

He fastened the other end to a ring on the rib and made off back to the buoy. The line proved to be a few metres short. Marius put on power, and began to drag *Molio* slowly towards the buoy. *Molio* had other ideas; she seemed to have formed an attraction for *La Mouette* and began swinging towards her. Kyla jumped to the stern and put her feet over the side to push her off. A woman came up from below and looked as though she might try the same thing. "Take care," I shouted. "Let her hit." Kyla swung her feet back inboard just as the ramrod pushpit slammed into *Molio*'s rear quarter. There was a sickening crunch.

Marius shouted, "*Molio*! Vous êtes attaché!"

"Cast off!" I called to Kyla. She let go the rope to *La Mouette* and I heaved on the long line now attached to the mooring buoy. The crash seemed to have brought *Molio* to her senses; she slipped easily away. Hand over hand I pulled her towards the yellow buoy but halfway over it became heavy going. I was dragging both boat and anchor, and the anchor was now dug in properly. One of the three lines holding *Molio* to the buoy was old and frayed; it wouldn't take much more of this. Marius saw the problem and came out again on the rib. Happily I'd attached a small fender to the anchor to act as a marker buoy. Marius swung round behind *Molio* grabbed the fender and brought it along-side. I hauled in, lifting the anchor with a cup of shell-sand onto the deck. With Kyla's help, it was now an easy matter to pull up to the buoy and make fast.

Marius turned back towards *La Mouette*. I called to him, "Fetch your crew and come aboard."

He waved. Soon he was on his way back with his sun-kissed partner, Chloé. As they arrived Kyla disappeared below, emerging a few seconds later with a bottle of Pinotage and four glasses. We sat on the coach roof in the evening sun. I toasted the French, all good sea folk and, most of all, their marvellous rescue. They smiled self-consciously. Kyla laughed and chatted away in French with Chloé. *Molio* swung easily on her mooring as if nothing had happened.

The soft breathing of Kyla and quiet lapping of waters calmed my dreams that night. I awoke feeling fresh and clambered out of my bunk to switch on the shortwave radio. Looking out the porthole, I noticed that *La Mouette* had already sailed; they would be homeward bound now, taking advantage of the favourable wind. I pulled on my jeans and sea boots, made tea and waited for the 05:36 shipping forecast. It didn't come. That was annoying but the day looked fine and the engine was operational again. The previous evening I'd traced the fault to an electrical plug that had become dislodged from a junction box at the back of the engine. Kyla had hung upside down through the forward hatch in the cockpit floor to reconnect it. Not to be outdone, I'd climbed out on the bowsprit and untangled the yankee furling line.

It felt like a toast and coffee morning so I lit the gas grill. Making toast on *Molio* required eagle-eyed attention as the bread went from untoasted to burnt crisp within seconds. Maybe this was because the pipe burner was hanging down at the back. But I was convinced the cooker waited until I turned away before performing its trick. I scraped the offending pieces. Kyla got up for some coffee choosing a bowl of leftover vegetables in preference to burnt toast. We tidied up and were underway by eight o'clock.

Clearing the land we found ourselves heading straight into the wind which had veered to SSW and strengthened. Kyla put on a black hoodie and found some waterproof trousers in the big duffle bag of spare clothes. We continued to motor until we had a good offing and then I went up on deck to hoist the main and mizzen, returning to the cockpit to unfurl the yankee and switch off the engine. Sailing as close to the wind as she would go, we made a long tack SSE to clear the Old Head of Kinsale. The sea began to build up, throwing *Molio* back. She lacked the punch I'd expected. The wind rose and the weather helm became heavier. I dropped the mizzen which eased the steering. Kyla pointed to another yacht which had turned back. We fought past the Old Head of Kinsale kicking up heaps of spray which was picked up by the wind and hurled with great accuracy into the cockpit. Holding the same tack we clawed our way across to the next headland, Seven Heads. The gusts were increasing now and I was concerned about our slow progress. We had made only seven and a half nautical miles in two hours of sailing and had eighteen more to the next harbour, with another ten to be added for tacks out from the land. The first tack would have to be taken soon as we were now closing with Seven Heads. I checked my watch and called to Kyla who was sitting in the cockpit looking white, "Could you fetch the radio for the shipping forecast?" She went below and brought it up, tuning the dial to 198 kHz long wave. Across the noise of the wind and boat came a clear message: *"There are warnings of gales in sea areas Sole, Fastnet, Shannon…"* Kyla was watching my expression. I kept it deadpan. "That's us." I thought rapidly. At *Molio*'s current speed we wouldn't reach Glendore Harbour before nightfall. As a boat and crew, I knew we weren't ready to ride out a gale at night along an exposed shore. The other possible sanctuary was Courtmacsheery Harbour just to our north but in these conditions there would be breaking water across the shallow entrance bar. It wasn't on. There was only one thing for it. "We are going to have to turn and run back to Kinsale." Kyla nodded that she understood.

As we came under the cliffs, the waves rose even higher causing *Molio* to thump down into the troughs and pitch green water over her decks. I was trying to get our exact position on the chart but couldn't seem to see properly. I took off my reading glasses and wiped them against my shirt collar only to find that one of the lenses had vanished. I threw them down in disgust. "Ready about," I called. Kyla stood at the yankee sheets. I pushed the helm hard over. *Molio* inched up into the wind, stalled with sails flapping furiously, and was knocked off the turn by a large wave. The thought crossed my mind, how the hell am I going to reach St Kilda if she won't even go about? The cliffs were now far too close. "Stand by to gybe," I yelled, loosening the running backstay on the lee side and bringing the helm hard over to port. Slowly *Molio* came further off the wind, picking up speed like a train as her sails bent in the wind. We were now running parallel along the shore. I looked out for rocks as I rammed down the opposite backstay lever and pulled in the mainsheet in anticipation of the gybe. A wave took her. "Gybo!" I yelled; the boom zipped overhead and crashed into the new tack. A wave caught us at the wrong moment and *Molio* rolled heavily to the side; there was a sound of pots and pans crashing down below. I spilled out the mainsheet and pulled back on the rudder to stop her turn, we straightened. "Leave the yankee," I called as we surged downwind with the waves running under us, fore and mainsail now goose-winged on either side, and a foaming trail in our wake. At last we were sailing.

The miles fell behind at a pace as we sped towards the Old Head of Kinsale. With the tide now running at maximum speed I could see an angry line of white water marking the notorious tidal race. It started under the outer headland of the peninsula and stretched for a mile or more to the south into the ocean. We gybed the yankee and pointed further out to sea to avoid the worst of it. As the gusts picked up further in power, *Molio* developed huge weather helm which I had difficulty holding even with feet braced and two hands on the helm. With bigger seas off the point I knew it would be hard to stop her broaching. The yankee was curved like a melon with the strain. It was past time to shorten sail. I asked Kyla to clip a lifeline onto the ring of her lifejacket which doubled as a safety harness and clipped the other end onto the guard wire running along the side of the boat before handing over the helm. For a slightly-built woman she was immensely strong, no doubt thanks to her yoga exercises. I showed her our heading and watched her for a minute. Those lessons in the dinghies had given her the basics. I decided she could hold *Molio* for the extra few minutes needed. I went forward to drop the main. The sail came down with a bit of pulling and I trussed it up in rough fashion along the boom, and then clawed my way back to the helm. *Molio* was making five knots on the foresail alone as we entered the outer end of the race. With breaking water on both sides, she began to roll alarmingly. I took the helm again and tried to hold her steady. There were crashes from below as more cups and dishes fell out of cupboards. I called to Kyla to slide the main hatch shut and close the companionway doors. If we took a large wave in the cockpit I didn't want it flooding below.

She got to the companionway and braced herself at the entrance against a steep roll. Clinging on to the coachroof, she looked below to assess the damage. "Martyn," she screamed, "it's full of water."

"Take the helm," I ordered and edged to one side so she could squeeze past me into position. Even as I contemplated imminent sinking, it felt wonderful to have Kyla by my side. I lunged forward to look below. The water was above the floorboards, sloshing about between the bunks from the foot of the companionway ladder to the fo'c'sle. Clothes, food, charts and anything that could move was swilling about with it. "Christ!" I shouted. "Where's the bloody water coming from?" *Molio* rolled heavily to starboard and the entire shelf load of cassettes above the port bunk broke free and fell into the water. With an effort I calmed myself and began to think rationally. If water had been entering from the time we left the shelter of Kinsale then the leak, whilst serious, wasn't critical. I went back to relieve Kyla at the helm. "It's not as bad as it looks," I reassured her, "but it needs sorting." It was the best I could come up with. She gave me a funny look. Things weren't working out quite as I'd hoped. There was no time to dwell on that either.

After a few more rolls we cleared the tidal race and were able to turn in towards Kinsale Harbour, easing the yankee sheet as we did. The gusts were now very strong with spray obscuring visibility and a big rolling sea coming up behind. I tried to catch the steepest waves exactly stern on. It was as well we were entering a harbour we knew. Rounding a point in the narrows the waves subsided and I was able to go below to start the engine. An experienced seafarer might sail in under such conditions without the engine, rounding up into the wind to pick up their mooring. One day perhaps, I thought, but right now we needed a mooring not heroics. I hoped the one we'd left that morning was still unoccupied but that couldn't be guaranteed. I twisted the key. Nothing. I scrambled up to the cockpit. "Kyla, can you to do that trick again with the wire connector?"

A look of protest crossed her face. "When will you fix it?" she snapped, then opening the cockpit hatch she leant backwards as if doing a backflip and lowered herself in, long curls of autumn gold disappearing into the oily chamber followed by head and shoulders. A few seconds later she reappeared with a smudge of oil on one cheek. "That's it," she said looking cross and pleased all at once.

I handed back the helm and tried the engine ignition again. This time it roared into life. I looked up and smiled. "Thanks, that was well done." I got a half smile in return. We came round the head of James Fort peninsula still travelling fast under one sail. Kyla spotted our yellow mooring buoy and brought *Molio* downwind of it before pointing her up into the wind and proceeding slowly on the engine. I managed a few turns on the yankee furling gear before we were on to the buoy. Kyla slipped the engine gearbox into neutral and I ran to the bow avoiding the flapping sail and lent out over the side. She had judged it well. We slowed almost to a standstill. I threaded a light line through the metal ring before the wind could blow us back from the buoy, fastening both ends to the Samson post. "That's us," I yelled over my shoulder. "Keep the engine on, she'll need heavier rope."

I found what I was looking for in the stern locker and went back to the bow hoping the light line wouldn't break in a gust. As I leant over the side for the second time, I felt *Molio* being bumped by another boat. I focused on my task: pulling up on the buoy with the light line, then leaning out as far as I could to pass the heavy line through the ring whilst trying not to lose my balance and fall in. After a couple of attempts I succeeded and wormed my way back to the deck.

A voice behind me said: "We intend to search your vessel." I looked up into the short muzzle of a submachine gun. The man holding it wore a black uniform, his face hidden behind the visor of a safety helmet. "Do you have any objection?" I was speechless with astonishment. A large rib with three other men clad in the same uniform was alongside and a fifth was in the cockpit talking to Kyla. Behind them a grey patrol vessel stood off menacingly. It had the word CUSTAIM beneath the bridge. I looked back at the guy with the gun. He certainly wasn't there to lend a hand.

"The first thing I am going to do is secure my boat," I replied taking the mooring rope past the yankee sheets still thrashing about above my head.

The guy from the cockpit came over as I tied off at the Samson post. "Having problems?" he asked the first man as if I had been a street kid trying it on.

Satisfied, I stood up. "Go on then, if you must. But you'll see we've had a rough passage." I followed them back to the cockpit.

The first one took out a large torch and went down the companionway ladder. The beam illuminated the chaos below. Food and clothing sloshed about in the water along with coils of audiotape and plastic cassette cases. The water level was now halfway up the sides of the bunks. "Jaysus! There's a fierce mess," he swore. He began rummaging about, opening all the lockers that hadn't opened in the storm and throwing their contents onto the bunks. Meanwhile the second guy wanted to know about the boat and my occupation. As I struggled to furl the yankee, I answered him as best I could. "We've come from Cork. I'm sailing her to Scotland. I live outside Edinburgh." The furling system was far too stiff. I heaved again hard so that the line cut into my hand. I was pretty close to exhaustion. I steeled myself to remain polite. "No I haven't been in the Canary Islands. This boat hasn't moved from Crosshaven in five years." Inch by inch it came in until finally the flapping sail was contained in a tight spiral around the jibstay. "No I haven't been in the Caribbean. No I don't have any contraband on board. Why not ring the marina. I can give you the number." I gave the drum an extra couple of turns so that the sheets formed a protective loop round the furled sail and then secured the coiled line to a stanchion. As I did this my face was only feet from the three black figures sitting in the rib. None of them offered a hand. Instead they stared back at me, guns cradled. One was talking rapidly into a handheld radio. The guy who had gone below climbed back into the cockpit. "Okay, that's us finished."

"What are you looking for?" I asked, curious to see if they would take me into their confidence.

"Just a routine check." And with that terse reply, he climbed into the rib and they sped back to the ship leaving behind only black boot marks on *Molio*'s silver grey deck and marks from their black rib on her white topsides.

"What do you think they wanted?" asked Kyla who seemed not the least bit fazed. I reminded myself that her father had been in the police; she was used to rough stuff.

"Maybe they just want to intimidate yachtsmen," I remarked coldly, concealing how shaken I'd been by their intrusion, more so even than by the problems at sea.

"You'd prefer criminals to just sail in here and offload stuff whenever they feel like it?"

I might have guessed she would leap to their defence. "They're doing a job but there has to be a better way," I muttered. Seeing the strain in her eyes, I suddenly realised how tired we both were. "Would you like some tea? We can clear up the mess afterwards."

Kyla smiled, "Yes, and put a shot of whisky in mine."

I put the kettle on using the one gas ring that worked and came up to sit on the bridge deck. This raised section at the front of the cockpit had become our favourite place on *Molio*. Fred Shepherd would have designed it to prevent waves that broke into the cockpit from flooding down the companionway into the cabin but its weathered teak surface was proving ideal for laying our charts, setting out drinks and food, or simply for lounging on, as now, sheltered from the wind by the cabin and overarching sprayhood. I stuffed a cushion behind my back, one of the few dry ones on board. "Would you like to hear a story?

She came over and sat beside me, snuggling close so that her golden red curls flickered in my face.

"The last time I rubbed shoulders with a navy frigate," I began, "I was just ten years old. My parents, three boys and our spaniel were on board *Primrose* for the summer holidays. We had come north from the Clyde through the Crinan Canal and reached the sheltered anchorage at Dunstaffnage Castle just to the north of Oban. Hauling up the anchor next morning, we motored westwards towards Lismore in a flat calm enjoying the hot August sunshine. The tiny Brooks engine took us along at a sedate two knots. Jerseys came off first, then shirts, until finally we were all in bathing trunks. As we approached the passage between the south end of Lismore and Lady Rock a light breeze sprang up. With the tide now turning in our favour we switched off the engine, hoisted the main and jib and sailed towards the Sound of Mull. On nearing the Grey Isles my father spotted a ship in the distance. Looking through the binoculars he noticed first the yellow funnel, then the sun glinting on one, two and, yes, three masts and astern of her he spotted two grey vessels. It was the *Britannia* with a naval escort. Instantly there was tremendous excitement on board. "Which way is she going?", "Are you sure?" Soon we could all see that the ships were coming closer. My mother's first thought was to change her clothes and she disappeared below. My father's first thought was to check that the RNSA burgee was flying free at the top of the mast and the blue ensign was ready for lowering from the peak of the gaff-rigged mainsail. As an ex-naval officer he intended to dip the flag in salute. The only problem was that the ensign halyard was jammed behind the topping lift. He brought *Primrose* into the wind, lowered the gaff, sorted it out, raised the sail and we were off again ready now for a smooth dip. My mother came back up in a dress with the wind-up cine camera and checked it was ready for use. My father told her to shoot only when she could see the whites of Prince Philip's eyes. My oldest brother, Greer, took the tiller and steered as close to the Grey Isles as he dared. The Royal Yacht came nearer and nearer until we could see all her flags: the Union Jack flew from a staff at the bow; the Lord High Admiral's flag with its gold anchor was at the foremast; the Royal Standard with heraldic lions of Scotland and England and a Gaelic harp was at the mainmast; the union flag was again at the mizzenmast; and a large white ensign flew from a staff at the stern. Robin, my next oldest brother, and I found a good spot by the shrouds. We gazed at the grand boats. I wondered what would happen next."

"Were you still in your swimming trunks?" asked Kyla.

"We boys were. Dad put on a shirt and trousers. In fact he even made some tea. For reassurance mostly I think – a bit like having a drink in your hand at a party. Talking of which I'll just make our own." I disappeared below and re-emerged with two mugs. "As we reached the Grey Isles, the Royal Yacht came past. She had slowed right down and couldn't have been more than a couple of hundred yards away. My father lowered the ensign slowly two-thirds of the way to the deck. Down came *Britannia*'s white ensign in reply. It stayed down for an extraordinarily long time. Dad got the three of us boys to line up and give a salute. I scanned every bit of deck for the queen but if the family were watching they must have been looking through a window. I couldn't see them. Eventually their ensign began to rise, slowly and majestically. Up to the peak went *Primrose*'s ensign in response. *Britannia* moved on. A fleet sweeper followed and then some distance behind it a frigate; she also dipped her ensign. Off Lismore, the Frigate disappeared towards Loch Linnhe but *Britannia* and the minesweeper turned in towards Duart Castle."

Kyla snuggled in closer, "That was a nice story," she said.

I nodded thinking back to that day again and remembering my awe. "Those huge warships and a beautiful Royal Yacht carrying the queen and her family, as if from a fairy tale, slowing down to a snail's pace and lowering their flag to us. And what were we? A thirty-foot wooden boat bobbing about on the waves with a family on board in their swimming trunks!"

"Are we living in a fairy tale too?" asked Kyla looking at me with a half-smile. "Will it have a happy ending?"

"That depends on us," I replied with a laugh. "I hope so." I shifted into a more comfortable position.

"Carry on with your story," she commanded.

"There's not much more to tell I'm afraid. We sailed on, heading up the Sound of Mull. The last thing we saw through the binoculars was a white companion ladder being lowered from *Britannia*'s starboard quarter. In the evening we reached Loch Sunart but that is another tale."

I'd almost forgotten why I'd started on those boyhood musings, but then it came back. It was about respect. I tried to explain to Kyla what it meant to have so much respect in a country. How even then – more than ten years after the end of the Second World War – there was immense gratitude for those who had served in the forces and for the men and women from every walk of life who had played a role in seeing us through the great ordeal. They were held in high esteem. That kind of respect may seem out of place today, perhaps a little too unctuous. But it arose naturally enough amongst those who had been through a hard time together.

At the heart of our society today is money. It has a different dynamic. We enjoy it. We want it. We envy those who have it. But we don't respect the wealthy. We don't respect the bank executives or the corporate bosses. We may fear them or admire them but they will have to do more than make money if they want to earn our respect. Our society is running short of respect. And what we experienced today from that customs frigate was barely concealed hostility.

Kyla picked herself up off my lap bristling, "Those guys had a job to do. For all they knew we had weapons."

"What, two people on an old sailing boat?"

"Sure, it happens. We could be carrying a load of drugs."

I knew Kyla was just supporting those on the frontline doing a tough job. She didn't believe in laws that criminalised youngsters for experimenting with drugs.

"It's true, but does that excuse their behaviour? Don't you think there's a better way – something other than cracking down hard with the full arsenal of state resources – satellite surveillance, naval support and so on? That's what we got caught up in. Their aims may be okay, but they use excessive force without any cause for suspicion and without respect for us as seafarers. It's a blunt weapon which treats us all as just numbers. If left unchecked that way leads to a police state."

"You are making it too black and white," said Kyla.

"Do you know that the UK Border Agency intends to impose e-Border regulations on us boaters? Every time we make a passage outside of territorial waters we will have to fill in a form 24 hours before departure with passenger and crew information."

"It might reduce human trafficking. Is that so bad?"

"It won't put off illegal traffickers. What it does do is make it harder for sailors to grab a safe weather window to cross the Channel, or to seize an unexpected chance to sail across in convoy, or just to change their mind because after all they are on holiday. What about the freedom of the seas? All gone. It's like putting one of Orwell's telescreens into each boat."

Kyla looked glum and I realised I was ranting. "Sorry, this stuff has gotten to me somehow."

"You said there was another way? I want to hear the other way."

"The other way is for government to take communities into their confidence, win their trust, and work with them. If it is some kind of illegal use of leisure craft, trafficking or whatever, then talk to the boating community – yacht clubs, motor boat clubs, canoe and kayak clubs, fishermen, ferry operators and so on. Hold open discussions in which the problem can be viewed honestly and from all sides. If it is a real problem that real people agree with, then you will win their support. They know the boats using each bit of the coastline better than anyone. They will recognise a stranger and any odd comings and goings before anyone else. They can tip off the authorities to dodgy behaviour. But they'll do so only if they trust the authorities. So the second way is about authorities respecting the community, working with local people, and reserving the iron fist for real criminals. Then when we see a border patrol vessel going past, we will want to salute it not shake a fist."

"I'm too tired to think about it," said Kyla.

I opened the hatch under the starboard seat and found the handle for the whale pump and put it into the slot on deck.

"I'll do it," she said taking it from my hand and sitting down one foot on each side of the pump. She worked it vigorously until a steady stream of bilge water began flowing over the side. I went below and waded forward to the fo'c'sle to open the hatch and bring in some fresh air. I found a bucket and began working my way aft, filling it with broken cassettes, spoilt food, magazines, paperbacks and anything else that could be chucked. Back at the galley I filled a bin bag with the rubbish. Then I fished about underwater for cutlery and crockery and rinsed each piece under the tap before laying it on a dry towel. The water level began to drop and pretty soon Kyla had the level below the floorboards. I went up to relieve her.

"Where did *La Mouette* go?" she asked, refusing my offer of help.

"They were heading back home. It's downwind all the way; I bet they had a brilliant sail." I went back below to continue cleaning up.

There was a gurgling sound from under the floorboards as the pump sucked dry. I climbed up to the cockpit again. "Well done; that was a great effort."

"How's it looking below?" she asked, handing me the lever.

"Not too bad. There are a few clothes to dry off. Sleeping bags are okay."

"Have you got any clothes pegs?" she asked.

The wind dropped towards evening and the sun came out. We took beers onto the foredeck to enjoy the last of the day. Kyla had changed into a tight pale sweater. Her hair was tied back and round her throat she wore a teal bandanna that matched her eyes. "What will you do now?" she asked broaching the subject we had been avoiding.

"*Molio* has to come out the water so I can investigate this leak." I patted the teak hatch surprising myself at the amount of affection I felt for the old boat. I so hoped there wasn't some hidden flaw that the surveyor had missed. "It means sailing back to Crosshaven."

"The Custom guys said there would be gales for the next 3 days. I better get a bus."

Next morning I was up even earlier having discovered that the shipping forecast was now broadcast at 05:20. The depression causing the gale was heading northeast and the wind was expected to moderate during the day. So much for the three days of gales. I dipped the bilges using a stick that I'd marked off in inches. *Molio* had taken about two inches aboard in the previous twelve hours. That was much better. I turned my attention to the engine. Kyla had been right to give me a look. We couldn't afford to lose our backup power at these critical moments. I examined the electrical connection. The wires ended up in a large rectangular plug that was pushed up from below into a plastic housing on the engine. The plastic tabs that should have held the plug in place were worn.

I found some soft rigging wire and set to work making a cat's cradle to fit round the plug, threading and tying lengths of wire. I netted the electrical plug in the cradle and secured it firmly in place. It would be considered a bodge at home but out at sea this kind of repair is part of the cruising man's craft. You learn to work with whatever tools and materials are on board. It even has its own name, 'jury-rigging'. Originally it applied to the workaround for a broken mast in which the crew of a stranded vessel rigged a jury-mast to get them home. Possibly the name derives from *joury mast* or 'mast for the day'. Now it applies to any temporary fix at sea. Out of all the different sorts of repair, ranging from concours restoration to the can't-be-arsed bodge, the jury-rig is to me the most satisfying; it brings together craftsmanship and seamanship in a single joyful whole that gets you and your crew out of trouble.

As I worked, Kyla came up on deck to inflate the Avon dinghy. She set up the foot pump and began to inflate the dinghy while looking about the bay. She was quiet and looked more rested. I took over after a while so she could pack up her things. About eight o'clock I rang Neil on my mobile to update him on the situation. He didn't hesitate. "If you can hang on 'til Wednesday, Martyn, I'll catch the bus to Kinsale and sail back to Crosshaven with you."

With the dinghy fully inflated, I pushed it over the side and secured it to a cleat. Then I went below and sat down on the bunk opposite Kyla. "The wind has moderated to force 5 or 6," I began, watching for her reaction. Not getting any, I continued, "It will be sunny and perfect conditions for running down the coast to Cork." It's only twenty miles; we would be there by afternoon.

Kyla frowned. "She might sink. Have you thought about that?"

"No she won't." I had more confidence in *Molio* than I could rightly explain. "She's sound as a bell; the survey confirmed that. Okay, she has a leak. I expect there's a seam needs caulking but there's no way she's going to sink."

Kyla was still frowning. "Huh, I hope so."

"Really, Kyla. The only reason we even noticed the water was because I disconnected the electric bilge pump yesterday; the reason I did that was because I wanted to assess how much she leaks. This is just what you'd expect from an old wooden boat."

"All right, sail us then but I want to be in Crosshaven by six. I've a plane to catch." She must have seen my disappointment for her face hardened. "Can't you see how exhausted I am? All I want is a quiet life where nothing happens. I've made all the wrong decisions and now look what a mess I'm in."

"We'll be there." I promised.

I started to put things away. As I worked I wondered again what was up with Kyla. A couple of days afloat shouldn't have knocked her out like that, even if they had been on the rough side. I couldn't see how her past decisions were to blame. The ones she'd told me about had been well thought out. In any case, I'd said I would get her to Cork on time. I would deliver on my promise and that would have to do for now. I jammed the cupboard doors tight shut with bits of folded paper and started the engine. With the decision made Kyla seemed happier. She went up to the bow to drop the mooring and then asked if she could take the helm as we motored out of the harbour. A fierce squall held us back at the entrance where we bucked up and down for a few minutes before winning free. After passing the Cardinal buoy off Bulman rock she brought *Molio* round to head eastwards, beginning our run down to Cork. I unfurled the yankee and switched off the engine. It hadn't faltered once.

With just the foresail set, *Molio* slipped along quietly at four knots buoyed up by the big Atlantic swell running on her quarter. Kyla gave me the helm and as the sun rose in the sky I began to relax. We coasted along the rugged cliffs with flights of kittiwakes, shearwaters and other seabirds for company. After a while I began to get a feel for steering *Molio* in a following sea. She was a heavy boat with a low centre of gravity which gave her stability. Fred Shepherd had crafted a fine bow which lent speed when cutting through the sea, and a long counter which added lift when large waves were coming from behind. The combination provided stability, lift and speed but at the price of sway and momentum. When a wave overtook her, *Molio*'s bow tended to sway off course. The trick was to catch the swing early but with a light touch. It felt good to work this out and I began to enjoy myself. As the morning turned to afternoon and the sun grew warmer, I could see Kyla relaxing too. She put a cushion behind her back, stretched her feet out, and lounged on the bridge deck in her sunglasses. Eventually she fell asleep. I put a spare tea towel over her face to protect it from the sun. Nearing Cork Harbour I gybed the yankee and sailed into the narrows. Once through I turned to port and furled in the sail, then motored past Crosshaven to the marina, choosing a visitor berth on the outer pontoon. Checking the ship's clock I saw it was half past five.

I nudged Kyla. "There's just time for tea before your taxi arrives."

Chapter 4

Fatal Flaw

Next morning I walked over to the boatyard owned by Packie O'Loughlin. These days he specialised in repairing and outfitting fibre-glass boats but he'd built his reputation in a bygone era constructing wooden yachts. He promised to help with the leak and we arranged to have *Molio* lifted out the following Tuesday. I walked back to *Molio* and stripped off my shirt. The heat wave had returned. I sat down at the chart table with a coffee and thought about the day's work. I wanted to fill the next few days with projects in preparation for the voyage home. A good place to start would be with the self-furling gear for the yankee. I went up to the bow and rigged a new pulley block that would reduce friction in the furling line. I also tightened the bobstay which tensioned the jibstay. It seemed to help. Next on the list was the kedge. I brought the Breton anchor on deck and secured it to a stanchion with a length of strong cord, making sure it would be ready for rapid deployment in the case of a dragging anchor, or, and I laughed coldly at the thought, for repelling unwanted boarders. I was still angry at the previous day's encounter with customs officials.

The world of leisure boating was not immune, it appeared, to the Big Brother kind of society that George Orwell imagined in 1947 and set in the future of 1984. As it happens, our capacity to monitor indi-viduals with electronic surveillance systems today, using, for example, cameras so small they may soon be hidden in a contact lens, goes well beyond what could be conceived back then. Technically, Big Brother has arrived. Orwell had imagined an all-powerful 'thought police' in

Oceania who arrested those guilty of 'thought crimes'. Today's battle for the mind is more subtle, relying on regular use of psychologists by commerce, and government for that matter, for softening society to its message. Even more subtle changes in society may be taking place as an unintended consequence of digital technology. Coded or tick-box thinking is proliferating because it fits with automated analysis. Forms, multiple choice questions, telephone menu options, frameworks for reporting are all substitutes for real thinking and communication. Online examples are everywhere – at school, at home and in the office. Minds that evolved to create 'natural' free-flowing textures of thought are being entrained, bit by bit, into the rigid formats of machine intelligence, or so I fear.

There are yet other kinds of control proliferating, such as a growing dependency on instruments as substitutes for our senses. Smart instruments can of course be an immense help, but on a small boat, nothing can substitute for the full sensory experience of being on watch in a busy shipping channel. The watch keeper relies on his or her senses to spot other vessels and estimate their course and speed, to listen for breakers or a foghorn, to look out for objects in the water and to keep an eye on weather conditions. He or she is reliant on their own judgment and ready to jump into action if required. Like most other folk I make use of technology all the time and so long as it is designed to help me, that's pretty much okay. It can even be lifesaving. An alarm on a GPS receiver alerts the skipper of a yacht to a dragging anchor. Knowing they are protected, the skipper and crew sleep more easily and are alert the next day. If fog descends, the same system will guide the boat safely home. Technology becomes a problem when we become overly reliant on it, even more of a problem if it is forced on us for the benefit of someone else. If it is introduced to enhance profit, acquire authority, manage 'troublemakers' or just to increase efficiency savings, it often impinges on personal freedom.

With the Breton anchor secure, I moved on to the next item on my list. As I worked, my mood gradually lifted. It hadn't been a brilliant start but then again it hadn't been a disaster. In the evening an angling boat drew close and tied up at the same pontoon. They'd had a good day's fishing and one of the lads brought over a big mackerel, much to my delight. I gutted it and cut a series of diagonal slices down the sides, rubbing in some pepper and garlic, and fried it for supper. A heron alighted on a small motor skiff moored alongside and eyed me up without success. On impulse I rang Cori. We were old friends who had worked at the same conservation office in Cambridge and got to know each other in the local pub. She'd dragged me along to clubs for crazy dancing and I'd dragged her along to folk concerts for 'real music'. Something might have happened but she chose an Australian. Tom was a steady, warm-hearted guy, happy in a nine-to-five job, the kind of man who wouldn't take risks. He'd found jobs for both of them in Australia and we'd lost touch, sort of drifted apart through distance and immersion in our own lives. And then she'd sent a Christmas card to say they were back and living in Scotland. She'd even given me a mobile number.

"It's Martyn here."

"So you are alive. What you doing man?" It was good to hear that voice again. It reminded me of pubs and clubs and almond brown eyes.

"I'm fixing up an old boat in Ireland actually."

"You're always up to something."

"Well what are you doing in Scotland?"

"Oh, I'm working with Government... in Stirling." She didn't sound as if she wanted to talk about it.

"That sounds good. No?" I asked.

"How's your romantic life Martyn?" I laughed. This was vintage Cori; always direct, whether above the belt or below it.

"I just found a new woman and then she left me." I told her a little about Kyla and her sudden departure. "I don't understand her, Cori, and I don't even know if I want to bother."

She listened without interruption. "Well what do you *think* you should do?"

"Maybe I shouldn't do anything."

"Come on. What kind of relationship is it? I can't tell you anything if you don't open up."

I told her a bit about the highs and lows, and the confusion.

"Leave her be Martyn. Look, I've seen a fair bit of life in my time and it can be confusing. Give her space." There was a pause. I looked out the porthole at the other boats. It sounded like good advice. "She knows how you feel, right?" Cori asked without expecting an answer. "So leave her to sort things out. Get on with your own life. What women really like is a man who knows what he wants."

"Hell, it's grand to hear your voice, Cori."

"I can't get away just now or I'd give you a hand, but come here any time you want. You can use the caravan. Tom won't mind."

It seemed to work. After speaking with Cori, I felt much lighter and I got back into *Molio*'s restoration with renewed energy. The first thing I did was to write a new list. I placed the 'heads' at the top on the general principal that it is worth getting unpleasant jobs out the way. Next morning, Baby Blake eyed me with some trepidation as I approached with an even larger adjustable wrench. I stripped down the extractor pump and took the seized plunger rod and discharge cylinder over to a lorry mechanic who freed it off with the aid of a welding torch and large clamp. By afternoon, the heads were operational.

My next job was to install a heavy duty switch for the engine heater plug so that I would no longer have to jam a naked wire into the battery terminal to start her up from cold. Another job was to solder a connection between the masthead aerial and VHF radio. That gave me access to local weather forecasts and meant I could call the coastguard in an emergency. As I finished one job it would be replaced by three others on the list. I replaced a seized pulley in the running rigging, cleared a blocked pipe leading from the self-draining cockpit, fitted stainless steel hooks to hold the cupboard doors shut, and added more sealant to the deck seams. When a rain shower came the next afternoon I noticed that the port side of the cabin was now dry and there were only a couple of drips above the starboard bunk. It felt like progress. Just when I was thinking of taking a day off, the Baby Blake backed up again. It was as if someone had stuck a cork in the outlet pipe. I grabbed my things and went to stay the night with Neil and Rosie.

In the morning, suitably fortified by a giant bowl of porridge, I felt ready for another round with Baby Blake. With some difficulty I removed the discharge hose. Sure enough it was completely blocked – not by a cork but by scale. Bending the tube back and forth broke off the scale and bashing it with a hammer accelerated the process. Eventually it was cleared all the way through and I fitted it back in place telling Baby Blake that it was no longer a baby, in fact it was older than me, and it was time to stop its tantrums. It seemed to work. I could now welcome guests aboard with a bit more dignity.

At high tide on Tuesday, I manoeuvred *Molio* between the arms of Packie's special travel hoist which was sitting at the bottom of a concrete slip. Slings were fitted and she was raised a few inches. As she was pulled clear of the water, a thick shining coat of tiny black mussels was revealed. They had grown to cover every square inch of the hull, which I'd cleaned only four months earlier. My theory that high pressure hosing would recharge the antifouling was spectacularly wrong. It explained *Molio*'s sluggish performance and her reluctance to tack. One of the yardmen appeared with an implement like a garden hoe and started to scrape off the mussels in inch-thick strips. I watched him fill six barrow loads.

"Sure that's the worse fouling I've seen in years," said Packie who was wearing a grey woollen jacket and tie, and keeping a watchful eye on proceedings. I felt a bit ashamed as boat owners do when a flaw in the care of their darlings is exposed. Over at the yard the boat hoist lowered *Molio* slowly to the floor. As she took the weight on her foot, water squirted from the seam between the lead and wooden keels. "Did you see that?" asked Packie, peering at the seam from under his seafarer's cap.

"What do you think it is?" I asked, already impressed by this man who had once built wooden yachts for the world's elite sailors.

"It's the keel... without a shadow of a doubt... the keel's loose."

"Can we tighten it up?" I asked hopefully.

"A loose keel like that rocking about in the waves will act like a pump. She'll pump water up through the keel bolts." Packie shinned up the ladder as if he were a sailor on a square rigger and pulled up the furthest floorboard in the main cabin. "There you are," he pointed at a large bolt with some rusty water oozing from the base. "That water there is coming up the shaft of the keel bolt. And just look at the rot, will you." He pointed to a patch of soft wood next to the bolt.

"How bad is it?" I asked, fighting back the panic.

"There's no telling how far down that will be going. Sure, I'll look her over in the morning."

I drove over to Neil and Rosie's house for a barbecue that evening which gave me a chance to offload my worries on Neil. "Packie knows his stuff all right," said Neil. "But there might be a bit of showmanship. Tell you what; I'll come down tomorrow after work."

It was reassuring to have Neil's steady support, for I was seriously worried. I hadn't yet learnt the tricks of the wily boatyard owner who takes an unholy joy in winding up gullible boat owners. It is part and parcel of their trade. One thought rampaged through my mind, interrupting the flow of carefully made plans like a boisterous drunk at a wedding. I'd sunk every penny I had, and every penny loaned to me by the bank, into this venture. There was nothing left to absorb another setback. I slept fitfully, dreaming of keels that rocked back and forth like the flaps of an aircraft.

Even the terrors of the night are tamed by a strong cup of Irish tea, especially on a beautiful August morning in the countryside. By the time I arrived at the boatyard, I had half convinced myself that all would be well. Packie was there before me, examining *Molio*'s lower seams. He straightened up as I walked over and nodded a greeting.

"Can we tighten up the keel bolts?" I asked, striking an optimistic note.

He pushed his cap back from his boyish face. "We can do that. It might help and it might not."

"Is there anything else we can do?"

"I had a wooden ketch in here five or six years ago – belongs to a doctor who lives over the hill there. She'd a long history of leaking and they'd caulked every seam tight. I dropped the keel a few inches, squeezed in twelve tubes of sikaflex sealant and bolted her back up. She's never leaked a drop since."

"*Molio* has aluminium-bronze keel bolts," I mentioned knowing their corrosion-proof reputation. I'd gone through the archive of information that Barry had sent me – old survey reports, photographs of repairs, letters from Fred Shepherd himself and some of his original design sketches.

"PJ here will tighten up the bolts for you," said Packie, nodding at a slight man walking over with a box wrench that must have stood two feet high with cross bars welded on top for purchase. I followed him up the ladder. If Packie was as lithe as a sailor, PJ was a jungle cat with the same fluid motion and economy of movement. He swung lightly down into the saloon, put the wrench to one side and began lifting the floorboards, seeming to have no difficulty in prising up the ones that were stuck fast.

"How do you do that?" I asked in admiration.

"Ah, you lift from the side here," he replied showing me the trick. "I'll just clear the table away." Pulling out a screwdriver he unfastened the base of the folding table. With its various lockers and sections, all in dense mahogany, it weighed a ton, but he lifted it into the fo'c'sle as if it were a camping table. *Molio*'s underbelly was revealed. "That's the wooden keel," he said pointing out the smooth base running along the bottom which I had regarded merely as the floor of the bilges. She's the back bone of the boat from stem to stern, and this is a bent floor, maybe American Elm." He pointed to a timber traversing the keel some three inches wide and four or five inches deep. "She's built strong all right. See there's a keel bolt running through each of them floors. They go right down into the lead keel."

Under his tuition I began to visualise how *Molio*'s insides connected to her outsides. PJ fitted the big wrench over the large nut nearest to the mast. He tightened and got half a turn on it. I heard someone coming up the ladder and, a moment later, Packie arrived to check on progress. He edged past to reach the mast like a man on a mission and thrust a screwdriver into the pocket of rot next to the keel bolt, working it in until it was about three inches deep. "That's not good news," he said fixing me with beady eyes.

"It's not?" I gulped semi-hypnotised by the man.

"There's rot in the stem of your boat, which will only get worse."

"It will?" I gulped again, aware that I was repeating everything he said.

"Sure it will. It's a fungus like and given a chance it will spread. These are structural timbers," he kicked at a cross member, "you need to get rid of that rot."

"Uh, can you do something about it?"

"Ooph," Packie exhaled slowly, shaking his head from side to side as if contemplating a dying patient beyond his help. "We might be able to help you I suppose. The first thing would be to unstep the mast. We'd have to take out the bulwarks and fo'c'sle woodwork to expose the stem, drop the lead keel, remove the floors and probe all round to see how far the rot extends. Then we could cut away the rot, make up a replacement piece, scarf it in, and reassemble."

It was even worse than my nightmare. I stared at Packie with my mouth open. I knew the job he was talking about would take hundreds of hours of skilled work and would end up costing nearly as much as the boat itself. This was it, then, the flaw I'd been worrying about all along, hidden in the single most vital part of the boat; an Achilles' heel weeping rusty blood, unnoticed by the previous owner, missed by the expert surveyor, overlooked by me. If Packie's assessment of the repair was accurate, and he had the reputation of being the best boat builder in Ireland, then it was the end of my dream as emphatically as if the Kraken himself were to rise from the depths and drag *Molio* under. I looked at him in despair. Was that really it?

PJ stirred uncomfortably beside me. It seemed to free me from the spell. I glanced back down at the small rough hole by the keelboat. How could that be so deadly? And what did Packie mean by taking out the bulwarks and fo'c'sle woodwork. It sounded like cowboy joinery not yacht restoration. I tried to imagine how the keel bolt would look if viewed with x-ray eyes. One of Fred Shepherd's drawings came to mind. It portrayed the boat from the side with her outer planking removed to reveal the main structural timbers and inner spaces. It even showed the little companionway ladder and the engine. I had found it enchanting and spent some time just absorbing the details. I could visualise it now quite clearly. It showed the mast coming down through the coachroof to stand on the stem, just like Packie said, except… I shut my eyes and thought about the drawing. That was right. The wooden keel sat above the lead keel and ran from the sternpost all the way to the stem. Everything attached to it including the stem piece up in the bows. The mast came down to stand on the wooden keel at the aft end of the stem piece. Only it didn't sit on it directly. There was another wooden piece there, like the base of a lamp, and it supported the mast.

I looked down at the foot of the mast where it rested on a massive block of wood. A few inches aft was the keel bolt with the rot hole. I knelt down quickly and peered at the bottom. Sure enough the massive block was not an integral part of the stem piece; it was a separate timber lying on top, just as the drawing showed. It was only a matter of un-stepping the mast and this block, complete with rot, could be removed without disturbing the other timbers or dropping the lead keel. What's more, it could be done at the end of the season at minimal extra cost, as the mast would be coming out anyway for winter storage. I glanced up to see Packie jotting some calculations in his notebook. Was he totting up the cost of repairs? If so, he was going to be disappointed. Over my shoulder I saw that PJ had moved down to the next keel bolt and was busy fitting the homemade wrench. "Take a look here Packie," I said, pointing to the base of the mast step. "This block is mounted on the wooden keel. It can be removed without disturbing the boat."

"Maybe you're right and then again maybe not," he hedged, look-ing a bit abashed.

"But you can see where the join is," I insisted pointing at it. "And it's shown in Fred Shepherd's plans."

"How are those keel bolts doing now?" Packie called to PJ, seeming to lose interest in the rot.

"This one's taken two turns."

"I t'ought as much," said Packie turning back to me. "That's been your problem, right enough."

I nodded, sitting down on the bunk, too relieved to feel angry. It was as if a huge shadow had just lifted and fled from my boat. Packie hurried down the ladder and disappeared into his office.

"That's them all then," said PJ giving a final heave on the aft nut.

85

"Thanks PJ," I said, still feeling a bit giddy. "That should make a difference all right."

"I'll be caulking up the bottom seams now. I'll show you if you like." PJ gave me a knowing smile which lit up his gypsy face.

"I'm going to sit down and watch the dogs in the park for a few minutes. I'll bring you back some tea." The need to clear my head was paramount.

As I walked past Packie's office, he popped his head round the door. "We'll put your boat in the water on tomorrow's tide. No hard feelings, now."

Chapter 5

In The Wake of Saints

My friend Stephen stood on deck, a streak of white in the beard but as tough as the steam engines that he played with in his spare time, and as dependable as the 10 o'clock Flying Scotsman from Kings Cross. One hand was thrust into the pocket of his blue cord jeans, the other grasped the sprayhood as he surveyed the busy scene. Neil came down to the marina and walked over to join us, ready to see *Molio* off for a second time. He had a courier parcel about the size of a beer carton.

"Here," he proffered the box. "It arrived for you this morning."

"Funny, I don't remember ordering any more gear. Maybe paint." I took the box and passed it over to Stephen asking if he could stow it below.

"You'll be fine now, Martyn. No problems this time."

"Next stop, Dublin." I confirmed.

"Just watch out for the girls in port, one look at you two hoary men and they'll be jumping aboard like flying fishes, sure they will."

"We'll save the ugly one for you," said Stephen as he came back on deck. We'd all three been drinking-friends in Cambridge.

Neil shook his head, "I wish I could come along."

I looked at him. "If there's a next time, you are coming. We'll make a seaman of you yet." I grabbed *Molio*'s stay and swung on board.

"Well that's as maybe, but just you remember boys, give a ring if you need any help. I can get over to Dungarvan or Arklow in no time." Stooping down he slipped off the last mooring rope and pushed the bow out into the harbour. With a wave he strode back to his car. There was another emergency to sort out at the wildlife park.

Putting the engine into gear, I steered *Molio* down the Owenboy River and out of the entrance to Cork Harbour, while Stephen stowed fenders and warps. With time beginning to run away from me, I'd decided to change tack and sail east towards Carnsore Point and then north up the Irish Sea. It was a shorter route and more sheltered. Rather than gallivanting about the wild and beautiful waters of the west, this was to be a business run with the sole purpose of getting *Molio* home. Stephen was a sailor, mechanic and University chum. If anyone could help me do it he could, but he had only a week off from work.

Clearing Roche's Point I switched off the engine while Stephen hoisted all sails, pausing to watch a pod of dolphins swimming close to the boat. Coming on to a bearing of 120° to pass Pollock Rock, the light southerly airs filled the sails and we began slipping along at four knots. Getting rid of the mussels had made a huge difference to *Molio*'s performance. I nodded to myself in satisfaction; St Kilda should be possible after all. Before long the wind died away, save for the odd puff from the east. We began to drift back towards Cork. There was nothing for it but to switch back to auxiliary power and motor towards Dungarvan Harbour. I checked the batteries after an hour of motoring and found that neither had been taking a charge so we stopped the engine once more while Stephen fitted the spare alternator. This sorted out the problem. Before long a breeze from the southwest got up and we ended the day on a glorious run along the coast, picking up a mooring off Helvick Pier.

Once we had the sails furled and the boat secure, Stephen offered to cook up some grub. I left him to it and went forward to find the mystery parcel. I cut the label that fastened the cardboard lid and proclaimed the contents to be fragile. Inside was a roughly made wooden box wedged securely with bubble wrap. I put it on the saloon table and found a large screwdriver to lever open the lid. Inside that was a dark blue t-shirt smelling faintly of herbs and surrounding something heavy. I lifted it out and carefully unrolled the shirt to reveal an antique ship's barometer calibrated in inches and millimetres. It was an exact match of *Molio*'s brass clock. Sellotaped to the face was a little square of paper with writing in a familiar tight hand in green ink: 'Consult me before sailing!' The brass was worn smooth from generations and gleamed from Kyla's polishing. I showed Stephen.

"What a beautiful thing," he responded, tapping the dial. "Hmm. Pressure is dropping."

I found three brass screws and fastened the barometer beside the ship's clock. I wasn't quite sure how to feel about this gift. Even so I put the t-shirt under my pillow.

Next morning the wind had settled in from the west. We slipped our mooring at 07:00 and ran along the coast with the staysail goosewinged on the opposite tack to the yankee. The breeze strengthened during the afternoon. We reduced sail progressively, finally lowering the mainsail on the approach to Kilmore Quay in a rising force 5 with rain lashing down. The engine started without difficulty but as we closed with the harbour it was difficult to make out the shape of the breakwater and I couldn't find the leading lights. "Damned if I can see them," I complained passing the binoculars to Stephen.

He stood up and stared intently, steadying his arms with the sprayhood. Water streamed from his beard. "Nope, not a sign of them, nor of the castle."

I turned the boat 180°, worried that our current heading would take us into shoal water. She heeled as a squall caught her on the beam. Just then, a fishing boat came steaming through St Patrick's Bridge from the east, turned sharply to starboard and headed straight for the end of the breakwater. "There's some luck," I shouted. "We'll follow her in." The fishing boat swept past *Molio* as I brought the engine up to full speed, determined not to lose her in the mist and rain. Rounding the end of the breakwater we passed between two concrete piers to enter a sheltered harbour with fishing boats rafted three deep on either side.

We continued towards a small marina at the far end with two pontoon arms. It looked as though it was jam packed with boats. *Molio* was slow to turn and impossible to steer in reverse but there was little option other than to go in and take our chances.

"Stephen could you get on deck with this?" I pulled the wooden boathook from the stern locker so he could push us off the sides if needs be. "Shout if you see a space."

A Wild Call

We came up slowly to the pontoons but there were no gaps in the tight cluster of masts. The rain was pelting down now and there wasn't a soul about to lend a hand. I began to edge down the left channel when a gust caught us, pushing *Molio* towards the pier. Looking over the side, I saw the bottom coming up quickly and realised we were drifting over a slipway. Ramming the gear level into reverse I throttled up. *Molio* responded instantly charging backwards into the line of fishing boats. In a trice Stephen leapt past me to the aft deck and pushed off with his beefy shoulder. I edged *Molio* forward but there was precious little turning room.

Just then there was a shout from the large motor yacht moored on the outer pontoon. "Over here! Come in here." An arm waved to us from the door of the bridge. I waved back in acknowledgement as Stephen used the boathook to turn *Molio*'s bow past the moored yachts.

"We'll go straight in on the port side," I yelled to Stephen. He nodded and ran to move a couple of fenders across. A figure in yellow oilskins and sou'wester appeared at the stern of the motorboat. He shouted to Stephen, who chucked him the bow warp. A minute later we were moored snugly alongside. Our rescuer disappeared and, after switching off the engine, we clambered below to get out of the rain which was bucketing down.

Later that evening the rain eased and we found a pub that served fish and chips. We sat down with relief at a small table next to an open fire and began to warm up. Stephen ordered two beers. I took a long pull of mine as soon as it arrived. The forecast was for persistent rain and northerly winds over the next few days. Not ideal, but we could make progress, especially with the help of *Molio*'s powerful engine. I turned to Stephen.

"I'd like to stop here tomorrow and sort out the charging problem. If we don't get to the bottom of it, we'll be stuck without an engine."

Stephen pulled off his fisherman's jersey, sweating in the heat. Our rain gear was already dripping from a peg. "I'll search about in the engine's electrics in the morning and see if there's a bad earth connection. Why don't you take the spare alternator to a garage and have it tested?"

Two days later we motored through St Patrick's Bridge with the batteries on full charge. Stephen had cleaned up the connectors in the main charging circuit of the boat and with the help of the friendly harbourmaster we'd found someone to test the alternators. Both were found to be working normally. It was only when we went to help our neighbour prop up his motor yacht on the slipway that we began to make progress. He had been chatting with one of his mates about our problem.

"Did you know that the ignition bulb itself is part of the charging circuitry?" He asked. "If you have the wrong bulb, the alternator may not start to charge."

I thought back over the past few weeks, "I did change the bulb a couple of weeks ago when cleaning off corrosion, but I kept the original."

"Worth a try then."

It was and it fixed the problem. Stephen wasn't sure of the logic but there was no denying the healthy charge coming from the alternator.

With Little Saltee Island astern, we raised sail once more, choosing the smaller staysail to accompany the yankee and putting a reef in the main. *Molio*'s bow creamed through the smooth water as we beat along the inshore passage to Carnsore Point. After clearing the southeast point of Ireland, the sea quickly built up and we started pitching into the waves coming down St George's Channel. We turned back into sheltered water to put a second reef in the main and to take in a few turns on the yankee. Clearing the point for a second time, the wind picked up even more. The combination of steep waves and wind brought regular curtains of spray aft to the cockpit until I was semi-blind from the near constant bombardment. Salt water penetrated right through my wet-weather gear, drenching jeans and sweater beneath, but at least the water was warm after a summer of baking sunshine.

The tall lighthouse on Tuskar Rock gave us our mark and we continued to beat south-eastwards, tacking back when a mile to its southwest. We tacked again, to follow a fifteen degrees bearing towards Lucifer Bank. As we swept past the lighthouse on the flood we entered some turbulence and *Molio* lurched suddenly causing me to lose my balance. Stephen grabbed me before I could fall and then clambered below to fit a safety harness, coming back up with another for me. We exchanged places at the helm just as a large wave caught us from the port side sending a wall of green water into the cockpit. It gushed out of the two cleared drainage tubes. The combination of powerful flood tide against a strong north-easterly breeze was kicking up steep seas that were tossing *Molio* about like a cork. I got into my harness and snapped the lifeline to the top guard wire, then turned to shut the main hatch. As I did water crashed onto the floor in the heads. It looked as though it was coming through the mushroom-vent in the cabin roof. It was seized wide open, another unfinished job. I shut the doors sealing off the cabin. We were going to have to ride this out in the cockpit. I grinned at Stephen who gave me a thumbs up. It was just as well that he'd cooked a mighty ship's breakfast that morning, for there was neither time not inclination for food now.

The motion eased a bit north off Greenore Point but we continued to take turns on the helm every forty-five minutes so as to hold *Molio* as close into the wind as possible. We put in two more tacks to pass Lucifer and Blackwater Banks, leaving them to port. I estimated our speed in a direct line was less than three knots. The sea was holding us back. I went below to consult the sailing directions again, wedging myself into the little bench seat at the chart table. Rosslare offered little shelter for a yacht and would be fully exposed in these seas. Wexford Harbour offered fine shelter but, with the sea breaking on the bar, it would be dangerous to enter, especially with our deep keel. The pier at Polduff would offer no shelter and the little harbour at Courtdown was too shallow. That left Arklow, over 30 nautical miles to the north, as the only possibility. It had a narrow entrance and there would be a big sea running, but with the engine we should be able to reach it before dark and then hold ourselves midway between the two piers on the way in. I switched on the ignition. The red light came on. A quarter turn more and the engine roared into life. That, at least, was reassuring.

With the engine helping, Stephen brought *Molio* onto a direct heading for Arklow Head and I furled the rest of the yankee. We made good progress for a time but, after passing the first can buoy south of Arklow, the engine slowed. I opened the throttle further and we continued for a few minutes. Then it started hunting, slowing down before surging with power only to slow once more. Soon the hunting grew worse. I checked the ship's clock. It was four p.m. That gave us several hours of daylight to sort things out. I let loose the yankee again and then revved the engine in neutral, thinking we might possibly have fouled a net. It made no difference.

Stephen had been thinking it out. "That's fuel starvation. All this heavy motion has thrown up dirt from the bottom of the tank."

"Can you clear it?" I asked, knowing it was a lot to ask but also knowing that the seemingly impossible would often yield when Stephen put his mind to a task.

"It would be difficult under these conditions. Do you have a spare filter?"

At this point the engine died completely. We were not far from the second can buoy which is four miles from the pier at Arklow. The wind had moderated but remained on the nose. The tide was running at over a knot, perhaps two, against us and progress was further slowed by the swell running south down the channel. Still, it should be possible.

"Not sure about the filter," I told Stephen, "but we can sail to the harbour. Conditions aren't great but we should make it before dark. The real problem will be sailing in. There's a big swell running and what's left of the wind will be blanketed by the piers. The worry is that we'll be thrown against the side."

"What other options do we have?"

"Not much. We could turn and run out to sea."

"We would still have the same problem in the morning."

"True. I'll call the coastguard and alert them to our situation and ask if they can tow us into the harbour in about three hours' time."

I called up on the VHF using channel sixteen and got an immediate response. They promised to give us a tow when we arrived. Ten minutes later a powerful launch appeared at the entrance of the harbour and turned towards us. "That's the lifeboat," called Stephen.

Within a few minutes they had arrived, standing some fifty metres off to assess the situation. The wind had moderated further, but the sea was over two metres high, causing both boats to heave and roll. The coxswain on the bridge called over on a megaphone asking us to drop the sails. Stephen went up to the mainmast, clipped his lifeline to the shrouds and set to work. I furled in the yankee from the cockpit. The lifeboat approached to within twenty metres and the coxwain asked us to let out the Avon dinghy to the maximum extent of the painter. I watched as one of the men in a bulky yellow suit jumped nimbly aboard the dinghy. I pulled him up to *Molio* and he scrambled aboard, hauling himself up with the mizzen shrouds with agility, despite his large size. He gave us a big grin. "I'm Roger. We'll soon have you in harbour."

He was as good as his word. Ten minutes later, we were attached to the lifeboat by an enormous eighty metre towing rope and heading towards Arklow Harbour at eight knots. As we burled along, Roger regaled us with stories of windsurfing and high performance dinghy sailing while keeping an eye on the hawser and an ear on the VHF. I made three mugs of strong tea. Inside the two piers the swell was running high. As the lifeboat came alongside to guide us through a final narrow entranceway, the waves threatened to knock us under its heavy fender rail. Even with eight strong pairs of hands it was touch and go, but finally we escaped the swell and were released into the calm inner waters of the old dock, where we tied up alongside a rusting fishing boat.

It could have been a different story if conditions had deteriorated and there had been no lifeboat at Arklow. Two centuries ago there was an average of 1,800 shipwrecks a year around the islands of Britain and Ireland. The seas are vastly safer today, in no small part due to the volunteer lifeboat crews who put their own lives at risk to save others. Duty? Altruism? Natural instinctive help? Call it what you want but few would doubt the value of their service. In their own unique way, they open up the freedom of the seas to any inhabitant of the British Isles who wishes to step into a boat and set off on a journey from the shore.

A night's rest revived us and next morning Stephen unscrewed the glass filter bowl. As he'd suspected, the filter and bowl were full of grey sludge. He tracked down a replacement filter in a small chandler nearby and fitted it. I tried the engine. It started and then died. Stephen began on a systematic bleeding exercise to track down the fault. He soon spotted a second fuel filter and eased off the metal bowl with a leather strap wrench. It too was filled with sludge. Fortunately there was a spare filter in *Molio*'s stores. With the second filter replaced, I tried the engine again. This time it roared into life with full power. We cleaned up and packed everything away before making ready for sea. By the time we had emerged from Arklow's sheltering walls, the sun was out and the breeze had died to a whisper. We decided to motor north to make up some miles and also to charge the batteries. In the late afternoon we arrived off Dublin Bay and slipped into Dun Laoghaire Marina next to the ferry terminal. An hour later we were set up with pints in the Purty Kitchen. I guessed Stephen must be thinking of leaving. He had a day in hand but there was no telling where *Molio* would end up next evening.

"Might be easier to catch that ferry this evening, eh?" I suggested.

"It's been great to let go of all that admin for a few days – grant proposals, staff performance meetings, teaching, university strategy. It never ends."

"Is it worth it?"

Stephen hesitated but not for long, "We are a team. We are building something in the uni. It's worth it."

Stephen and I were a team now I thought. His mechanical wizardry and muscle power had got us here and set me up for the second leg to Scotland. "Is it what you want?"

"Not exactly, but close enough."

We finished the pints and walked down to the boat to get his bag and then over to the ferry terminal on the far side of the marina. After seeing Stephen onto the ferry, I turned to look for *Molio* but she was lost in a crowd of masts. For a moment I felt alone, out on a limb, equally far from my friends in Cork and my old cruising grounds in the Clyde. There was only one recourse: I went back to the Purty Kitchen and ordered a double whisky. Soon I was thinking about the next stage. By the time I arrived back at *Molio* the exhilaration of the voyage had taken hold again.

In the morning, I went shopping for fresh provisions and stowed the purchases carefully below. I took *Molio* over to the marina's fuelling pontoon and topped up with diesel. A moderate westerly breeze was forecast, which would give plenty of shelter along the east coast of Ireland. I checked possible anchorages in the sailing directions. My plan was for a short passage, as much to escape the extortionate marina charges as to test myself at sailing solo. The skipper of a neighbouring boat cast off my ropes and I powered *Molio* astern out of the narrow gap between two pontoons. Luckily she turned the correct way. I engaged forward and we were off round the breakwater and out into Dublin Bay. It was empty of shipping, leaving plenty of time for stowing fenders and hoisting sail. A couple of hours later I rounded Lambay Island and, closing with the mainland, anchored in three fathoms within the sheltering arms of Loughshinny.

I was up early next morning to beat north along the coast with just the mainsail and yankee. I spent a couple of hours experimenting with the wind vane self-steering system, a wonderful invention that required no motors or batteries, only the power of the wind and sea. Once I had it tuned correctly, it freed me from constant duty at the helm. By that time there were no other sails visible, as most pleasure boats in the Irish Sea are clustered round the marinas. I relaxed and took advantage of the calm waters to tidy up the boat. I was just contemplating making a cup of coffee when a helicopter came into view, flying up from the south. I watched it for a few seconds before going below to put on the kettle. When I came back up it was much closer and I could see, from the striking colours, that it must be an air-sea rescue helicopter. As it approached it began to circle slowly, perhaps curious to take a look at *Molio*. I hoped they would go away soon so I could enjoy the quiet sounds of the sea.

Although it is considered good practice to keep the VHF radio switched on at all times in a boat, part of the joy of sailing for me is getting away from the buzz of technology, so *Molio*'s set was switched off. The helicopter buzzed around a couple more times. The kettle was beginning to whistle and I went back down to make coffee. Coming back up the steps I noticed, to my satisfaction, that the chopper had flown off and was now about a mile astern. As I watched, it reduced altitude until it was hovering just above the sea, swivelled to face me, switched on twin spotlights and started flying straight for me at speed. This guy wasn't sightseeing: he wanted to communicate.

I scrambled down below and switched on the radio. I put out a call on channel sixteen. "Helicopter, helicopter, helicopter. This is yacht *Molio* position one two zero degrees fifteen miles from Dundalk Bay. Over."

Immediately the reply came back, "Yacht *Molio*, this is Irish Coast Guard Search and Rescue. Switch to channel six seven. Over."

"Six seven. Over." I switched channels but by this time the helicopter was hovering immediately over the cockpit and the racket was indescribable. I could just make out a voice. Once it stopped, I pressed the transmit button, "Irish Coast Guard, I cannot understand you because of helicopter noise. Can you move back a bit?" I was getting worried. Could there have been an emergency at home? Even if there had been, I reasoned, surely they wouldn't send a helicopter. I'm not James Bond. I just don't rate that kind of attention.

The helicopter retreated fifty metres. "Yacht *Molio*, I say again we are conducting a training exercise and request permission to lower a man into your dinghy. Over."

That was reassuring. These guys were always having fun training and I was all for it. "Yes, I would be delighted to receive him. What's his name? Over."

"This is Captain Robert Murphy. We'll be winching down Liam Woodley. Stand by." There was a pause and then the VHF crackled with life again. "Keep as close to the wind as possible but hold your present course and speed. Out."

"Message understood. Out." I went back up to the cockpit as the chopper closed in until it was hovering forty feet above the dinghy. The sound was deafening. *Molio* was pinching into the wind a bit and only making two knots, but rather than change course now, I let her be. The door of the helicopter slid back and a helmeted figure climbed out backwards and began to descend, swinging gently from side to side on the winch line, until landing plumb in the middle of the inflatable. He unhooked, gave a big grin and a thumbs up, which I returned, then he re-hooked and was taken back up. I gave the pilot a wave as he pulled back and turned to head south.

As the noise abated, the easy rhythm of life on board returned. I noticed that the wind had slackened and hoisted the mizzen and staysail. *Molio* made better progress continuing on her journey north through the morning and afternoon. We arrived off the lighthouse at St John's Point in the evening and, soon after, I recognised the mile-wide mouth of Strangford Lough. A powerful tide sets through the entrance, but our arrival coincided with slack water so it was a simple matter to start the engine and motor in. After passing Angus Rock, I headed for the first anchorage about a mile up the narrows, a five mile throat that leads from the Irish Sea to the large sea lough. It was a quiet spot with an open view between the wooded banks. It was late when I finally sat down to enjoy a supper of Irish potatoes, carrots and tinned meatballs. Afterwards I took a glass of merlot into the cockpit to enjoy the fiery glow lingering in the night sky.

Awakening next morning to the screeching of excited terns, I climbed up to the cockpit and watched them swooping and diving for fry. A heron on the shoreline was waiting patiently for bigger fare that might venture too close to its dagger-like bill. I glanced at the clock. It was six-fifteen. The tide would begin to flood in at eight o'clock, effectively sealing the exit for six hours. I pumped out the bilges: four hundred and twenty-two strokes – it was more than I liked. Breakfast was a hurried hunk of Irish brown soda bread covered in organic butter and honey with a large mug of tea. I dipped the diesel tanks and topped up one from a 20 litre jerry can, picking up the seven o'clock forecast on the VHF. The day would begin with a light variable breeze that would increase southerly four or five. Hastily I plotted courses and distances on the chart, which I slipped into a cellophane pocket to keep in the cockpit. The engine started without hesitation and I went forward on deck to haul up the anchor, using the old-fashioned winch attached to the mast. By the time I had it secured on deck I was concerned to see that it was after eight. I put the engine in gear and headed for the entrance, estimating my exit time at about eight-thirty. Usually the tide runs fastest midway between low and high water. In fact the rule of twelfths is that the amount of water travelling each hour after slack water is 1,2,3,3,2,1 twelfths of the total in the 1st, 2nd, 3rd, 4th, 5th and 6th hour respectively. In other words the fastest streams take place during the 3rd and 4th hour after slack water. Thirty minutes from the turn of the tide put me in the one bracket, I reasoned, so the tide could hardly be racing yet. What I had neglected to check was the disparity between low water and slack water.

As I entered the main channel, the tide was running fast, in fact very fast. *Molio* was hardly making any progress against the inrush. I pushed down the throttle and began edging closer to Angus Rock. The closer we got, the faster the tide became. I kept pushing down a bit more until eventually *Molio* was going flat out, with the power of forty-eight horses shoving her hard into the rush of water. Although there was no wind to speak of, and the surface of the water was like flowing glass, it was not the same as motoring fast in a calm sea. The tide rushing through the narrows swirled and gyrated, creating turbulent spirals under the surface which caused *Molio* to lunge and swerve alarmingly, as if some beast were clawing at her, trying to drag her down into its underwater lair. We edged up to within twenty metres of Angus Rock, where the tide was falling over itself as it plunged past. In its wake, gannets and gulls were diving in a frenzy. We were making barely a quarter of a knot against the land. Slowly we made up to the rock, kept going, got past it and continued towards the entrance, picking up speed as we did. Soon Angus Rock was well astern and I was able to bring *Molio* on to a northeasterly heading, to intercept the South Rock Light Vessel. It was another lesson for me. The tide does not wait. Not because it's being personal, or in a hurry, but because it's under lunar control and when it comes to planetary forces it's best just to fit in.

In a brisk southwesterly *Molio* ran north all day under the yankee and mizzen alone, needing only occasional attention from me. I crossed the entrance to Belfast Lough in the late afternoon, and rounded Islandmagee into Larne Lough just as the sun dipped below the clouds. A friendly yachtsman, out with his family for an evening race, guided me on to an empty mooring. I listened especially carefully to the forecast that night to check the conditions for crossing the North Channel to Scotland. A light westerly was expected. The barometer was steady.

Next morning I was on my way by six. I hoisted sail when clear of Larne Lough but the wind was so light that I continued under power, heading northeast. After one hour I passed the notorious Maidens, a pair of rocky islets looking as deceptive and dangerous as their reputation amongst mariners. From there I steered on a bearing for Pladda Light on Sanda Island at the south end of Scotland's Mull of Kintyre. It was, I reflected, pretty much the exact same route that St Molio must have taken in the family galley some fourteen centuries earlier, crossing from his father's side of the channel in Ireland to his mother's in Scotland, where he lived as a hermit on the Holy Isle.

In the afternoon, I passed close to Paddy's Milestone, an isolated volcanic plug marking the outer edge of the Firth of Clyde. Also known as Ailsa Craig and the Sea-Fairy Rock, it had been visible from my boyhood home in Ayrshire whenever the weather was fair. When I saw the gannets massing off its familiar cliffs, it suddenly felt as if I was coming home. All afternoon the feeling grew stronger and I swear *Molio* could sense it too. She seemed to surge forward, throwing a foaming turquoise wake carelessly aside as she made for the high hills of Arran. Perhaps she sensed its charms, this most-favoured of isles, heralded by the minstrel Caeilte of Irish mythology as *Arran of the many stags, where the sea strikes against her shoulder*. When a breeze blew up from the west, I freed the yankee and reached north up the east side of Arran to Holy Isle where, tucking inside the shelter of Lamlash Harbour, I dropped anchor in five fathoms. I was back in home waters and this time with my own boat.

A number of text messages arrived, as friends told friends, forcing me with little protest to raise my glass in numerous toasts. Amongst them was a call from Kyla. She had found a wooden boat specialist to look after *Molio*. "If anyone can fix her leak, this man can. He is a distinguished companion of the ancient order of leaksmiths." I rang Adam Way at his yard in Lochgilphead and arranged to lift *Molio* out of the water at Ardrishaig.

It was colder next morning, reminding me that the summer would soon be drawing to a close. I sailed across to Holy Isle and ran north, hugging the shore. This was St Molio's Isle and I wanted to pay my respects. As we passed the northwest end of the isle I saw that the old farmhouse had been converted into a Buddhist centre. Much as I admire Buddhism, and especially the life and teachings of the Dalai Lama, I was uncomfortable at their presence on an island hallowed by an early Christian saint. I decided to return there with time for a proper visit at the earliest opportunity. I didn't want to jump to hasty conclusions. Passing through the northern entrance between Arran and the Holy Isle, I hoisted the mainsail and ran up the east coast of Arran, passing beneath the northern hills that resemble a sleeping warrior. According to legend he has lain waiting for his call to arms through the millennia to the present day. Crossing Kilbrannon Sound I entered Loch Fyne and sailed north past Tarbert to Ardrishaig. Searching with my binoculars, I spotted a man with curly hair and lean frame standing by a tiny concrete slip just beyond the main pier. I furled the sails and approached under power easing *Molio* alongside.

Adam jumped on board. "Hello, I'll just take your ropes." No fuss and no shouting, he had the relaxed boyish manner of the true pro. After securing *Molio* he turned back for another look, assessing the combinations of boat, waves and pier. "How about moving a fender to just off the starboard bow," he pointed to where *Molio* was in danger of touching as she swung in the waves. "That should keep her safe until the crane gets here." He smiled with an infectious fruit-gum grin that seemed to say "I love hauling things about, don't you?" I hoped Kyla was right about his skill with wooden boats.

"You have a yard in Lochgilphead?" I asked, puzzled, as the head of Loch Gilp dries out for a mile at low tide.

"We're in the industrial estate. We'll put *Molio* on the low loader and have her lifted into the yard. I think she'll fit." He nodded once to reassure me and then leapt ashore.

I looked at the truck with the low loader which was reversing along the pier. "She's heavy," I shouted. "You'll need strong supports."

Just then a crane started up and lurched down beside the slipway. It began lowering a hook over *Molio*. Adam tied the canvas strop to the mast before lending a hand with unfastening the rigging. With a burst of engine power, the mainmast eased out of its socket in the deck, swung over the slip and began descending to the ground, suspended from a point above the first spreader. The base touched first and as the hook continued to descend, the mast began to bend... and bend. I looked at Adam. He looked at the crane driver. The solid wooden mast, with a diameter of ten inches at the base, looked like a bow. And then it was down. The mizzen lifted out easily. Next it was *Molio*'s turn. All eleven tons of her were plucked from the water like a toy and suspended by a thread. Half an hour later *Molio* was sitting snugly on the back of the low loader and being driven to her winter home.

N

Lewis

Harris

North Uist

Outer Hebrides

Part Two

South Uist

Skye

Portree •

Loch Carron
Plockton
Kyle of Lochalsh

Isleornsay •

S C O T L A N D

Rùm

• Mallaig

SEA OF THE HEBRIDES

• Fort William

Coll

Tobermory •

Sound of Mull

Tiree

Mull

• Oban

Ardinamir Bay

------- This part of the voyage is
------- not described in the text

• **Ardfern**

Crinan •

START & FINISH
Cairnbaan
Ardrishaig

Burnt Islands

Tarbert

Bute

Fairlie

Jura

Gigha

Kintyre

Arran

Firth of Clyde

Islay

Holy Isle

• Campbeltown

0   25nm

Rathlin

Mull of Kintyre

Sanda Island

Chapter 6

Glorious Day of Salvage

With the long-awaited arrival of summer, the trees of Argyll were wearing new summer outfits: the lovat shawls of silver birch contrasted with the verdant robes of oak and the emerald cloaks of alder. *Molio*, too, was showing off a new coat; a thick chestnut dressing below the waterline to keep gribbles and mussels at bay and a forest green cape above, capped by teak deck and coamings. I watched as the crane lowered her gently toward the calm surface of the canal basin at Ardrishaig. Her nut-brown underside reflected in the water below. Closer and closer they moved until the two hulls hovered an inch apart as *Molio* swayed ever so gently above her natural element. Imperceptibly, the two boats moved closer until they touched, creating a circle of thin ripples that spread outwards. There was an audible sigh from *Molio*, at least it was audible to me and perhaps to the gulls as they called out to their friends. Adam jumped quickly aboard, pulled up the floor hatch in the cockpit and peered at the timbers in the stern. "Dry as a bone," he called out.

During the winter he had removed the rudder and prop shaft to fit new bearings; it had opened up the aft part of the boat to closer inspection. As he walked back and forth from the homemade boatshed to the tiny caravan that doubled as office and tearoom, he passed *Molio* umpteen times per day. He began to get to know her, not as you or I might, but as only a builder of boats really can. He saw how her Devon builder had put wood and screws onto the bare plans drawn up by her master designer, how he had fashioned and fastened timbers to add strength and where, despite the care and quality of materials, weaknesses might be found – the pockets of unventilated air in the hull and the channels that might conduct rainwater through the deck. Freshwater and airlessness were invitations to damp and rot. In a stroke of boat-builder genius he worked out that seawater was entering her hull at a seam between the deadwood and horn timber in front of the rudder, travelling vertically up along another seam to a third seam beneath the mizzen mast step, from where it appeared inside the boat, before travelling down the top of the horn beam to the bilges. He drilled two tubular holes across the seams about half an inch in diameter and inserted softwood plugs, which expanded on contact with water thereby sealing off the leak: a surgical repair that had cured that particular ailment. In passing he had treated and filled the pocket of rot in the block where the mainmast was stepped, entirely dismissive of Packie's dire prognostications. "I soaked it in cuprinol for a week and squeezed in filler. It's minor. Forget about it." Kyla's hunch about Adam was proving well founded.

Acting on instinct again, he had jammed a knife into the hull under the lowest port-side garboard plank which sits immediately above the wooden keel that runs all along the bottom of the boat. He probed about. Sure enough, there was a soft section in the keel that the surveyor and Packie had missed. He'd removed a seven-foot length of the garboard and suggested that I come on over to take a look. I drove across from the other side of Scotland on a wet February morning to find *Molio* under a light blue rain cover with a gaping black hole in her nether regions. He showed me an ancient slab of black elm to which the garboard had been attached. "That's the wooden keel," said Adam. Taking a wood chisel from the side pocket of his blue overalls, he rammed it into the keel, burying the steel up to the hilt.

My stomach churned. It was like witnessing a post-mortem. "Hell," I gasped, "that looks terminal."

"Not a pretty sight," agreed Adam.

"Is the whole thing rotten? Is she finished?"

Seeing me wriggling on his hook, Adam took pity. "This is an old repair. Someone scarfed in a length of hardwood here. It looks like purpleheart. Anyway, they left a gap which has allowed water sitting in the bilge to drain down between the wooden keel and the garboard. It's allowed freshwater in and that's rotted the keel."

"Can you fix it?"

"The problem is that the rot has increased the gap. If the lead keel isn't seated tight, it might pump water back up in a storm."

This was sounding more and more like Packie talk I thought, aware now that I'd just been softened up by Adam. I was beginning to learn the ways of the boat builder and the fine art of loosening the purse from the grasp of tight-fisted owners. It was a subtle combination of skill, cunning and showmanship that must go back into the mists of boat-building time.

I pulled myself together. "If it was repaired before, surely you can make a better repair now?"

My appeal to his building credentials worked. Adam nodded, conceding the point. "The main problem is that the repair was poorly made in the first place." He looked over his shoulder and called to someone operating a band-saw in the shed.

A guy with a ponytail and thick, knitted sweater emerged. It was hard to place him. He might have been a yard worker all his life. He might have been one of life's dropouts who'd found his way back into the world again with boat work. He might have been a professor seeking more meaning from life than the mental gamesmanship of the academic. As he walked up I saw him appraising the boat and us in a couple of swift glances. Professor, I decided. "Nice boat," he said.

"Mike, we're thinking about cutting out this old repair and scarfing in a new section. What do you think?"

Mike got down on his knees and peered into the slot, pushing the chisel blade about. "Looks like the original keel is made from elm. This other stuff is harder. Should be possible right enough."

"What are your waiting for, then?" asked Adam.

"It's your turn to make tea," responded Mike.

Molio was going to be just fine with these two boat gurus. I'd left them to it and driven back home, content now that my plans to reach St Kilda in the summer, and perhaps to take Kyla with me, were back on track. One good thing about teaching is the generous holidays.

Kyla had come up to Scotland at Christmas for a couple of weeks. She arrived on the platform at Waverley Station, wearing a black body-hugging coat with knee high boots, which had the ticket inspectors vying for her attention. We explored castles and coastlines and she delved into the history of the Scottish Borders. I was careful to give her plenty of room just to be herself.

Closing the floor hatch in the cockpit, Adam shimmied down the companionway ladder and lifted the cabin floorboards. I clambered aboard and peered over his shoulder. "Still some water coming in here," he reported, "but hopefully she'll take up in a day or two." The timbers of wooden boats contract when they dry out on land, which often results in leaks for a few days on launching, after which the wood expands and they seal together. We stepped the masts quickly so the crane could get on its way, tightened down the rigging and moved *Molio* to a handy berth alongside the concrete wall of the basin.

"How about a sandwich?" asked Adam. I followed him up to a grassy bank where we had a view of Loch Fyne stretching like a long sliver towards the open sea and the Mountains of Arran. "Nice day for sailing right enough."

What a contrast, I thought, sitting on the grass munching a plough-man's. For all the buzz of city life, I'd trade it every time for a sandwich, a grassy bank and a view of the sea. I was looking forward to some sailing. If anyone could judge *Molio*'s seaworthiness, it was the man munching a BLT beside me.

"Is she ready for the open sea?" I asked.

He looked down at *Molio* as she rested easily in the water.

"Mike's done a power of work. Scarfed in a new piece for the keel, replaced the hood end fastenings and reinforced the floors. Considering her age, she's in great shape."

"I plan to take her to the Hebrides this summer. It's been a long while since I sailed that way."

"She'll look after you all right."

Two days later, I motored out of the sea lock and into Loch Fyne. As luck would have it, there was a light north-easterly. I hoisted sail and let the yankee and mizzen carry me slowly south down the loch with the ebbing tide. Families of guillemots swam out of the way and gannets from Ailsa Craig circled above. Occasionally an explosive 'choof' marked the spot where one had dived for a fish. I debated putting out a mackerel line for supper. A friend had mentioned that mackerel were running up the loch this year having somehow evaded a pair of trawlers patrolling the lower reaches. He feared that the modern boats were so efficient that the mackerel would soon go the same way as the herring in the 1970s. Instead I decided on a pub meal in Tarbert, which was just a few more miles down the loch and where there was a natural harbour with perfect shelter. The village lies between two sea lochs which cut into the long peninsula that extends from Crinan south to the Mull of Kintyre. A millennium ago the Vikings had their longboats hauled over the isthmus separating the two sides. As I neared the entrance to East Loch Tarbert, a small ferry carrying a dozen cars came out from the harbour and set off across Loch Fyne, heading for Portavadie. I scanned the seas beyond the ferry with my binoculars. There it was. The small lighthouse on a low-lying island called Skate. The last time I'd sailed into Tarbert, I had been coming from that island and at the head of a small flotilla. That was twenty-five years ago, but the memories were etched in my mind.

I was about to leave for an extended period in Africa so my father and oldest brother, Greer, had suggested that I take the family boat, *Pippa III*, for a cruise. She was a Ballad, a thirty-foot cruiser-racer of fibreglass construction with a royal blue gel-coat on the topsides. I set off from Fairlie on a sunny June morning. On board were my buddy Chris (whose bushy red beard and pugnacious grin made him the spitting image of his ancestor, the explorer Sir Samuel Baker), his wife Anne, my wife Laura, and our baby girl Isla. We were approaching Skate Island at the mouth of Loch Fyne, sailing slowly from the south on a dying evening breeze. The island is well-named – round and flat like a giant skate, about one hundred metres across at its wings. Where the spike of its whip-like tail might have been is a rock that only just breaks the surface at low tide. In behind is the anchorage of Ascog Bay, offering good shelter if the wind is from the north or east. Anne called our attention to a boat lying off the island, propped up at an odd-looking angle. Coming in close we saw that it was a submerged motor yacht with just the tip of the bow and part of a varnished cabin above the water, together with two masts. We stared mesmerised.

"What do you think?" asked Chris as we drifted past.

"Looks recent to me," I replied, noting a glint on the varnish and a lifebuoy floating in the water still attached by its line. We ghosted past the wreck, sticking to the deep-water channel before entering a small gut on the west side of the bay, known locally as Skate Hole. We dropped anchor on a white sandy bottom just visible through three fathoms of clear water. A local fisherman was mooring his skiff nearby. He shouted across that the wreck was two days old and something about insurance and keep away, but at that moment Isla began bawling for her supper and the rest was drowned out. I looked at Chris who shrugged. We weren't going to pay attention to that kind of thing.

Later that evening after downing a few drams we decided to row over to take a look. Rounding the headland we could see just a couple of masts standing above water in the fading light. "Tide's full," said Chris rubbing his beard. "But she'll be high and dry at low water."

"Are you thinking what I'm thinking?"

"Low tide's at five-thirty in the morning."

When my alarm went off at 04:45, the rain was drumming on the cabin roof. I groaned, regretting the tumblers of whisky that had fuelled last night's wild talk of salvage using old sails to patch stove-in planks, and human chains to pour buckets of water overboard. As the evening wore on the ideas had grown ever more fantastic until it was well after midnight. All that bravado came down to one simple equation now: would I drag myself out of my comfy sleeping bag into the cold wet morning to look at a motorboat on a rock with a big gaping hole in its bottom, or would I sink down into my warm nest and fall back to sleep? With a few more hours' kip, oh let's see now, maybe in three or four hours' time... I caught myself falling asleep just in time, unzipped the bag and put a leg on the floor. Okay, I thought, I'll sneak up on deck and take a peek. Outside, the rain seemed lighter and the sky was brightening in the east, suggesting dry weather to come. There was a smell of seaweed on the air. The surface of the sea was calm and the tide was well out. Towards Skate Island two masts were just visible, but the rest of the wrecked boat was hidden by a point of land. A heron flew overhead. I felt excitement beginning to pour through my veins like a spring tide on the turn. I came down into the cabin and put the kettle on. Grabbing some clothes I gave Chris a shake in his fo'c'sle bunk. "Time to go," I whispered urgently.

There was stirring in his sleeping bag. "Do we really have to," he asked groggily.

"It's a beauty of a morning and the tide's right out. Tea's coming up." I moved back to the galley and heard him climbing out of his sleeping bag. Nobody else stirred. Little Isla, only two months old, was happy zizzing in the land of Nod. I scrawled a quick message for the girls.

Ten minutes later, Chris and I rowed quietly away from *Pippa* with Mars bars and apples stuffed into our pockets. Once we were fifty yards off, I pulled the start chord on the seagull outboard. It coughed and stalled twice before settling down to work. Chris brought in the oars and we sped towards the island. As we rounded the small headland off Skate, we craned our necks expectantly. There she was, our prize, a forty-foot motor-sailer with the broad beam of a fishing boat. Her creamy green hull was graced by seven bronze portholes on either side. Her beauty took our breath away. The bow was perched on a rock that had tilted her partway over on one side. Even now, at low water, the starboard side was mostly underwater and obscured by a thick matting of seaweed, which pressed up against the edge of the deck like a mane of wet hair. The port side, on the other hand, was almost entirely above water. At the front, the boat's name was carved into the top plank, *Palinode*, 'a poem or song that replaces an old one'. Owing to her angle, the stern was low in the water and there the sea was almost reaching the top of the aft coaming. Just a few more inches and it would begin to pour into the cockpit. We circled slowly looking for a hole or stove-in planks.

"Can't see anything wrong with her," said Chris. "But she could have a hole under the weed".

"Let's go on board," I suggested, bringing the dinghy up to the stern. We climbed up and clung to the stanchions to edge round the cockpit, which was full of seawater. A whale pump stood uselessly in the corner. Chris went along the deck to the bridge to look about, while I secured the dinghy to a cleat. I took the companionway steps leading down from the cockpit into the saloon, letting the water fill my boots. It was dark inside, much darker than I'd expected, and the air stank of diesel. I pulled out my torch. The water was inky with fuel oil. Plastic bottles and food containers floated on the surface, along with fenders and cushions. Everything was covered in black slime, which shone in the torchlight. I descended another step and as the water level came up to my thighs, my feet slipped. I dropped the torch, which was tied to my wrist, and hung on to railings with both hands. The water must have been five feet deep in the aft cabin and I did not want to go under. Finding the starboard bunk with my feet, I hung onto whatever I could and began to work my way forward. The surfaces were so slippery that I needed all four limbs in contact to keep balance. At the front end of the saloon the water was shallower. A passage led forward. I waded down this and into the galley where the water was down to my knees and from there into another cabin. There was no sign of external damage in the forward part of the boat, but it was difficult to be sure, as much of the inside hull was covered with perforated foam material. I clambered on to the fo'c'sle bunk, opened the hatch, and climbed gratefully into the fresh air. Looking down to the sea from the bow, I could see the barnacled rock that was holding *Palinode*. It was now just awash.

Chris came forward from the bridge. "Any sign of damage below?"

I shook my head. "Nothing major at the front. Can't tell about the stern because it's full of oily water."

"Bridge seems fine. New engine controls, compass mounted forward and binoculars hanging by the door. Everything's soaked of course. She's got a hand pump in there, a massive whale gusher, and…" he paused for dramatic effect, "it's working." I glanced at him and he looked back at me with a raised eyebrow that clearly said, 'Why not?'

"We will have to be quick. The tide must have turned by now." I hurried back to the cockpit. The top of the aft coaming had been five inches above the wavelets. Now it was no more than four. The tide had definitely turned. Looking out over the expanse of ocean, I could imagine the sea beginning to flood up Loch Fyne, tons and tons of it, building up a colossal momentum that would raise the sea level in the loch by ten feet or more. Even if we managed to pump out some water, we would lose her if the waves started to lap over that coaming and down into the open cockpit. Unlike on *Molio* there was no barrier to stop the water pouring from the cockpit into the aft cabin, as it must have done on each occasion that the tide had turned and started to flood up the loch over the past two days.

I heard a clanking noise from the bridge. Chris was at work. I sat down in the water of the cockpit, put both hands on the handle of the second pump and began to work it back and forth. I felt it stiffen as it started to work. After about fifteen minutes there was no apparent change. I called out to Chris, "What do you think?"

"By my mark, the level is down one eighth of an inch."

"Is the water draining out by itself?"

"Let's give it all we've got for another fifteen minutes."

We pumped furiously. After a while Chris called out, "You're not going to believe this. The water is down half an inch."

"That's not much," I grunted in time with the pump.

"If we can lower it by half an inch, we can lower it by a foot."

Chris is a mechanical engineer. He knows about these things. I began to pump even harder. As I did, I could see the tide creeping up the outside of the coaming. The sea was now three inches from the top. Bent over the pump all I could see was the lumpy grey surface of the open sea stretching mile after mile towards the dark Isle of Arran floating on the far horizon. I felt impotent in front of all that ocean. Ten minutes later the tide had risen again. "The sea is two inches below the coaming," I shouted. There was no reply, just the donk, donk, donk of the pumps. It had become an all-out race and we were losing. We went at it furiously for another 30 minutes. It wasn't so much a question as an equation. Could we shift sufficient water out of *Palinode*, create

113

enough buoyancy, to lift her stern and to lift it at a faster rate than the rise of the incoming tide. I remembered the rule of twelfths. The tide was coming in more rapidly now.

"We've dropped the level by three inches," shouted Chris.

"Water is slopping in," I shouted back.

"Every inch pumped is a ton of water out and a ton of buoyancy in," he shouted back.

I plunged my arm underwater and found the carpet on the cockpit floor. I rolled it up and put it across the stern coaming, sat on it and pumped furiously. It seemed impossible but all our pumping, all those tons of buoyancy, had failed to shift the boat by one iota. Water started to pour in over the stern coaming. I ran forward to the bridge and grabbed a second carpet. "We're losing her," I told Chris unable to conceal the anguish in my voice.

"Increase the pumping speed for five minutes," Chris responded. I've rarely seen him look so grim. "It's all we can do." He pulled out his Mars bar, took half in a single bite and started pumping at incredible speed. I leapt back to the cockpit, threw the carpet on top of the first, sat on both and began pumping, matching Chris's burst of speed. We were pumping so vigorously now that we both feared that the pump diaphragms wouldn't take it, but they held. After five minutes the water was still coming in, but in slops, and no faster than before. Chris shouted to ask how it was going. I wasn't sure. A minute later, Chris yelled again: "How is it Martyn?"

"Just keep at it," I shouted back. We continued the furious speed of pumping. For some reason, I felt not the slightest fatigue and nor, I believe, did Chris. There was no denying it; the water was barely slopping in now. "Chris, we're doing it," I shouted. "She's lifting. Keep pumping flat out." Slowly, barely perceptibly, yet inexorably, *Palinode* began to rise. Ten minutes later, the water level was two inches below the coaming and hardly a drop was coming in. She was righting herself. I shouted the news to Chris. He let out a mighty cheer, the first of many that marked great landmarks in the salvage, but this was the most exciting. At that moment we realised for the first time that we really could save this boat.

"Water level inside is down by six inches," reported Chris.

"Water level outside down by four," I replied.

"Better get her kedge out in case she begins to float."

Chris was right; the last thing we needed was for her to float further up the rock. "Let's give it one more burst to be sure".

Ten minutes later, we left the pumps to hunt for ropes. We tied the lengths together and fastened one end to the boat's second anchor, a thirty-five pound CQR. We rowed fifty yards from the *Palinode* and dropped the kedge into deep water before returning with the 'bitter' end of the rope. Climbing back on board, I put a turn around the base of the mizzen mast. Chris heaved on the line and the *Palinode* slewed around about ten degrees but remained stuck fast. Looking out to sea for a moment, I began to think about wind and tide. The current would work *Palinode* further up the rock but the light easterly might help us in the other direction. That was it, I thought. Use the wind. "Let's get the sails up," I called. "We can sail her out of here." For the next hour we pumped and rigged alternately. There were sails in the stern locker, together with half a dozen roller collars for the gaff-rigged main-sail. We found some blocks and tackle in a second locker forward of the bridge. Between bursts of pumping, we assembled the gear and worked out the best routing for the sheets. The purpose, the adven-ture, the total engagement in the moment, was not dreamlike then, but unthinking normality. It was how life was meant to be lived. We raised the tan sails one after another, jib, main and mizzen, and as they opened in the breeze, it was as if our spirits opened with them. From the deck, *Palinode* was no longer a wreck. She was a boat, a powerful motor yacht, and we could feel the life returning.

There was more pumping to be done, but we had time now to think and plan. We thought of sheeting her sails in tight and attempting to sail along the deep channel into Asgog Bay, to find shelter and a place to anchor. It would not be easy, even in a good tacking boat. As we discussed the options, it dawned on us that we really had salvaged the *Palinode*, and that brought responsibilities. We needed to take her to the harbour in Tarbert. The wind helped to make up our minds. It was coming from the east. We could sail across Loch Fyne and then have

Pippa tow us into harbour. Chris went back to man the big pump. I was pulling in the dinghy on its painter to go and fetch *Pippa* when the miracle happened. *Palinode* swung free of the rock. She sat quietly in the deep water as if nothing had happened.

A little while later, I returned with *Pippa*. Leaving her in the capable hands of my wife who now had Isla strapped to her front, I re-joined Chris, giving him a couple of bacon and egg rolls prepared by Anne. He devoured them like a bear awaking from hibernation. With *Pippa* circling fifty metres off, like a watchful mother duck, Chris hauled up the kedge as I pulled in the sheets. The sails filled. *Palinode* began to make way. Still heavy with water, we edged her well clear of the island, before turning into Loch Fyne and putting her on a course for Tarbert. As her bow came round there was another great cheer from *Palinode*; this one shared by the girls who shouted in unison and jumped up and down on *Pippa*. From there on we took it in turns to steer and pump. Halfway across Loch Fyne the pumps sucked dry. Half an hour later she was still dry. The *Palinode* was sound as a bell. And for a few sweet hours we were the masters of a beautiful motor yacht sailing up Loch Fyne.

As I steered *Molio* towards Tarbert I remembered how much Chris and I had wanted to keep *Palinode*. It had been a grand adventure but we wanted something more than fun. Amazingly, the owner offered to give us the boat and we'd thought of turning her into a research vessel like Jacques Cousteau's. We tried to find a way but it didn't fit with other plans or, at the end of the day, with the owner's wishes. But it did indicate a new stage in my thinking. The best adventure is more than an escape: it contains a higher purpose.

Just two months after the glorious day of salvage, I set foot in Africa again, this time with my family. Living a hundred miles from the nearest village, each day brought its own crop of adventures and added to this was a driving purpose. I was out to acquire new knowledge about the deep ecological rules underlying biodiversity. It was my goal and passion while at play in the Eden of Africa. It came as a surprise to discover, a few years later, that something was still missing.

The knot that held together the different parts of my life was rarely visible. In certain locations, at unspecified moments, my spirit awakened. It might be in a remote wilderness as the sun came down at the end of a hot day and the herds wound their way onto their evening meadows or it might be among a roomful of scientists in a crowded meeting as we strove to find common understanding. There was a widening of awareness coupled with a sense of spiritual connection. It had something to do with a wider balance and inclusiveness and the life moving within me. Seldom have I felt that connection more keenly than when cruising in the Hebrides of Scotland, where the island-filled seascapes are permeated with a long history of seafaring. Signs of the past abound – castles, ramparts, ancient forts, brochs, stone cells, monasteries, clachans, Vikings' graves, and post-Ice Age caves that guarded the remains of exotic animals like Arctic fox, lemmings and reindeer. To voyage in such a setting is to travel as the wild geese on their autumn migration, as the Atlantic salmon taking to their spawning rivers, or the basking shark seeking the summer blooms of plankton, as free as only the wind and tide can be. Now, as I felt again those tides of freedom moving about me, there was something else at large. Unseen forces quite different from those that confronted my father's generation were bringing change. They had started to challenge that wider balance and inclusiveness that I loved. I hoped that time had stood still in the western isles and that the wonderful cruising grounds of my boyhood were unchanged. I needed that west coast with its communities of independent and self-sufficient islanders more than I cared to admit. I looked down Loch Fyne to the mountains of Arran, picking out the profile of the mythical Sleeping Warrior. Surely the west was still free?

Chapter 7

The Sea Gypsy

Entering the outer bay of Tarbert, I held my course until spotting the beacon that marked the narrow entrance into East Loch, the sheltered inner harbour used by the fishing fleet. Bringing *Molio* into the wind, I furled the sails and motored through the narrows. Most of the boats were out fishing, leaving only a couple of whale-nosed trawlers moored by the processing sheds. Further down, a wooden trawler lay against the south pier, with a row of tyres strung along its side as an invitation to other craft. Opposite the boat were some new pontoons stretching out from the marina on the north side. They virtually filled the loch including the area off the old pier where we used to anchor. A man was working on the foredeck.

"Could you take my line?" I shouted to the fisherman.

He walked to the side of his boat and held out a hand. "We'll be going out in an hour, mind."

"Is there nowhere to anchor?"

He spat over the side. "You'll need to ask the marina about that."

I thanked him and made secure. Down below I turned to the back page of the ship's logbook, where I kept a list of useful phone numbers. There it was, Willie Leitch, sailmaker, Tarbert. My main reason for stopping the night here was to arrange the repair of some sails. The luff wire on *Molio*'s second jib had rusted through about a foot down from the head. I didn't have either the crimping tools or heavy sewing machine for stitching the anti-chafe covers. Some of the other sails could use a bit of patching too. It was a good feeling to be returning to the same family business that my father had used fifty years before. I rang the number on my mobile phone.

"Willie here."

"Hello, it's Martyn speaking. I'm on board the ketch *Molio* over at the pier with the fishing boats."

"What can I do for you Martyn?"

"Do you have a mooring I could use?"

There was a pause. "Do you know Deuchlands? It's the northern bay. Well if you come in from East Loch you'll find a large yawl on your right. In between her and the wooden sheds is a red buoy that belongs to Skerryvore. You can take that one."

Drifting up in neutral a few minutes later I located the buoy, heaved it on deck with a wooden boathook, and made fast. This corner of the harbour was out of the way of the busy thoroughfare of yachts and fishing boats. On three sides oak trees hung their boughs low over the water; on the fourth a rocky islet shielded the view from the marina. I breathed deeply, enjoying the fragrance of lush new foliage. Time enough to see to the sails in the morning. The signal on my mobile phone indicated two bars. I stood on the cabin roof and rang Kyla. She picked up.

"Listen, there's a family of swans just arriving." I held the phone over the side so that Kyla could hear the hissing of the cob. "Did you hear them?"

"Mmm, they sound hungry. Where are you?"

"I'm in Tarbert, in a little corner amongst the trees. Did you get the train ticket by the way?"

"Might have."

"I'll be on the platform to meet you." I rang off with a smile.

Next morning, I dipped the bilges and entered the new level into the log. *Molio* was still making water despite her repairs. I removed the main and mizzen, bagged them up for Willie, and dropped them into the cockpit. Then I rowed across to a rickety ladder set in the rocks, and climbed ashore. I walked along the shore road to the sail loft. It wasn't open yet, so I walked on to the marina. Hundreds of boats were packed along the pontoons almost as far as the dark wall of the south pier which sported a diesel tank, ice maker and several large crates of fishing gear. North and south. New and old Tarbert. The harbour and community were divided. With fishing on the decline, it looked as though the leisure industry had staged a takeover. Even the harbour office had moved from the pier to the marina, which seemed peculiar. I walked into the portacabin and found myself in a bare office with a plastic counter and two stands of leaflets. At the back, a woman was busy on her computer. I waited but she didn't look up.

After a while I coughed, "Do you have a map of the harbour?" Getting a blank look, I added an explanation. "There's been a lot of change since I was last here, what with the new pontoons and all."

"I think there is one in an old brochure." She searched in a drawer and retrieved a tourist pamphlet which had a small diagram of the harbour.

I thanked her and scrutinised the mini-map. It wasn't much help. "Where can visiting boats go?" I asked.

She pointed out the visitors' pontoon and four moorings. "You'll find the fees on the next page."

"Wow!" I exclaimed looking at the price listed against a thirty-six-foot vessel. Even without electricity or use of showers, both of which cost extra, this would set me back more than a night in a B&B. It was the nearest thing to extortion I could imagine. "Whereabouts can we anchor?"

She gave me a glance that I won't forget. "There is no anchoring in the harbour," she informed me, unable to disguise the curling of her upper lip.

I stared for a moment, mouth wide open. When I finally understood what she meant, I closed my mouth and walked out of the door. I was used to the timeless hospitality of the West Highlands and ill-prepared for this intrusion by a grasping culture. It was, moreover, the first time in my yachting life that someone had attempted to make me feel shabby. It was a good lesson. I knew now how a tinker must feel when denied access to his traditional camp. The natural harbour at Tarbert, an inner sea loch, provides perfect shelter in deep water. Like other havens dotted along our coasts, it had always been open to visiting boats, either for tying up at the pier for a short period or for anchoring overnight. Hospitality to strangers is a Celtic custom and a seafaring tradition and, until now, a proud part of our shared maritime heritage. The life of the cruising yachtsman or woman may be akin to that of a sea gypsy but we find no shame in that. We seek to bring something bright and cheerful wherever we anchor. Most of us will pass the time happily with anyone who is curious about sailing and we could not, I think, be thought of as tight-fisted when in the hotel, pub or shop. If someone was in need, most yachting parties would be quick to offer help in whatever way they could, just as they might seek the help of local people in their own hour of need. On what pretext, I wondered, did these Tarbert officials bag this sea loch for themselves? Closing off an ancient right to anchor is an intrusion on custom that is neither hospitable, Highland or even friendly. It gave me a sinking feeling. It looked as if new forces were already at work in the west, and beginning to challenge the age-old custom of granting hospitality to strangers.

I walked back to the sail loft and climbed the outdoor stairs. At the top was a door which I pushed open, crossing a dark anteroom into a large open loft with wooden floors and whitewashed stone walls. Ceiling joists were propped up by ship's masts and on the far side were four deeply recessed windows, which looked out over East Loch to south quay and the castle above. Sails were piled on all sides and a row of sewing machines stood guard along the back wall. To one side, reels of multi-coloured braid were stacked on shelves next to a desk covered in sail cloth. On the wall behind, in the place of pin-up girls, were photographs of yachts under sail. It was quiet. So quiet that for a moment I didn't notice the big man in the far corner hunched over a sail, needle in hand, in Zen-like meditation. He hadn't noticed my entry either.

"What a beautiful loft," I sighed.

He looked up with the innocent eyes of the righteous: for all the world like Desperate Dan, ready to help the latest victim of injustice.

"Ah, sometimes it seems too big and sometimes it seems too small. It's too small for the topsail of a tall ship."

Inwardly I rejoiced at this soft-spoken wild man working quietly in his loft. The shiny new marina with its business-school management plan slipped from my mind. "I remember coming here in the nineteen fifties, with my dad, to fit a new tent cover for the cockpit of our boat. She was a Falmouth Quay Punt. Would it be the same place?"

"No, it was smaller then. We rebuilt this larger loft after the fire in the nineteen sixties."

I looked out the window and made out *Molio*'s masts close in by the trees. "Thanks for the mooring; it's a lovely spot."

"I watched you coming in. I was glad to see you missed the bank." He really did look relieved. Willie put down the needle carefully and stood up. There didn't seem any need for introductions or a handshake. "Shall we take a look at your sails?"

We walked along the road to where I'd left the Avon dinghy and Willie rowed us out to *Molio*. For a large man he was surprisingly nimble. Large and fast, I thought, the ideal combination for sailing a dinghy in a gusting wind. It turned out to be something he loved to do. On board, Willie pulled the jib out of its bag and eyed it up. "That will be no problem," he assured me. Then he pulled the mainsail out of its bag and held a section up to the light. It was mottled where the material had thinned. "Ah, and I thought it was just a tear."

"She's on her last legs I'm afraid."

"Yes, and my Mum could use a new tea strainer." He examined the repair I had made with my daughter's sewing machine and cocked an eyebrow at the bits of coloured tape sewn into the leach hem.

"She's a bit like Joseph's multi-coloured coat." I said. "That one was last summer. I think maybe her life is coming to an end."

"I think so," said Willie placing the sail gently down. "We can patch it up for this season and then, in the winter, I'll make you a new one with a burgundy sail cover. It will look smashing." He looked up at an open skiff that was travelling towards us at speed. A couple of guys on board were looking intently at *Molio*. As they approached Willie shouted, "We're making adjustments to the sails." The boat turned and without a word headed back the way it had come. I could see the man driving the outboard scowling and muttering to his companion.

"What did they want?" I asked.

"Oh, that was the new harbourmaster and his sidekick," replied Willie. "They are wanting fees from every boat now."

"But this is Skerryvore's mooring."

"Yes and they are getting five hundred pounds a year for it. But they're not content. They're always looking for more money."

"They could have come on board for some tea. It might have cheered them up."

"This used to be a friendly place. But this man has driven away four of my customers who won't bring their boats into Tarbert anymore. I told the harbourmaster it was wrong. 'You can't charge for the same mooring twice.' Do you know what he said?" Without waiting for my reply, Willie continued, "'You're old-fashioned. This harbour,'" Willie nodded at the beautiful sea loch that could be glimpsed through the four windows, "'is our business now. We are managing it despite people like you and it's thriving.'"

"When I was at their office this morning," I responded. "I asked where I could anchor. They said, 'Nowhere'."

Willie's face darkened, "This is a harbour of refuge. Nobody has the right to deny a boat sanctuary." I noticed for the first time that his cap had Coast Guard written across the front.

We re-bagged the sails and took them ashore. Willie climbed out of the dinghy, picked up the bags as if they were full of feathers, and ambled back to his loft. Returning to *Molio* I decided to go back over the deck to look for spots where rainwater had been entering. It would impress Kyla if the boat were dry. The seams that I'd caulked were holding up but several wooden plugs that covered the deck-fastening screws had loosened. Some had even popped out. I found some sealant and started on the suspect plugs above my bunk. As I worked a noisy pair of oystercatchers kept me company.

The traditional right to anchor in a sheltered harbour is known as a 'right of common'. Even where land or loch is owned by someone, the 'right of common' allows others to use the resource for a specific purpose. A famous example is the right to pasture one's animals on common land. This right might be restricted to local 'commoners', but the essential point is that traditional users of the resource have a legitimate right to its continued use. You can tell a lot about a country from the way it manages its commons. Securing the right of users to manage their resource is one more step in a hierarchy of actions that builds freedom in society.

The greatest wrong inflicted on the people of England was surely the enclosure of common land, which took place over an extended period from the sixteenth to the nineteenth centuries. It ended the communal grazing tradition and precipitated eviction, unemployment and conflict. In Scotland, the common people of the Highlands suffered enclosure and eviction on an even larger scale, especially in the latter part of this period. Instrumental as these land reforms have been in shaping our nation, it is the coastal resources that I wish to reflect on.

British seafarers have traditionally been granted the right to anchor in almost any loch or bay offering shelter without let or hindrance. Beyond that is the idea of a harbour of refuge. These are places offering exceptional shelter where a boat can seek safety if overtaken by a storm or otherwise in need of urgent assistance. Traditionally, the government sought to maintain such places for the welfare of British and foreign vessels and even invested in them. Tarbert would surely have qualified as a harbour of refuge. Yet these customary rights which went back centuries, and which enabled all seafarers to anchor in the shelter of natural harbours, appeared to have been usurped in the past few years by the new marina business model. Part of the problem with common resources is a difficulty in managing them sustainably. People are reluctant to limit their own offtake to within sustainable levels when the resource is open to abuse by free-riders – people who cannot resist taking more than a fair share. In the case of an anchorage, the problem would arise if one person started to lay out many moorings. This hadn't happened in Tarbert; the problem only arose with the coming of the marina. This expropriation of common rights represents a loss of freedom for the boating public.

Take another example of a common resource from around these waters – commercial fishing. In the nineteenth century the Firth of Clyde fishing fleet peaked at a staggering one thousand vessels. Unsurprisingly, there was anxiety about overfishing, particularly for fishermen living higher up Loch Fyne who would be the first to suffer when stocks collapsed. They were fully aware of the consequences of overfishing. 'No herring, no wedding' was a popular saying of the time. Overfishing of the Clyde herring was a classic 'tragedy of the commons', which pitted boat against boat, man against man, and community against community as the resource was overexploited and became harder to fish. The government was urged to intervene but tension continued to rise culminating, in 1853, in the loss of an Ardrishaig fisherman who was shot and killed by a naval gunboat while fishing illegally. Rules were relaxed after this. The alarm about overfishing became muted. 'Fish for profit and damn the consequences' became the accepted attitude of the fiercely independent skippers. Although boats and gear continued to evolve, herring were so prolific, and the migratory population spread out over such a large sea area, that another century was to pass before major declines occurred. When the population crashed it was not just in Loch Fyne but as far as the North Sea.

It is hard to understand why fishermen would demand the lifting of government restraints, only to end up destroying the source of their livelihood and that of generations to come. But how much choice did the skippers really have? Were they out-of-control freebooters unable to restrain themselves, or victims of the government's system of fisheries management? Could it be that the top-down system of governance that controlled the fishery drove the skippers into over-fishing? I cannot claim any expertise to answer such questions. But overfishing, like its cousin overgrazing, is by no means an inevitable outcome of a communal system of resource use. The solution lies in reform of local governance. Elinor Ostrom won her Nobel Peace prize for developing social tools that helped communities to manage their common resources in ways that ensured their sustainability. These same tools should be applied to the management of natural harbours, with the wider boating community fully represented along with local users in any development planning.

In the evening, the temperature began to drop. I put away the tools, found my fleece jacket and went hunting for *Mollymawk* in the dinghy. She was a forty-five-foot French ketch built along fishing boat lines, which belonged to a friend who now lived aboard. I wondered what it was like spending a winter on your boat. I found *Mollymawk* next to a brightly painted tug on a pontoon used by several larger vessels. She looked a treat with varnished coachroof and Devon cream hull. As I bumped alongside I spotted Ben walking along the pontoon with a hippie couple who waved as they continued on to the tug. A big grin lit up his face which, despite the beard, had the innocence of a Botticelli cherub. He took the painter and tied it off while I climbed onto the pontoon. Pulling back an awning that sheltered the bridge, he invited me aboard. "Welcome to *Mollymawk*," he beamed, this time with an owner's pride. I followed him down the ladder into a vast saloon where a wood burning stove radiated warmth. On the opposite side, a fixed sofa surrounded a pinewood table. I noticed that a couple of books on philosophy had been tossed carelessly to one side next to a box of children's games.

"I thought you might be on your own here but I see you've got friends," I nodded in the direction of the tug.

"They're great and the children get on together like there's no tomorrow. There's a community of liveaboards here and we help each other out. "

"Where do the kids sleep?" I asked.

"They have a cabin in the stern. They love it. So do their school friends. It's like a dream come true for them."

I remembered my bunk on *Primrose* with stickers on the planking and secret places to hide sweets. It brought back a rush of childhood memories. I told Ben about my first boat. A canvas canoe that I'd built at school. The great thing was being able to go wherever I wanted. Mostly I messed about along the beach, trying to keep up with the waves, spearing flounders in the shallows and, on one occasion, rigging a sail made from a broom handle, a large sack and a couple of crosspieces.

Ben had a proper canoe in the Native American tradition and knew about the many adventures to be had. "It's getting the right mix. I want my kids to have the skill and judgement necessary for handling a boat

126

safely in strong winds and enough self-reliance to improvise and have fun."

"We used to row about here looking for a big old seal with one eye called Simon."

"He's here still. Well maybe it's the son of Simon," said Ben, eyeing up the grey patches in my beard.

"Grandson probably," I laughed.

"Talking about fish, how about the pub?" He closed off a vent in the wood burning stove and I followed him back up the companionway ladder, past the tomato plant and onto the pontoon. A short walk took us to the Vic where we found an alcove furthest from the noisy TV. We sat down with pints and ordered food. I kept remembering incidents from the past.

"One time we arrived here in *Primrose*," I told Ben. "It was late so we tied up alongside the fisherman's pier. Dad put a bucket in the cockpit with a note, THREE HUNGRY BOYS TO FEED. Next morning there were a dozen fish in the bucket and others strewn about the cockpit."

"The fishermen are a good crowd still," said Ben. "It's the marina that is bringing problems."

"Willie said it was supposed to be run for the benefit of all local people but it was a joke."

Ben nodded, "We've had an outbreak of CODS." Catching my raised eyebrow he explained, "Corporate Office Domination Syndrome. I think you've tasted some already. When the trust built the new pontoon, the one that juts out close to the fishing pier, they didn't even consult the fishermen. When challenged, the harbour master didn't budge. 'If a fisherman can't control his boat, he shouldn't be fishing.' They are fed up with him. He doesn't dare go onto the pier now."

"In case they give him a hard time?"

"In case they throw him in."

"A harbourmaster that can't go onto his pier; what kind of madness is that?"

"The town is split between those who love its traditions and have an eye for the natural beauty of the harbour, and those who just want to make money. That's the way of things round here."

Later that evening, I lit the oil lamp on *Molio* and pulled out the log of *Primrose* from 1956. Back then, the community of seafarers – the sailors and fishermen – was closer knit. I was looking for a passage that my father wrote which had stuck in my mind:

August 24th

Barometer 28.75

Here the wind freshened more than somewhat and she took a bit of holding as we crossed the entrance to Loch Striven. We were creaming along. The bow of the dinghy was well up and we were leaving a wake like a destroyer. The wind kept veering between north and northeast so we were constantly hauling in or letting out the sheets, luffing up or bearing away, and all the time we were thrashing along, going like the hammers. Judging from Tarka [my grandfather's motor yacht] *we were making a good eight knots. If anything it felt faster than Tarka with both engines flat out and all sails set. Greer* [aged eleven] *was eager to take the tiller. It took all his strength to hold her as we crashed along in a strengthening wind. A succession of fishing boats passed us coming down East Kyle from Loch Fyne. All waved including one skipper who flashed his lights on and off to draw our attention, and then stepping out of his wheelhouse, took his hat off and bowed extravagantly, grinned, put it back on and gave us another great wave, along with all his crew. We waved back madly. Coming up to Colintraive we turned in and dropped the hook by a moored yacht. It was quite dark by the time the sails were furled and stowed, the burgee lowered and the riding light hoisted.*

Primrose wasn't so different from the Lochfyne skiffs that the fathers and grandfathers of those fishermen had sailed. They loved those skiffs – almost as much as a man loves a woman. That passion is captured in the lines of George Campbell Hay's epic poem *Seeker Reaper* written aboard a Lochfyne skiff, perhaps surrounded by diving solans as the gannets thereabouts are known, at the entrance to Kilbrannan Sound:

She's a reaper, she's a river, she's a racer,
she's a teerer thon. It takes the wind tie pace her.

She's a leaper. She's a gled roar wi the sea before her face.
She shoothers bye her anchor chain, she canna lie at peace.

Boating is different now. The divergence between recreational sailing
and fishing has continued to grow to the point where little unites the
chartered splendours of the marina and the heavy commercial fishing
vessels, other than the modern comforts – private cabins, hot showers,
video and electronic navigation – that both now share. The two communities have drifted apart as well. Yet in times of peril, seafarers of all
brands will come to each other's rescue. It is their ultimate bond.

With the weather set to deteriorate, I determined to make ready to
sail for *Molio*'s summer moorings at Fairlie. My plan was to go home for
a few weeks to attend to some consultancy work and then to sail north,
making for St Kilda if the weather looked settled. First I would show
Kyla some of the more sheltered waters of the Clyde. I collected the
repaired sails from Willie next morning and rigged the main and mizzen, admiring the large patches he'd sewn neatly into place. As *Molio*
sailed through the deserted narrows to the outer bay, it was easy to
imagine an earlier time when sail still ruled. In Tarbert's heyday seventy fishing skiffs jostled daily in these narrows, their great brown sails
masking each other's wind, until one by one they won through to Loch
Fyne and began their chase for the silver darlings.

Chapter 8

Molio's Cave

I awoke from a heavy sleep to the sound of my office telephone downstairs. I checked the alarm; seven o'clock. Bit early for a phone call, especially on Saturday. I rolled out from under the downy and thundered downstairs naked, grabbing the phone at the fifth ring.

"Are you the owner of the green ketch moored at Fairlie?" The voice was formal but apologetic, like a doctor preparing to pass on bad news.

"Yes," I began, my mind in a whirl. We'd had gale force winds overnight, but surely nothing that *Molio*'s mooring couldn't cope with? They'd come from the east which was unusual. I knew that the steep slopes above Fairlie tended to funnel easterlies down the glen and out across the bay in a vicious mistral. Even so, she'd weathered plenty of easterlies on that mooring. "Yes, that is my boat." I braced myself for what was to come. Collision. Stolen. Sunk at her mooring?

"I have to tell you that your boat and mooring are out in the bay."

"Out in the bay?"

"Way out." The tone was contrite but the message was clear.

I stammered my thanks and hung up. Out in the bay. How could that be? How could *Molio* just wander off on her own? I needed to act fast, but what could I do? I found *Molio*'s logbook and opened it. At the back was a list of important contact numbers. There it was: Stewart McIntyre, Cumbrae Yacht Slip. Stewart would help. He looked after *Molio*'s mooring just as he had *Pippa*'s all those years ago and *Primrose*'s before her. I dialled the number. A groggy voice answered.

"It's Martyn. Sorry to ring so early but I've just heard that *Molio* and mooring are dragging out of the bay at Fairlie."

"Wit do you expect me to do aboot it?"

"Could you get over and take her in tow?"

"Ma boat's oot the water. Without ma boat I'm buggered."

"Okay, okay. I'll get on to the coastguard." I hung up. As soon as I did the phone rang. It was the secretary of Fairlie Yacht Club. He said that three other boats had dragged and there'd been two collisions. *Molio* had dragged into deeper water but then stopped on the outer sandbank. With luck she would stick there until I reached her. He was driving down from Glasgow and promised to alert the coastguard before leaving.

I strode across the hall to the spare room and shook Kyla's arm gently. She stirred.

"Sorry to wake you but we have to leave in ten minutes. *Molio* is dragging her mooring."

In the kitchen I switched on the kettle before running upstairs to find some clothes. By the time I came down again, Kyla was fully dressed and making hot chocolate in a thermal mug.

"Ready to go?"

"What kept you?" she smiled. It was only three days since she'd arrived but already it felt normal having her around the house. She had some time off in the school holidays and we'd been planning a few days' sailing.

Two hours later, we crested the hill above Largs in my old Passat estate and descended to the coastal road that brought us into Fairlie. I turned into a narrow side street which led down an incline to the start of the yacht club jetty. Hastily scanning the bay with my binoculars all looked normal. There was the familiar cluster of boats bobbing up and down on their moorings, twisting in the gusts spinning out from the shore, but no sign of *Molio*. I looked beyond the boats to the outer sandbank, marked by a green navigation buoy. No boats there. With my heart in my mouth, I began to scan along the coastline of the Isle of Cumbrae, which was shrouded in mist rising from a line of angry white horses.

"Isn't that *Molio*?" asked Kyla, nudging me and pointing to a yacht at the far end of the moorings close to the Hunterston coal terminal.

I lifted my binoculars in that direction and there was the unmistakable outline of *Molio* – twin masts, green hull, graceful counter at the stern, blunt business-like bow with the bowsprit raised at a slightly cheeky angle. My breathing eased. "Yes. It is. She's on another mooring."

My mobile rang. "Did you find yer boat?" asked Stewart with a hint of laughter typical of the old Puffer hands.

"After I thought I'd lost her."

"Ah," he guffawed, "I did wonder about that. See yon mooring? That belongs to the other ketch. She's twelve ton. Aye she's the heaviest in the bay. She'll hold *Molio* tight as a Glasgae tart."

"Thanks Stewart. How did you move her without a boat?"

"Jacky boy owed me a favour. We went out in his fishing boat. Found *Molio* on the sandbank and put a line on her. I jumped on but couldn't release yon mooring because of the weight on it. She'd dragged both mushrooms across the bay. Christ, how did she move them? Onyways, eventually we worked out a plan – I lassoed the mooring and we hauled it up onto Jacky's boat. That bloody mooring is perfect. We towed *Molio* o'er. Wasnae easy, mind. She was right up our arse in the gusts. But we got her on tha ither yin."

"If I had a medal to give, you'd have it."

"I wasnae going to lose yon boat on one of ma moorings."

"What's your favourite dram?" I asked.

"Highland Park" he shot back.

"There's two bottles coming your way, one for yourself and one for Jacky."

"Och, that will be mighty fine."

I thanked him again and rang off. Knowing *Molio* was safe was a huge relief. I stood there for a while looking out at her. Seeing me in a kind of trance, Kyla took the mobile and rang the coastguard to give them the news and to ask for an update on the weather. She lifted her eyebrow. "They say force four, occasionally six, moderating later." I looked across the bay of white horses. The gusts were ferocious. In one dark fury, wave tops were lifting off in sheets and being flung across the sea. "It's more than that out there. We'll need to wait."

"You can take me for breakfast, then."

We drove the half mile to a bar and restaurant at the nearby yacht haven and walked in the glass door with a gust of wind. A big bearded fellow in yellow Bermuda shorts was talking to a crowd of spellbound onlookers. The white dreadlocks tumbling over his shoulders gave him a Billy Connolly look except this fellow was still in his twenties. There was a puddle of seawater spreading out from under his chair. I caught the end of his tale.

"...dragged the anchor right past the terminal."

"Our boat dragged her mooring all the way from Fairlie to Cumbrae and back," said Kyla who has a weakness for bearded men, especially ones dripping with water in fancy restaurants.

He eyed her up and down, beaming in satisfaction at the latest addition to his circle of admirers: "I was coming over from the Wee Cumbrae when I saw the white water off Fairlie. The engine went on the blink so I put out an anchor and called the coastguard. They towed me in."

"The forecast is four to six," said Kyla showing off her new nautical lexicon "But it may be more."

"Is that right," leered Bermudan shorts. "Well the cox on their rib said it was gusting eight or nine off the terminal. I'm waiting this one out." He knocked back a glass of the finest, grinned at his mates, leered at Kyla and went off to find some dry clothes. We found a table with a view of the sea and ordered breakfast. We were both starving. Kyla gulped down Cullen skink like a cormorant swallowing eels as I tucked into an English breakfast of bacon and eggs. Over coffee we decided to go for a walk up the hill. The sun had come out and, in the shelter of a wooded glen, it was hot and deceptively quiet.

By mid-afternoon the wind had moderated but it hadn't steadied. Calms were now interspersed with squalls. Through the binoculars, *Molio*'s masts looked a bit steadier. We went down to the jetty for a closer look and found that *Molio* was now lying exactly downwind. We inflated the Avon, taking our time. It seemed quieter so we loaded the dinghy with stores and I rowed out from the shore with Kyla in the stern. We had about a mile to go. As we left the shelter of the houses the wind caught us, driving the dinghy forward. I shipped the oars and we made a lively two or three knots downwind. A stronger gust took us, spinning the dinghy sideways on, and propelling her at four knots. I experimented with the oars. It required powerful strokes to turn her stern into the wind but it gave us added stability. The waves were now about six inches high, and not yet a threat. We passed the other boats, but that still left a further 500 yards of open water before we would reach *Molio*, who was prancing in the gusts all on her own. The waves began to build up. Out past the terminal they could swamp the dinghy or lift her enough for a gust to get under and flip her over. Neither of us was wearing a lifejacket. The strongest gust so far seized us. I fought for control with the oars. It wouldn't do to miss *Molio*. The mooring rope stretched out from the hippo buoy to *Molio*'s bow at a shallow angle. It made a tempting target. But once I'd grabbed it I knew the wind would drive the dinghy under the rope and that I'd end up on my back trying to hold on. It would be better to come into the side near the stern where *Molio*'s deck is closest to the water. I prepared myself to grab her gunwale. There would be one chance. Kyla looked comfortable in the stern. She trusted me. I aligned the dinghy with a few swift strokes, determined not to betray that trust. Suddenly the gust left us. We sat flat in the calm lumpy water with not a breath of wind. Looking back over Kyla's shoulder, I could see the next squall line two hundred metres off. I put my back into rowing and reached *Molio* before it arrived.

"Quick, Kyla, you first." She jumped nimbly aboard. I passed up the stores at speed and threw bags and oars into *Molio*'s cockpit, before clambering aboard myself. As I secured the dinghy properly to a steel cleat on the counter, the wind struck, pushing *Molio* hard until she bucked at the restraint of the mooring line. It held us tight. I sat down for a moment to catch my breath. Kyla opened the companionway doors and slid back the hatch. The cabin smelt sweet as summer hay. She lit the small burner on the galley and put on the kettle, restoring our normal shipboard routine. I set about preparing *Molio* for cruising the next day – hoisting the burgee on the mainmast and the ensign on the mizzen, opening seacocks for the heads, and dipping the diesel tanks. There is always something to do on a boat, at least there is on *Molio*.

In the evening, Kyla sang some of her favourite Scottish ballads with a fair interpretation of the lowland Scots dialect. There was an easy camaraderie aboard, which I didn't want to break. Later I lay awake on my bunk thinking back over the day, alert to sounds and movements of the boat. The wind strengthened briefly at about midnight, finally dying away in the small hours allowing me a few hours' sleep.

The sun rose on a transformed bay, breathless and still, and as it rose higher, both man and beast in the great panorama of hill and sea that is the Firth of Clyde basked in its warmth. I was looking forward to a lazy day. Kyla was still sleeping, head buried under piles of golden-red hair which tumbled over the side of her bunk like some glorious fern draped over the boughs of forest tree. I wondered what revelations were appearing in her dreams. I left her to sleep and took a mug of tea into the cockpit to relish the majesty of the morning. A family of mallards swam over and began feeding around the mooring buoy. Herring gulls cast about, looking for any sailors throwing leftovers overboard. One settled in the water thirty feet behind *Molio*. My eyes settled on the whale pump which was set into one side of the cockpit. It had been taking more and more strokes to get the first squoosh of water over the side. Here was this morning's task. With the maker's diagram to hand, I dismantled it and replaced the diaphragm. By the time it was reassembled, a light easterly breeze had picked up. I hoisted sail and prepared to let go the mooring.

Kyla's head appeared from below. "What a beautiful day," she enthused. "Shall we go up the Kyles of Bute to that place where you caught the skate?"

"Can you steer?" I offered her the helm.

"Just a minute."

She went below, reappearing with sunglasses and hat. I showed her the passage between a row of moored yachts and the outer submerged sandbank, followed by a turn that would take us out to deeper water. From there we sailed north along the eastern side of the Isle of Cumbrae and out into the main Firth, where we passed a playful group of dolphins, the first I'd seen in the Clyde. The breeze died away. Reluctantly, we switched on the engine to motor northwest, passing

Rothesay to port before entering East Kyle. As the land enfolded us, we were drawn into a world of rolling hills and narrow sea passages. The tide swept *Molio* north to the Burnt Islands, a group of three small islets surrounded by fast flowing tidal narrows. It was the home of gulls, ducks and geese which dive-bombed trespassers unmercifully. On one island was a prehistoric vitrified fort and on another I'd found the rank-smelling den of a mustelid – mink perhaps.

"It's the kind of place where BB's little grey men might be found cooking up minnows on the shingle," I remarked.

Kyla smiled. "Will there be sea faeries too; little ones riding on fishes backs?"

We anchored off the larger islet from where Kyla set off in the dinghy to explore. I began to think about making dinner. A little while later I heard her voice floating across the water. Looking up I saw a seal's head bob to the surface just beside the boat. It seemed to be following her. When she came back on board she was glowing with excitement. The seal, it turned out, had followed her all around the island.

"She thinks I have a big rubber bottom and wooden paddles. I told her not to be so silly. Then she showed me a little bay with fish and lobsters."

We spent a couple of days in this idyllic spot. Kyla set about overhauling the gas stove and even got the second ring to work. This was a particularly impressive effort as I had been unable to free off the seized control knob in Ireland. She polished the clock and ship's bell with brasso wadding before turning her attention to the brass handles on the companionway doors. She found an old jar of Bois Vivant, a turpentine wax polish that the previous owner had left on board, and polished the saloon table and mahogany fittings, creating an entirely new atmosphere below decks. She also found a large bottle of teak oil and began nourishing the exposed surfaces in the cockpit. "You must treat the whole deck," she ordered. Kyla loved wood and *Molio* basked in her attention.

Not wanting to be shown up for a slouch, I made a new ensign pole from a section of stout garden cane and rewired the echo sounder. Each of us found favourite perches: Kyla's on the starboard side of the bridge deck, or lying flat out aft of the mainmast; mine standing on the companionway ladder, or sitting on the port side of the cockpit. It reminded me of watching the chimps at Edinburgh Zoo as they perched on their favourite branches and platforms. So when Kyla asked me that evening why I felt so at home on *Molio*, it wasn't hard to explain.

"When I visited the Gombe Stream Research Centre in Tanzania, an old rafiki took me into the forest one evening and through a dense thicket to a vantage point where we could see Gremlin, a large female chimpanzee with her baby, Gimly, and two six-year-old twins, Golden and Glitter. As the sun lowered towards the lake, the chimps moved from a large fig to a smaller tree with large limp leaves and began to make nests. Soon Mum was lying on her back, body stretched out, one arm flung behind her head, the picture of relaxation. Her mahogany eyes turned to look at us with a sad expression, as if she was remembering some much-missed member of her family. Little Gimly sat on his mother's tummy making all kinds of expressions with his rubber mouth before curling up beside her. Fifteen feet above, Golden and Glitter made their own nests. The first stars came out, darkness fell and the three nests swayed in the night gusts that rushed towards the lake."

Kyla came and sat down beside me. "Don't stop now," she said putting her head on my shoulder.

"Don't you think the love of trees and the love of wood lie deep within us," I intoned whilst untangling a lock of hair that had fallen onto my lap. "*Molio* is more than just a boat to me: she is part of the primeval forest."

"Well we girls like to be on terra firma," replied Kyla without hesitation. "We prefer stone houses with big kitchens. You see, Martyn, they remind us of our ancestral cave."

On the second day, I put out the fishing line hoping to catch cod for our tea. There were nothing but tiddlers. As a boy, my brothers and I pulled up plenty of big fish at the Burnt Islands. It was one of the best fishing spots in the Clyde and the seabed was littered with cockles, scallops and starfish. The ideal time for fishing was at the high tide following a full moon. As the spring tide rushed up the Kyles, with the speed and power of a large river, it brought unimaginable numbers of zooplankton for the filter feeders. Most of them fed at night, avoiding the risk of exposing soft body parts during the day, when the fish predators could spot them. Except that under a full moon their delicate white flesh was still visible...

Mussels, cockles, gents and dams
And pale luminescent clams
Lie open for the silken moon
Defences down in tidal swoon.

Wagging tails in their haste
Fishes rush up for a taste,
Snatch the tongues without a care
Mantles sweet they rip and tear.

The moon she gasps at each bite
Weeps a moondrop in the night,
That each shell clasps, as waters swirl
To shield the Mistress in her pearl.

It was an angler's paradise but, like everywhere else in the Clyde, the fishing at Burnt Island was a shadow of its former self. Most people blamed the removal of the three-mile ban on commercial fishing in 1984. It is hard to imagine why any government would agree to such a retrograde step. It is a deep mystery to me that it remains easier to this day to introduce wise and sustainable systems of natural resource use in the poorer countries of Africa than in the UK.

Rummaging about for alternative fishing lures, I discovered a ten-year-old bottle of cava that Barry must have tucked behind the life-jackets for a special occasion. Kyla and I opened the heavy bottle and drank a toast to his foresight. It was a warm evening so we took it up to the cockpit and watched Venus come out low on the eastern horizon, followed by the stars one by one as the sky darkened. Kyla showed me the summer triangle overhead and the eagle constellations which she had learnt when camping in the far north. She snuggled up beside me. Tentatively I put my arm round her.

After a few minutes Kyla closed her eyes. "When I was small Gran used to comb my hair. It was always in a complete mess. I used to complain but I loved it really."

"Was that your Cornish Gran?" I asked.

"I loved staying with them. I knew all the neighbours in the street and the fishermen on the beach. I would sometimes roam along the coast to the next cove just to see what was going on."

"I can imagine you as tomboy. Did you collect cockles?" Not very likely, I realised, but I had remembered collecting cockles as a boy and leaving some particularly fine ones in my coat pocket, only to find them again a few days later from the awful smell.

"I collected fossils and curious stones. Grandpa was an artist. He knew about the fossil beds and took me up the river to look for otters and kingfishers. Those holidays were the best."

Lying in my bunk that night I imagined Kyla as a feisty little girl popping in and out of her neighbour's homes for a chat and drink before running down to the beach to meet the fishermen returning with their catch. As I drifted off to sleep there was a squeal from the heads: "There's phosphorescence in the loo."

On the third morning, we weighed anchor and continued round the Kyles, stopping briefly at Tighnabruaich for some fresh provisions. Picking up a breeze off Kames, we hoisted sail and were soon making five knots on a close reach. We came into a swell off Ardlamont Point which stayed with us as we crossed the open entrance to Kilbrannon Sound and then eased off as we continued south in the shelter of Arran. In the late afternoon we tightened sheets to enter the northern channel to Lamlash Harbour and dropped anchor in four fathoms, not more than a hundred yards from the jetty on Holy Isle and two hundred from the Buddhist monastery.

As it grew dark, electric lights sprang to life in the monastery. We lit the oil lamp, rather than switch on our own electric cabin lights, as it felt more in keeping with the saint that had made his home on the island all those centuries ago. The little flame shone bravely, lighting up the cabin with its warmth. Kyla wanted to hear again my boyhood story about the Holy Isle and my serendipitous connection with St Molio.

"We arrived at this exact same spot late one summer in *Primrose*. On board were my father and mother, two older brothers, our black and white spaniel Nick, and me. I was about seven, I think. Back then there was just a white-washed farmhouse at that end of the island. I think it must have been recently abandoned. In the morning we rowed ashore with Nick, who needed a good run, having been cooped up in the boat all the previous day. Nick rushed about smelling the good smells and we set off to explore. As we crossed the rough pasture near the farmhouse I stumbled on something strange. I bent down and picked it up. I was amazed to find I was holding a tortoise, a beefy little chap about six inches long, with a lovely arching shell back. His head and feet were tucked right in. Everyone was astonished, including Nick. What could a tortoise, a native of the warm Mediterranean lands, be doing here? Dad said he wouldn't survive the winter if I left him. So I popped him in a fold of my large, home-knitted jersey. I thought he would feel safer there but he began to wriggle. I peeked in-between the folds and saw that he had made a mess. I couldn't blame him, so I just put up with it. We picked some grass and once we were back on board I put him in a cardboard box as a temporary tortoise home. We thought about different names. But there wasn't any question about it really. I called him Molio, after the Celtic-Christian saint who made his home here." I broke off briefly to explain that St Molio had lived in a cave further towards the south end of the island, and that we could go and look for it in the morning. "We kept Molio the tortoise in our garden at home in Ayrshire for years, together with a companion that we bought for him. He was a friend and mascot really."

Kyla was looking at me through those large eyes that made my tummy do turns. "So what kind of friend was he?"

"I didn't think about him much. He reminded me that some things can be exotic and mysterious but still poop in your jersey."

Kyla wasn't to be put off by my attempt at humour. "So did you feel connected to St Molio?"

"Not especially."

"Then why did you call your tortoise Molio?"

"I don't know. Maybe I couldn't think of anything better."

"Then why did you call your boat Molio?"

I sat there looking at her. "I don't know Kyla. I don't understand myself that well. It just felt right." I knew that wouldn't satisfy her, so I tried again. "I couldn't imagine his life. Sitting in a cave for years and years, it sounded excruciatingly boring. Even so I remained curious about him. I was just a wee tyke but I knew St Molio stood for something, he kept pursuing something he believed in."

Next morning we took breakfast in the cockpit and enjoyed some of the fresh food from Tighnabruaich – yoghurt, blueberries, bananas, brown bread and honey. I looked carefully at Kyla. Her eyes were bright and clear, with no sign of tiredness. I let myself believe she was getting better. After a bit we rowed ashore and carried the dinghy well up the stony beach to just below a small hut. Our plan was to climb to the top of the island, starting out from the north-end. Holy Isle is about two miles long and half a mile wide, and consists essentially of one large heather-clad hill rising to just over a thousand feet. It is steep on the east side facing out into the Clyde, but has a flat shoreline on the western side, which is confined to a narrow strip except at the north and south ends of the island. We set off along the shorefront for the north end, passing a small flock of Soay sheep in chocolate brown coats keeping cool in the shade of the jetty. A little further on, we came to a wood of native trees, which had evidently been planted in recent years. It was doing well with the aid of a deer fence. Seeing the wood developing so robustly was a reminder of the ecological devastation pressed upon the Highlands and Islands even today. Grazing pressure alone maintains a treeless desert over much of the land.

We walked up a tiny drainage line to the top of the first rise where we came across two groups of Eriskay Ponies. They were enjoying the cool breeze blowing across the exposed eastern face of the island. We sat on a boulder to watch them frisk about, evidently delighting in the same free life as the wild horses I'd seen in Mongolia. Not wanting to disturb them, we circled round before continuing up the hill. Near the top we had a view of the beach with our dinghy. The tide was coming up faster than I'd anticipated and we decided to forego the rest of the climb. Kyla led the way down the steep slopes of the western side, her red curls disappearing under the tall fronds of bracken until reaching the footpath at their base.

A small side path took us through another thick stand of bracken rising above our heads. We found the cave on the far side of a small clearing set into the base of an ancient sandstone rock face. Tresses of flowering woodbine hung down in front of the wide mouth acting as a screen to obscure the dark interior. It was so simple, more of a shelter than a true cave, almost forty foot wide and thirteen foot deep in the centre. The sunken floor was partly bare rock and partly a covering of dry sandy soil, with evidence of recent use by sheep. The roof rose from the back at forty-five degrees. In Africa, I would automatically have looked for Bushman paintings on such a surface. Here too we found art: various graffiti from pilgrims through the ages and many unexplained indentations. I'd learnt from looking at Bushman rock art that the best way to see it is to sit patiently. You look, wait and look again. After a while your eyes begin to see more, helped by the changing patterns of light. So we waited, warmed by the sun and made drowsy by the perfume of honeysuckle, until the first stories from St Molio's Cave revealed themselves. Kyla made out three heraldic crosses in one corner, broad and confident, on a pale seam of rock. Below them, almost invisible, were some spidery vertical lines that might have been the remnants of Viking runes.

When I first began thinking about St Molio on this voyage, there was little to go on. Facts were sketchy and digging about for new ones meant going back a long way. He never was in the mainstream of history and what little I did glean to begin with was hardly promising material for an inquiry into freedom. He had lived on an uninhabited island as a hermit in a monastic cell and had stayed there for a very long time. On the face of it, that's about as far from freedom as most of us can imagine. Yet it was a lifestyle that was freely chosen. I persevered. All along I had this notion that he would have something to say to me.

St Molaise was not a pauper. He was the son of a Scottish princess and an Irish prince who became the first bishop of Leighlin, a diocese in County Carlow, Ireland. The name Mo-laise, which is pronounced Mull-Ay-she, is an affectionate shortening of the proper name Laserian with the *Mo* prefix that means 'beloved'. Putting it all together, Molaise can be translated as 'my beloved gleam of light', akin, perhaps, to the gleam from a candle that brings light into the dark night. I wonder if his mother and father gave him that name. Molios is the affectionate term that the local folk of Arran used, and this has become shortened yet further, to Molio.

The early missionaries of the Christian Church in Ireland and Scotland were respected not just for their preaching and literacy, but also for their powerful connections, which naturally included the authority conferred on them by the Church. Molio was no exception. His father, Cairel de Blitha, was a prince of the Dál Fiatach peoples, descendants of the legendary Ulaid. They held land in Counties Antrim and Down in Ireland, which lie across the water from Stranraer in Scotland, and further south on the Isle of Man. Their chief royal and religious seat was at Downpatrick. Perhaps this is where Molio was born in 566 AD. At that time, the Dál Fiatach were ruled by King Demmán mac Cairill who might have been fostered as a youth by the family of Molio's mother. Relations between the Scottish and Irish families were indeed close. Yet when Demmán's brother, Báetán mac Cairill, took the throne six years later, he sought to extend his power into Scotland, which must have created tension and some difficulty for Molio's family. This might explain Molio's various moves back and forth between Ireland and Scotland as a boy.

Molio's mother, Maithgemm, was the daughter of King Áedán mac Gabráin who ruled Dál Riata, an ancient kingdom stretching from Skye in western Scotland, south along the Inner Hebrides, to northern Ireland. It is a beautiful name. Maith has its roots in the Gaelic 'mhaith' translating as 'good'; it also has the meaning 'noble' which would be appropriate here. Gemm or Gemma, as she was sometimes named, is less easily traced; it doesn't appear in compendiums of names from the early mediaeval period, nor does it have roots in Irish or Scottish Gaelic. Nevertheless, Maithgemm might be waiting in the wings of British history, for greater recognition. Recent research suggests that the legendary King Arthur was one of King Áedán's sons. It would make him Maithgemm's brother and Molio's uncle. It may be stretching things too far to imagine Molio as a boy eavesdropping on discussions between King Arthur and the Knights of the Round Table (located near Stirling Castle according to this new interpretation) but he must at least have heard numerous discussions on politics, intrigue, battle, and leadership.

The portion of Dál Riata in what is now southern Argyll and Bute was dominated by Áedán's own people, the Cenél nGabráin. One of their royal strongholds was at Dunaverty which lies at the southernmost tip of Kintyre, not far by boat from Arran. The welcome that Molio's grandfather gave to St Columba and the other nascent saints on their arrival in Scotland, would suggest some level of religious awareness in his family, as well as political astuteness. St Columba set foot in Scotland at Dunaverty in 563 AD. He went first to Eileach Naoimh, one of the Gavellach islands south of Mull, and then famously to Iona, which was gifted to him by King Connal mac Comgaill, Áedán's uncle. From here, St Columba and his twelve apostles brought Christianity to the Gaels of West Scotland, amassing, in the process, one of the greatest religious libraries in Western Europe. In later centuries the vulnerability of the monks and nuns was ruthlessly exploited by the Vikings, but the birth of Christianity in Scotland took place in more peaceful times, within the safety of the protection offered by St Molio's family.

According to one source, St Molio came to Scotland at an early age, presumably to live with his mother's family. He received instruction as a youth on Iona from St Murin of Fahan and must surely have met St Columba, either at that stage or later, since he was thirty-one when Columba died in the church on Iona. Molio went back to Ireland for his main education, returning later to Scotland to take up the life of a hermit as a young man, possibly as a teenager. The main means of transport in those days was by boat and his family had a fleet of them.

The Antrim coast is but twelve miles from the southern tip of Kintyre at its closest point so there were surely regular crossings, given the family connections and the common Gaelic culture on both sides of the channel.

As a young man, St Molio was in an enviable position: educated, well connected and with prospects in Ireland and Scotland. Apparently they didn't interest him. He chose instead to follow the disciplined path of the early Christian missionaries in the West Highlands. In this he was also well prepared, being trained in the gospel, familiar with the simple monastic lifestyle and well known to royal and religious leaders in Argyll. He could have joined the Iona monastery, but, apparently, St Molio had a calling for the hermit's way of life. I wonder what his powerful family thought about their dear 'gleam of light' opting for this life of solitude and servitude. In any event, they appear to have respected his decision as there is no suggestion of a falling out. In fact, it is likely that his mother's family helped him reconnoitre potential locations for a hermitage, travelling about by boat or on horseback. They would have known of the nearby cave on Holy Isle, or Inis Shroin, 'Island of the Water Spirit', as it was then known. Presumably they discussed its suitability with the local shepherds and farmers. No doubt St Molio's family kept a watchful eye on their young hermit.

Archaeologists have found that Molio did not live rough within an open cave. He built a wall at the front of the shelter, some eight feet high, to seal off the cavern, creating, in effect, an enclosed monk's cell. This he paved on the north side with flat stones, managing somehow to place a heavy stone slab in the middle of the paved area, measuring roughly six feet long by two wide and two deep. It was known in the nineteenth century as the saint's bed – an altar perhaps?

Kyla and I walked down the rough stone steps that led from the grassy entrance to the sunken floor. The paving stones had survived, but the altar, if present, was buried. This northern part of his home had been improved by cutting a drain into the rock floor at the back; it came across to the front through the middle section to meet the foot of the stair. There it continued under the flagstone to the outside. I hunched down to take a closer look.

I tried to imagine what it was like as a home. Presumably St Molio constructed a wooden door, or at least screened the entrance with a hide, to keep out the rain and wind. It must have been dark when he first entered. Some light would have filtered in through the doorway at the top of the stair, but not much. A little more might have penetrated through a vent in the wall. It reminded me of the time that I was invited into a Maasai home in the heart of their manyatta in southern Kenya. The walls and roof were one foot thick and made from cow dung, ash and the earth taken from termite mounds. We ducked into the entrance, glad to escape the heat and glare of the African plains at midday. Stooped over under the low ceiling, the first two turns took us past the calves' chamber. After that it was pitch black. I stumbled along behind my colleague in a crouch until we reached the living quarters. I knew we were there only because of the murmur of voices around me. My colleague took my hand and guided me to a stool where I sat down. Slowly vision returned. I made out a figure crouching by a small fire place and blowing embers to life. One by one, the rest of the family became visible, smiling and chatting to each other as their features came to life. Soon I could see quite normally. A glass Coca-Cola bottle was embedded upside down in the thick roof, like a prism set into a ship's deck, bringing a ghostly shaft of light into the room. I imagined St Molio living with the same combination of dim light and heavy, enclosed walls.

At the back of the cave to the right he had his fireplace, which was made from a natural indentation in the rock. Smoke would have passed between two stone uprights and behind a flat stone mantel to a natural chimney, formed by the meeting of two courses of stone; from there it would be carried up and out of the entrance at the top. In the southern corner, under three feet of soil, the archaeologists had found a mass of kitchen refuse. It contained layers of black matter with limpets, oysters, and bones that had been split open to obtain marrow. St Molio had evidently enjoyed a varied diet of shellfish, beef, mutton, pork and venison. Most of the bones were from young animals, perhaps supplied to him by his 'parishioners' on Arran. Outside, at the beach in front of the cave and near to a freshwater spring, a large stone had been levelled. A crude step or recess had been fashioned on one corner. It was known locally as the judgment stone. Perhaps that is where he taught.

After some ten years of solitude, prayer and devotion to the people of Arran, St Molio departed. We don't know why. Perhaps the community as a whole had come to accept his teachings, bringing his mission to a natural conclusion. Perhaps he awoke one day with a new calling. Perhaps the death of St Columbus prompted a re-evaluation. Perhaps his family persuaded him that it was time to leave. One can imagine the wrench he must have felt as he gathered his few things together and carried them aboard one of the family boats. Life would never be so simple again.

St Molio was soon back at his father's home in Ireland where he turned down the chieftainship of his clan, the Dál Fiatach, demonstrating once again an impressive commitment to his faith. Instead of applying his wisdom to ruling his people, he set out for Rome where he studied for fourteen years before being ordained by Gregory the Great. He returned to Leighlin in County Carlow and entered the monastery. In time he became Abbot, with responsibility for fifteen hundred monks, and gained fame for settling the long-running Easter controversy. Bishop Molio died on 18th April 639.

"Doesn't it remind you of Columba's cave by Loch Caolisport?" asked Kyla who was lying on the grass at the cave entrance, shirt pulled up to tan her midriff. It was well muscled I noticed, no doubt from her daily practice of headstands and cartwheels; its light tan matched the copper tones of her hair. "I suppose St Molio here was doing the same thing?"

Immersed in my contemplation of Kyla's tummy, I'd forgotten what we were talking about. "What was that?"

"Preaching the gospel. Taking on the old superstitions that terrified people. Shaking the ground from under the Druids."

"Maybe he was a big guy with dreadlocks."

"Like the Birdman of Pollok?"

"Exactly, but why would such a cool guy choose the life of a solitary hermit? He could have joined Columba's gang?"

"This is the wilderness of the Old Testament," she nodded

towards the north. "These remote islands and seas became their Judaean Desert."

"St Molio came here to find God?"

Kyla rolled over to look at me as if I were an imbecile. "St Molio believed in this new Christian faith." She repeated herself to make sure I understood: "He really believed, okay? In those days the people round here, people everywhere for that matter, were pagan. They might have heard about St Ninian or St Brendan but Christianity was confined to pockets of faith that centred on a few scattered monastic cells like this one. The Arran folk would be full of superstition – stones that could cure, curses that could kill, Gods in human form – their lives were ruled by it. The ancient Druids were in charge and they were full of scary shit – secret powers and human sacrifices. That's what St Molio was up against: centuries of superstition and pagan control. He had to stand up before all that customary power with something new, and not flinch. That's what makes him great. With his new faith, he blew it all away. Centuries of belief in the pagan world just blown away. Can you imagine that? It must have been a total liberation. It was what… like the sixties but supercharged. Supercharged Woodstock. We can hardly conceive it. Everyone was included in this new message – rich, poor, minorities, outcasts. People loved it. They would die for it. Nothing could stand before it – nations, empires, other gods, they all bowed and made way. St Molio wasn't just a candle. He was on fire." She subsided in the grass, appalled at my ignorance.

"I thought you liked Druids?" I nudged her with a wink.

She smiled, "Come on. We'd better get going." She stood up and went over to the cave entrance, fingering the tresses of woodbine one more time: "Nature makes it beautiful here."

On the way back to the dinghy, we passed some boulders with paintings of Buddhist deities. The saturated colours and exotic themes made me wince. They felt so out of place in this temperate land of the Gaels, this ancient land that resonated with a thousand stories from its past – Scots, Picts, Irish Saints, marauding Vikings, kingdoms won, kingdoms lost, generations scraping a living next to the sea, with nothing left to mark their time but the subtle Celtic music and the engravings of rare knots and triskeles worked into lichen covered stone. There are few places where such history withstands the sword of progress better than on the Holy Isle. Would it not be possible to celebrate the modern pilgrim's arrival on this island with a more resonant monument – perhaps that subtle fusion of art and Christianity found in a Celtic cross? There is such a spirit of goodwill and high ethics in the Buddhist community here that I believe it could be done. Perhaps the lama could bring back the ancient stone cross taken from Holy Isle to Arran many years ago; find the lost site of the thirteenth-century monastery in the north of the island and place it there? On this holy island, where a sensitive soul might hear the distant ringing of a monastery bell carrying the prayers of the early saints across the ages, with their universal message of faith, peace and comfort, surely there is room for all beliefs?

Who should be outside the wee hut guarding our dinghy but Lama Yeshe, dressed in Tibetan brown robes and sandals, eyes twinkling with merriment beneath his American baseball hat. Any feelings of rancour about the gaudy paintings vanished. We began discussing the environment, sitting down together to enjoy the evening sunshine.

"What is your opinion about the ecology of our Holy Isle?" Yeshe asked, bringing us down to earth with something practical and local.

It was a question I'd thought about before – the problem of animal overabundance – but in other places with different plants and animals. "Your sheep and horses will increase in number year on year until something limits them. There are no large land predators in Scotland anymore, so they will probably become limited by food. That means competitive grazing, poor body condition and winter mortality. That's what happens on the island of Hirta, one of the islands away to the northwest where your Soay sheep come from."

"As a Tibetan we know about husbandry. We wouldn't want animals with ribs sticking out."

"Well it might not come to that. A red deer could swim to Arran from here but somehow I doubt that your animals will leave. If you are a sheep on an island without wolves it's your teeth that will give way first. When they are smooth and flat you cannot grind the forage. Even if the winter is mild and the summer grass is green, you still grow thin.

So you either have to let nature take care of things and put up with thin animals or remove surplus stock from the island."

"I've noticed that the horses here are divided into three groups," replied Yeshe. "Each group has a stallion. Last year they had few foals. I feel that natural processes are beginning to take effect, beginning to slow down the population growth."

"You are right; that is another possibility. In Africa, elephants stop breeding entirely when their numbers outstrip the food supply. I think the sensitivity of breeding to low body condition depends on the species.

"We will wait and we will watch. We don't want guns here if we don't need them."

"Are you taking meditation retreats this summer?" asked Kyla who had spent two months on a personal retreat at the Samye Ling centre, an experience which hadn't quite worked out the way she'd hoped.

"We are. I have just finished teaching. There is much to do." For a moment he looked tired. "Is that your boat out there?"

"We came over from the mainland yesterday," said Kyla.

"Imagine, sailing with just the wind," he sighed. "It is so free," he sighed again. "Sometimes I would like that, to leave everything and go sailing."

"We love it," said Kyla, to my amazement.

"Would you like to come with us?" I asked, without really thinking, but happy to show him the ropes if he wanted to come.

"Ah, no," said Yeshe. "It is not possible." He looked at his watch – a magnificent golden timepiece. "I must get back to the monastery now." He got to his feet and smiled hugely. "It was lucky for us to meet." He smiled again and turned to walk back along a small footpath.

Kyla wanted to do some sketching in the little pad she carried about. I closed my eyes for a few minutes. When she was done we pushed the dinghy into the sea and clambered in. Kyla rowed us out to *Molio*. Once on board, I went below to make ratatouille with a courgette from Tighnabruaich, tinned tomatoes, garlic, aubergines, onions and dried herbs.

Sitting in the cockpit afterwards with a glass of wine, Kyla said: "You need a tortoise for your sail."

I smiled, nodding my agreement. I didn't need a dolphin or a proud lion as some triumphant emblem: a tortoise, Kyla's tortoise, slow and steady by nature, to match my yen for slow-boating. That would do me fine. "Will you make me one?"

"Might do."

I looked into her eyes and smiled again. "That would be great," I croaked. I was contented then, more contented than I could remember in a long time. It felt precarious.

Chapter 9

Mull of Kintyre

Molio surged south-westward, sails taut in the breeze blowing up the North Channel between Ireland and Scotland, bows thrusting through the Gulf-fed waters. Off Pladda at the south end of Arran the wind backed a few points and strengthened. A sizeable swell began to build. I thought of putting into Campbeltown Loch. It was a sensible option offering plenty of room and good shelter; it would give Kyla an easier down-wave motion too. But I was high with the rhythm of boat on wave, higher still with the flying red mane beside me. I was looking for another wild spot to contain the elements roaring inside me. I elected for Sanda Island off the south end of the Kintyre peninsula. Kyla would be interested in the remains of Saint Ninian's chapel. Maybe the seals would sing for us. As we approached, the powerful ebb tide setting through Sanda Sound kicked up a nasty sea. Green water began surging down the deck and sheets of spray were crashing into the cockpit. Kyla looked uncomfortable despite my confidence. I regretted my decision. At least I'd timed our arrival to coincide with slack water: the tide eased off as we came up on Sheep Island which lies close in on the north side of Sanda Island. With a few wallows, we turned into the sheltering bay on the north side of Sanda, motored a hundred metres into quiet water, and dropped anchor next to a red motor launch not far from the old stone pier.

The last time I'd visited there had been just an abandoned farm next to the pier. Looking through my binoculars, I could see signs of renewed life. The stone-walled farmhouse had a fresh coat of paint around the windows, and one of the outhouses had been converted into a restaurant. Judging from the number of small craft tied up at the pier, it was doing well. We decided to explore first and rowed across to the shingle beach, pulling the dinghy well up the foreshore. We set off in an easterly direction along the shore and soon came upon the site of St Ninian's Chapel. It was not much bigger than Molio's cave but the remains of an outer stone wall that enclosed a scattering of gravestones suggested a larger and more permanent settlement.

"I would be quite happy living here," said Kyla. "I don't need the internet; I don't need any stuff around me. Give me a community of nuns and I would be happy."

"Well, I wouldn't be happy to have you in a nunnery," I replied. She didn't smile. Despite our intimacy in the last few days, I could read the danger signals. We continued our walk to a vantage point that looked out across the eastern entrance to the bay, which was filled by flat rocks that were barely covered at high water. I watched some grey seals pulling themselves out of the surf.

"Perfect place for seals," I began hopefully. There was no response. Something was definitely brewing.

"How is your tummy?" I asked.

"I'm not made for the sea. I'm happiest in a cottage with a stone wall, trees and neighbours."

Instead of asking her if she'd had enough sailing, I was busy mapping out the next part of our voyage together. "You'll get your sea legs soon. I know some sheltered anchorages further north with woods and cottages." There was no response. I suggested a drink at the bar. We walked back in silence, following the way we had come.

The atmosphere inside was warm and cosy. A mixed crowd of sailors and trippers were seated at pine tables enjoying some fine looking food. I ordered two bottles of dark Orkney beer at the stone bar and pulled my stool over to Kyla's. I took a long pull and relaxed.

"Lama Yeshe should have come with us. This is the life."

Kyla didn't answer. She was looking across at the far table where 'Bermuda Shorts', the big yin we'd met at the yacht haven near Fairlie, was entertaining a tour group. He noticed her watching him and waved to her. She turned to look at me. "What do you know about it? Yeshe is committed. His life is full of meaning."

"Nah, you heard him, he wanted to go sailing," I replied, feeling a bit riled. "He should have put his burden down for a day and come with us. He could have used a bit of fresh air, a bit of freedom on the water."

"Freedom? This isn't freedom. It's escape. All you ever do is escape. Africa, Mongolia, and now your precious boat. Escape, escape, escape. Lama Yeshe doesn't escape. He lives for his beliefs. You're not a patch on him."

I blinked at Kyla, wondering why she was so angry. "You need to lighten up. Here we are. Right here, right now. We're anchored at the doorway to the Hebrides. We can go anywhere from here. Islay, Gigha, Ireland. You choose. We're like those gannets we saw diving off Arran. We are free agents. We can choose our fate."

"You just don't get it," she shook her head. "I need to go home now."

"But you only just got here," I stammered. "Let's sleep on all this and talk it over in the morning."

"I need to go home now," she repeated as if she hadn't heard me.

"Kyla, I'm not going back to Fairlie now. I'm sailing north with limited time. I thought we agreed all this."

"I just can't cope with your heroics Martyn."

"I'm sorry it was a bit rough out there today," I nodded in the direction of Sanda Sound, "but we were never in any danger. *Molio* is a very seaworthy boat. We'll take it slow and I'll keep to sheltered anchorages."

"Take me to Campbeltown then. It's not far."

"If weather permits I plan to sail round the Mull tomorrow. If you still feel the same way then I'll drop you at Tayinloan where you can catch the Glasgow bus." I wasn't at all happy about this sudden change of plans but at least it felt like a compromise.

Kyla wasn't listening. She was looking across at Bermuda Shorts. Without warning she knocked back the stool, got up and walked over to the far table, green eyes flashing, head high, tossing her mane like a grand racehorse. Bermuda Shorts rushed to pull up an empty chair. Kyla sat down beside him with a smirk and started chatting and laughing as if nothing had happened. With difficulty I remained at my seat and waited.

After about ten minutes Kyla returned. "Brucy will take me to Campbeltown in his motor yacht. He'll pick me up from *Molio* this evening." Perhaps noticing the look of disbelief on my face, she added: "I can't be spending time with a man who just plays."

I stood up. "I think dinner is over."

Back on board I busied myself with routine tasks while Kyla started packing. I checked the anchor cable and our position, put an extra tie round the mainsail and lowered the ensign. Slowly my anger subsided. Although it was high summer the sky was now darkening. I decided to hoist the riding light. High water was after midnight. Ships might arrive at slack tide from any direction – the Clyde, Loch Ryan, or the Sound of Jura. Retrieving the lamp from its hook at the back of the sail locker I placed it on the bridge deck. It was a lovely thing, like a mini lighthouse. I removed the burner from the glass housing which protected the flame and doubled as a dioptric lens to focus the light beam, topped it up with kerosene, lit and adjusted the flame and waited for it to settle. When it was burning evenly I screwed the burner back into the glass housing and carried the lamp forward to hang from the forestay. I put stabilising guys out to the pulpit on either side. The lamp glowed softly in the twilight like a guardian sea faerie on watch in the rigging.

I stood beside it for a few minutes and looked out over the rocky islets to the southeast; a seal on the flat rock began singing. It was a song of wild places and broken hearts. It was time for me to find my own way again. I went below and made a cheese sandwich and took it back up to the cockpit. I resisted the temptation to take a drink. An hour later I heard a boat's outboard start up at the pier. It headed out to the red motor launch, presumably to take the tour party back on board. Then the engine revved up again and grew steadily louder. I looked out the porthole and made out the bulky figure of Bermuda Shorts at the rear of a rib. It was dark now, but I knew his face would be grinning. I went below and told Kyla her lift was coming. She stopped for a second to look at herself in the small mirror above the galley sink, frizzing her long curls. Green eyes glinted in the light from the oil lamp. She knew she was breathtaking.

"Bye, Martyn. I'm off then."

I felt the anger ignite again but controlled it. This part I already knew.

"You look so good together. You're bound to be happy."

I saw the hesitation, then she was gone. It wasn't my finest moment but I'd had enough of Kyla. As the noise of the engine faded in the distance, there was just *Molio* and me, and the tide. It tugged at the boat as if wanting to carry us out to sea.

Unlike the wind, the tide never rests. It ebbs and flows day and night, marking out the passage of time, marking out the passage of life, urging us to loosen our ties to land, free our bonds with security, catch the outgoing flow and set off on a voyage of discovery – before it is too late. Some cannot wait. They are off at the first opportunity, with no plan, no purpose, content to drift along with the current of the day. Others think deeply. They ponder on all that might go wrong. They are filled with such apprehension that they are blind to faith and fortune. They never will catch a tide. I wondered where I lay in this tidal story. Wherever it was, I knew now was the time to catch another tide.

I pulled out the charts and studied the passages and currents one more time. I had four more weeks. Maybe I could make it to St Kilda if I got moving. It would mean rounding the Mull of Kintyre in the morning. This steep foreland sits at the southwestern tip of the long Kintyre peninsula jutting out into the North Channel, opposite the Antrim Hills in Ireland. A strong tide rips rounds the headland, giving the Mull a fearsome reputation. That suited my mood. I picked up the 'Wee Blue Book' – an early edition of the Clyde Cruising Club's Sailing Directions – and looked for the entry. My father had marked the warning in red ink.

*The passage from Campbeltown round the Mull of Cantyre is one which requires great care, owing to the tremendous seas which arise in the race off Deas Point (Sron Uamha), when wind and tide are opposed. In favourable weather, of course, a rowing boat could go round, but in bad weather it is **very** bad, and an ugly sea gets up* *in a very short space of time, when even a fairly large boat is bound to take a good deal aboard. Thus, in small craft, unless provided with a watertight cockpit and the means of securely battening down all hatches, there is a very great element of risk.*

The wind had backed further and was blowing a steady force 5 from east northeast. Waves were building up in the Sound of Pladda and circling into the anchorage, to set *Molio* rocking. Her cupboards banged open and shut. One by one the motorboats left, heading for the safety and comfort of Campbeltown. Once the red motor launch had gone, I stopped thinking about Kyla.

A fiery dawn suffused the sky behind Sheep Island as I drank a steaming mug of tea in *Molio*'s cockpit. The wind had died in the small hours, leaving a lumpy, confused swell and the sound of breaking waves that marked the tidal race in the Sound of Sanda. Tinny alarm beeps from down below alerted me to the coastal forecast at five o'clock. I went below to switch on the VHF. It was iffy: "...becoming cyclonic, force 4 or 5; slight or moderate sea state; thundery showers, fog patches, moderate or good visibility, occasionally very poor". Despite the calm conditions, I put on a safety harness. On deck, I secured the dinghy with two painters astern before raising the mainsail, tying in a reef at the same time. The boom jerked from side to side as *Molio* rolled in the swell. I set about hauling up the anchor, turning the big winch on the mainmast. It came up with plenty of mud, which I scrubbed off before lashing it to the deck. At 6 a.m. I sailed quietly out of the anchorage, patched sails catching occasional breaths of southerly air. With the help of the dying ebb, *Molio* moved steadily west. The sun came with us, dancing in our wake in a line of golden stepping stones. Ahead lay the Mull shrouded in mist. Ten gannets flew low and fast out of the mist, passing within yards of *Molio*.

As they passed and headed east towards Ailsa Craig, I thought of Kyla, despite my resolve. It was as if we had bonded at some level through our mutual love of nature. But love was not on my mind. On the Beaufort scale of human anger, my annoyance at being turned away on the motorway had been something like a force 4 moderate breeze with 'fairly frequent white horses, small branches beginning to move, dust and loose paper raised'. At Kinsale there had been warning signs of severe weather but what came eventually was a brief buffeting and then the squall had passed. Last night was worse. Kyla's outburst was gale force 8 by my reckoning, with 'high waves and breaking crests, whole trees in motion, cars veering on the road and progress seriously impeded'. On a small boat there are only limited options in a storm: you can 'lay ahull' by downing all sails, battening the hatches and taking whatever comes your way; you can 'heave to' by backing the jib and riding it out with a bit more comfort and control; or if you have sea room you can 'run downwind' under bare poles, with ropes streaming astern. It's exhilarating but arguably more dangerous. I'd chosen the last option and those heavy seas had passed harmlessly beneath me. Now that I was on my way again, I'd no intention of turning back.

Over in the southwest the sky had grown dark. The tide was pulling harder, sweeping *Molio* under the towering Mull. It stood as a brooding giant, shoulders hunched, head shrouded by cloud, braced against the invading seas. The water slapped idly at *Molio*'s side and we slipped into the stilled cauldron, unnoticed by the gods. A guillemot, handsome in its black and white suit, dived and then surfaced alongside the cockpit as if attempting to warn me off. The darkness spread from the south reaching out towards us. I remembered reading stories of white squalls coming unexpectedly out of nothing, to roll a sailing ship on its side. If Poseidon so chose, he could churn this sea into a seething tempest. I furled the yankee. As visibility contracted around me, sounds seemed to be magnified. The sea sucked and gurgled alongside. A gull's cry echoed off the cliffs. The swell boomed as it entered a sea cave. A heavy roll of thunder began far to the south, a growling in the darkness. It quietened to a continuous mutter. I kept looking for tell-tale signs of a squall. Eventually I ran forward and lowered the mainsail, lashing it quickly to the boom. The thunder came again; closer now. Peal upon peal rumbled across the sea. A memory stirred. Could it be ship's guns? Closer and closer it came, echoing from the cliffs around me. Could it be a naval exercise? I recalled one time as a boy, when sailing with my father, we heard the navy practising. I glanced at the Admiralty chart. Ten nautical miles to the south was a note, *Firing Practice Area.* Thunder bolts exploded around me, shaking the air, making me giddy and confused. My father had told me that when a battleship fired its sixteen-inch guns, the shells roared past at twice the speed of sound. "Your head rings and your heart leaps. When the fleet opens up in naval battles the air shudders from the broadsides. One salvo follows another in a continuous scream that comes from all directions, on and on, until you can think of nothing else, just the great guns firing."

Later Mum showed me a letter about an amphibious landing operation in which my father's destroyer, *HMS Bleasdale,* took a hit while standing off the beach in support of the commandos. There were wounded sailors in a critical condition lying on the deck but they were exposed to fire from machinegun nests. As Ship's surgeon his place was below preparing to receive the injured, but instead my father went out on deck and carried the wounded to safety. Only then did he ask orderlies to bring them down to the makeshift operating theatre for surgery. He was awarded the Distinguished Service Cross for his actions.

Like so many others who fought in that war, my father had a deep sense of duty. It ran through his life like a golden thread – beginning with his rugby team and school, both of which he captained, then for his fellow sailors at war, for his wife and family in peacetime, for his medical partners in their Ayrshire practice, duty to his many patients, and duty towards his country. He had a deep love of Scotland and was immensely proud of his forbears, but he loved his fellow man whether in England, Wales, Ireland, the Commonwealth or beyond. He showed them nothing but friendship and loyalty. He was an extraordinarily selfless man. I think he shared that with many of his generation.

The tide carried *Molio* steadily north towards Gigha and the Sound of Jura. And as we swept northwards, the thunder slowly faded. Instead of the dreaded squall, a steady breeze picked up from the south. I unfurled the sails. Soon *Molio* was making five knots on top of two knots of tide. The brooding violence withdrew further until it was no more than a memory on the distant horizon.

Chapter 10

Fiddler's Green

The best anchorage in Loch Crinan is sandwiched between Eilean Da Mheinn, 'the island of the young goat', and the bluff to its east, on which the Crinan Hotel now stands. It offers perfect shelter from the storms driving up the Sound of Jura, and has surely been used by sea-farers over many centuries, perhaps millennia. As I entered in *Molio* there wasn't a single spot free. The natural harbour which stretched before me in a wide arc was overrun by moorings. A sign made it clear they were managed by the local boatyard. There were at least fifty, leaving no space for a boat to anchor. It looked as if the CODS infection had spread from Tarbert. I turned *Molio* round, threading my way between the boats, and headed back out and round to the west side of the island. Rows of bright pink mooring buoys traversed this secondary anchorage as well. By saturating the anchorages with moorings, CODS ensures that visiting boats have no option but to take one and swallow the excessive charge. Economists have a name for this kind of scam: they call it 'creating rents'. The resource is controlled and the price is inflated. It's the kind of fix we associate with high prices at petrol pumps and for certain life-saving drugs. To the man in the street, it is exploitation. Looking about, I realised that none of the moorings on this western side were taken. They were all of the same type, shiny and without a sign of weed. I guessed they were newly laid and that the Crown Estate, which owns the seabed 'resource', was now poised to hand them over to the boatyard. It was that magic moment of transition with nobody in charge. I picked one up with a chuckle.

This casual grab of a public right has got me riled. These havens and sanctuaries have been used by generations of sailors on their annual journeying. Now some likely lad has put out his hand and taken them for his own. It's not just about natural harbours either. If you think about it, almost every manifestation of personal freedom requires some essential resource that sustains it: farmers require seed and water to grow their staples; herders require pasture for their livestock; public broadcasting requires access to airwaves or the internet; and skateboarders require streets and skate-parks. History is full of cases where a custom of fair use of essential resources has been usurped by the powerful, who laid claim to what had been commonly or publicly owned.

Although it might easily pass by unnoticed, the commandeering of open access to a sheltered anchorage in Loch Crinan is just one more episode in a centuries-old rip-off of land and coastal resources. We may live in an old democracy in Britain, one that began to take shape in the thirteenth century, but land-ownership is not party to it. Land has always been governed by a law of the jungle, in which the powerful appropriate what they can, whether as local barons taking from their countrymen, as Colonial powers taking from indigenous people, or as wealthy investors buying from the poor. Take the Crown lands of Great Britain as an example of a vast resource appropriated by the powerful. Acquisition of land in England began with the Norman Conquest, and continued to grow over the next half millennium in one of the longest land grabs ever recorded. James VI mined the same rich vein in Scotland with the seizure of numerous estates and consolidation of royal power in the Orkney and Shetland islands. He then combined his Scottish lands with those of England and Wales to form a vast golden pot under his personal union of crowns.

It did not end with annexation of the land: people who got in the way of the barons were dealt with as worthless possessions, and moved off the productive areas. In the West Highlands of Scotland, in the early 19th century, some of them were moved onto tiny plots of land by the sea where they sought a new source of livelihood. In the words of the writer Neil Gunn:

The landlord had driven them from these valleys and pastures, and burned their houses, and set them here against the sea-shore to live if they could and, if not, to die... Yet it was out of that very sea that hope was now coming to them... The people would yet live, the people themselves, for no landlord owns the sea, and what the people caught there would be their own.

Just a few years later, a new landlord did emerge to claim the sea for his own. For it was not just the land but also the maritime resources off our coasts that were claimed by the Crown. By the time Gunn penned his classic, the maritime resources were not managed by the monarch, but by the Crown Estate Commissioners who acted on behalf of the Government. Using its royal power, Government took away the common right to harvest and manage local resources, and gave it to foreign fleets or sold it in the marketplace like any other commodity.

The Crown Estate owns or has major shares in residential property, listed buildings, shopping centres such as Fort Kinnaird outside Edinburgh, and chunks of rural countryside such as the Glenlivet Estate in the Cairngorms. On the marine side, they own virtually the entire seabed out to the 12-nautical-mile territorial limit and the majority of the foreshores between the high and low watermarks. This means that they own salmon-fishing rights, aquaculture sites, wild shellfish harvesting, wildfowling rights and other renewable natural resources. They also own offshore mineral resources such as oil, gas and coal. They oversee the laying of cables and pipelines, license work in ports and harbours, and they lease moorings and marinas. In other words they have immense, almost sovereign power and responsibility over our coasts and offshore waters.

The Crown Estate is supposed to hold stewardship of the marine environment as a core value, and in the past they have indeed acted for the common good for instance in leasing moorings to yacht clubs. As social groupings of users, the clubs exercised their own democratic form of management that catered for members and visitors alike and, with a few exceptions, were devoid of excessive profit motive. Commander R.G. Mowat made this point in the Clyde Cruising Club Sailing Directions: '*Although the Club is a Clyde organisation, its information and its hospitality are at the disposal of all fellow cruisers from kindred clubs else-where who may visit the West Coast of Scotland.'* By and large, this tradition-al allocation of moorings has worked well. But times have changed. Under its new commercial manifestation, the Crown Estate today is exercising its sovereign power in a different way. By licensing large blocks of moorings that fill natural harbours, they are unilaterally end-ing a right to anchor that has been open for centuries as part of the medieval right of navigation.

Freedom to sail, freedom to roam, free as the nomad, the gypsy, the tinker, the traveller, or the music-festival goer... it takes us back to a time when we were not bound by rules of place. Like the great whales, the Atlantic salmon, the caribou, the swallow; humankind has an instinc-tive urge to roam. To travel, to settle, to travel again. It is our heritage.

Taking a mug of coffee into the cockpit, I sat back on a cushion to enjoy the sun and the rare sight of a dozen wooden yachts plying back and forth across Loch Crinan. It was the classic boat weekend. Two pilot cutters were making for a nearby navigation buoy. Egyptian cotton sails ballooned before a brisk sou'westerly, thrusting the heavy working hulls through blue seas. Rounding the buoy, the boats tacked close into the wind; their progress curtailed, they now nodded slowly into the oncoming sea, like stately swans. A crowd of small motorboats rushed after them, creating zigzag wakes in their eagerness to photograph the dozy giants. It reminded me of elephants being paraded round the ring of a circus, slow and dignified amidst the excited spectators. The cutters and their retinue disappeared behind the headland. Not long after, a puffer appeared from the same direction in steam-driven silence. I imagined it as a dumpy duckling wishing to be a swan with sails and sea-swept decks. It ghosted behind Eilean Da Mheinn, leaving a smudge of black smoke drifting over the water, and the stirring sound of a pipe band striking up on the central deck.

I got out the oars from the fo'c'sle and went for a row round the island, partly to look at the boats and partly for the exercise. Mostly it was to expunge the past. I went round twice and felt calmer. The dark-ness of Sanda and the Mull finally lifted. It felt good to be on *Molio*, looking out over a beautiful loch, on my way north.

In the evening I went ashore to see what was happening at the festival. I pumped fresh water into the galley sink, stripped off and washed myself with a flannel. Then I emptied my bag of clean clothes onto a bunk and picked out a heavy cotton shirt. The inky blue colour was a bit severe with black jeans but it would do. I stuffed a jersey, midge repellent and a camera into my pack and looked at myself in the hand mirror. A tired man looked back. He was tanned from his time at sea, except for the eye creases. Maybe he should shave his beard? Start out with a new image? I shrugged and climbed into the dinghy.

The Crinan Hotel was heaving. Both bars were jammed and guests were overflowing on to the sides of the canal basin. A party was being held on the deck of the puffer as it docked on the far side, next to a row of classic yachts. I walked over to take a look at these painted and varnished ladies. Some were older than *Molio*. Their teak decks were scrubbed, sail covers pressed, ropes hung in perfect coils, and the brass work shone in the evening sun. Even the fenders had smart blue covers. *Molio* didn't belong here. She would have looked awkward with her imperfect paintwork, algae-stained coamings and uneven deck caulking. Her fenders didn't match and her sail covers were patched. Her place was out in the wild Hebrides, tugging on her anchor chain and swinging to the tide with gulls and seals for company.

The men wore festival t-shirts and shorts that were too tight. They looked more like Pavarotti than James Bond. The women had changed out of their sailing gear and were relaxing in revealing tops and cropped trousers, managing to look smart and sexy at the same time. Everyone had a flush of sun on their face and a glass in their hand. Kyla would have caused a sensation here, I thought. With more than a trace of envy I noticed the intimacy between the couples: a nodding smile, the casual arm draped over a shoulder, a neck massage to ease tension from the afternoon's race.

I wandered over to the candy-stick lighthouse on a promontory across from the hotel and looked out over the Sound of Jura to Scarba. More beautiful boats were moored nearby or had anchored well offshore. The pride of the fleet was a three-masted superyacht that must have been two hundred feet long. It was a replica of the 1903 Schooner *Atlantic*, which had held the record time for a passage by sail from New York to Cowes for a century. My own favourite was a Bristol Channel Pilot Cutter with a fanned counter stern. She was dressed from stem to stern in signal flags, which contrasted gaily with her sombre black hull. Another boat to set the wanderer's heart thumping was a double-ended motor ketch with a deep sheer, like the early RNLI lifeboats. The wooden deckhouse and gaff rig gave it a workmanlike appearance which reminded me of *Palinode*. But for sheer elegance, it would be hard to beat *Truant*. Low, sleek and fine like a hunter's arrow, with a bowsprit at its tip. William Fife had put all his cunning into the design of this forty-foot gaff cutter, built for one purpose alone – to go faster than any other in the 8-metre class. She was a rare Scottish beauty. *Truant* and *Molio*, racer and cruiser, were friends having stood next to each other all winter at Cairnbaan. I'd seen the care that her owner took in preparing her each season.

"Looking good isn't she?"

I turned to greet David, another wooden boat owner who wintered his Buchanan sloop, *Snoopy*, at Cairnbaan. Despite his relaxed manner, there was a brooding intensity about the man. "She's a dream. I wish *Molio*'s paintwork was one-tenth as good."

"Were you racing today?"

I shook my head. "I'm just passing by, on my way north."

"That's what I'd love to be doing. I've been stuck in Cairnbaan for weeks, working on *Snoopy*'s gearbox. We're ready at last. If I'm not out the canal by tomorrow, they'll be charging me by the day – and that's on top of the thousand pounds for the boat park." He looked really annoyed. I waited, giving him a chance to get the whole thing off his chest. "I had to get a new battery from the boatyard here today. The old one was getting past it. I couldn't risk not being able to start the engine. The bloody mark-up in their shop is fantastic. I asked the owner if I could use a mooring whilst getting the gear on board. He told me I would have to pay if I so much as picked one up. The charging is relentless. There is no stopping it. Everyone is on the same game. It's like…" David was lost for words he was so annoyed.

"Piracy?" I suggested.

"Have you heard, they've just established a Kyles Marketing Board. Imagine that: turning *our* wonderful Kyles of Bute into *their* business."

"Nothing is sacred," I agreed.

"Our dear wee places are just marketing opportunities to the commercial boys. If they could find faery folk, they'd market the wee unfortunates too."

I sympathised with David, but the idea of exploiting faeries was funny and I couldn't stop a guffaw. He looked up in annoyance. "No, no," I assured him. "I'm agreeing with you. I was thinking about marketing faeries. First off they'll do a *SWOT* analysis. *Strengths*: Faeries are attractive to a wide variety of markets. *Weaknesses*: Faeries are unpredictable. Visitors can't be guaranteed viewing times. *Opportunities*: Let's see now, faeries are a largely untapped marketing opportunity. It may be possible to negotiate with the Head Faery for better visiting hours. *Threats*: If annoyed, faeries may cast a spell causing everything to go wobbly."

"I've got a mooring in Tayvallich," David's face relaxed at last. "Maybe I'll fit boat legs for the winter. I don't plan on being back in Cairnbaan next year."

"How about a pint?"

"I've got to go – I'm looking after my Mum just now."

I watched him make his way through the guests to the car park. The sun was drooping over Jura. It was time for a drink. I wandered over to the lounge bar and squeezed my way through a press of bodies to the wooden counter where I ordered a pint of Best from the Italian barman. As luck would have it, a party of sailors sitting opposite chose that moment to leave. I edged over and sat down, hanging my pack on the next chair. There was just enough room for a pint and *Molio*'s logbook on the small round table. I took a long swallow, turned to a fresh page and began to bring my notes up to date. Occasionally I looked up to catch a glimpse of the canal basin between the bodies. When my glass was half empty, a large man with a shock of black hair that was swept up at the front in an Elvis style quiff, came over and sat down on the other side of the table. He placed a battered case on his knee from which he extracted an old fiddle, the colour of treacle. Without looking up, he lifted his bow and began to play. I've heard fine fiddle playing before but I didn't seem to hear this music at all. It entered without resistance, lifting me into another world as if I were an old trout being guddled by a wily crofter. There was an evening to be had here. I went over to the bar and ordered another pint. Archie from Campbeltown, as the barman informed me, was just warming up. As I sat down again, he started on a jig. It picked me off my backside and flung me down a Scottish hillside. Catching myself up I leapt from hummock to hummock in time with the rhythm all the way down to the bottom of the glen. I ran on to a rushing burn and danced with the small notes, hopping from one stone to the next, before racing up the far side keeping time with the sweeping bow.

"Hello Martyn," the warm breathy voice was inches from my ear. I turned.

"Cori, Christ, what a bloody miracle." I stared up into almond eyes, laughing at me so hard they almost fell into her dimples. Behind the smile was a proud face, with long dark hair parted down the middle like a Native American.

She smiled, holding eye contact, "Are you sailing your old boat then?"

"I am," I tried and managed to stop gawping. "I'm heading north. What in the world are you doing here? I mean I'm really glad to see you." I moved over to the wall seat so she could sit down. "Where's Tom?"

"Didn't I tell you? We broke up around Christmas. I'm living in Oban now with Danny."

"Huh," I gasped. "And how's Danny doing?"

"He's great. His school friends take him out on the boats. Even I'm learning to sail." She smiled at me, still holding eye contact.

"How's the music scene in Oban?" Cori had been a vocalist for a country-rock band in Melbourne. I knew she would have checked it out.

"How are things with you and Kyla?"

"Can I get you a drink first?"

She picked up my glass and tasted the beer. "I'll take a pint of this."

As I came back from the bar she put her mobile phone away. She was exactly the person I wanted to be with tonight, even if we were making a good job of avoiding things. She looked fantastic. How did she do it – cope with a job, an eight year old and a new town – and still find time to be herself. Her hand touched mine as she took the glass and drank deeply. "That's just what I needed. Bloody hot day."

I dragged my eyes away from her in a feeble effort to hang on to some street cool and stuffed *Molio*'s logbook into my pack. Archie had taken a break from fiddling. He came back now with a pint of stout in his hand, put it down, picked up the fiddle and dived straight into another electrifying jig. The audience loved it. Outside friends were chatting. Couples were holding hands discretely. Inside, the atmosphere had grown thick. All of a sudden the bar was an animal's den, a lair for intimate huddling.

Cori leant over with her mouth an inch from my ear.

"Are you in love Martyn?"

It was growing dark. The Scottish gloaming was upon us. Nymphs would soon be coming out of their hiding places. Now was the time to go home if you wanted to avoid mischief. "We had a row," I yelled back into her ear. "Kyla left with this younger guy. I'm so pissed off with her. I don't even want to talk about it." I sketched the events of Sanda, anyway.

"You're okay, you know." She took my hand for a few seconds. I noticed the warmth of her palm. Her nails were long on this hand but short on the left. She must be playing guitar. "I know the kind of stuff Kyla's been through. I've been through something like it myself. Only she can deal with it; you have to let her go."

I nodded, it was pretty much what I'd concluded.

"I'll tell you one thing. She'll be back for you. I'd bet on it."

"Maybe," I nodded again. I didn't know how I felt about her coming back. I was for the Hebrides now, mentally prepared to throw off my old skin and forge a new identity. I didn't want any more of Kyla's confusion. If I was honest, I was still seething with anger. Why the hell, then, did Cori's words reassure me?

"If you bury that anger for a minute, you'll see it's a great blessing she left you."

I blinked. "Oh yeah?"

"She wasn't going to sort herself out on *Molio* cooped up with you now, was she? That has to be her priority. So why would you want her to stay?"

I laughed and this time Kyla really did slip from my mind. "Cori, I'm so happy you're here."

Cori leaned closer still until I could hear only her voice in my ear and her breath coming and going.

"Tell me about your dreams. You always have interesting dreams."

I put my mouth to her ear and spoke about sailing when I was a boy, about the freedom of the islands and lochs, about what it meant to live in the west, the land of the Gaels and to breathe the moist Atlantic air each morning. She turned her head and leaned in again so her ear brushed my lips. Around us, faces were flushed. A couple began dancing. Somebody whooped. Archie responded and, impossibly, stepped up his music again. The sweat dripped from his brow as he plunged into a reel. Half the bar was moving with the music. Cori was swaying in time.

"Will you dance?" I asked.

She was on her feet at once. We bopped about next to Archie, happy just to be near each other. When she talked all I could make out was a soft voice and fluting laughter. The reel closed and Archie relaxed into a slow air, a lilting lament that I recognised as an old pipe tune. He seemed to exist in his own world, as if isolated from the throng around him, yet somehow he remained bonded to us. Could he be watching out the corner of his craggy eye? Loss and love welled up in the music. I opened my arms. Seeking what? Love? Reassurance? She moved close, lifting her eyes to mine, lips parted in a happy smile. I took her waist as she put her arms around my neck, folding in, pressing her lithe body hard against me. Time lost all meaning.

Out in the night, the pale summer twilight lingered above Scarba. Boats slept in the bay. The tide tugged at weeds on the rocky ledge below. A gentle breeze dried my forehead and kept the midges away.

It was the highland gloaming and Puck was laughing in the oak grove behind us. Cori stood in front, leaning back against me, head lying in the fold between neck and chest. My arms circled her yet I found myself thinking of Kyla. Hell, why was I always confused?

As if reading my mind, Cori turned in my arms one more time. "I have to go. I'm needed at home." She kissed me long and hard.

Chapter 11

Ring of Bright Bubbles

A light easterly wind carried *Molio* north across Loch Crinan and then northwest past the mouth of Loch Craignish into the Dorus Mor, the 'tidal door' to the west. It was open and *Molio* whizzed through on the outpouring, gurgling, whirling, laughing, tumbling flood. On the other side, I steered her towards the passage between Rèisa an t-Sruith and Rèisa Mhic Phaideanat, two small 'islands in the tidal race'. Being accustomed to slow boating in light airs, I was disconcerted to find headlands flying past. I followed a course down the middle of the boils and rips, keeping pace with two porpoises, and fighting back the fatigue brought on by lack of sleep. I had to stay vigilant to prevent *Molio* being swept sideways over reef or shoal. The mist lifted slowly, revealing the Gulf of Corryvreckan, the 'speckled cauldron' that fills the passage between Scarba and Jura. I could feel the pull of the flood as it turned westward towards this infamous maw of the Hebrides, which offered, in one gulping passage, either a fast gateway to the outer isles or, in the wrong conditions, a tumbling wall of rising waves that could tip and swamp an open boat. The morning's forecast had alerted shipping to a deepening Atlantic low moving northeast towards Scotland, bringing strong easterly winds of force six to gale eight, poor visibility and rough seas. I kept *Molio* moving north, passing between Luing and Shuna, the 'Heather' and 'Fairy' isles.

Halfway along Heather Isle a shaft of sunlight lit up its fringing wood, flashing a note of welcome in the darkening west. There was a pool at the north end, Ardinamir Bay, which would offer perfect shelter in a gale. I furled the sails and waited in Shuna Sound for the tide to rise and put more water over the shallow bar at its entrance. While drifting, I took the Wee Blue Book up to the cockpit and checked again the tricky entrance. It might seem perverse to use the 1951 edition of the Sailing Directions when I had the current edition lying open beside me, but the early edition has excellent hand-drawn sketches of the anchorages which were prepared in the early nineteen hundreds by Murray Blair, and updated over the years by members of the Clyde Cruising Club. The sketches indicate rocky promontories with hatching, reefs with enclosed wiggles and areas that dry at low tide with stippling. They even mark areas of visible weed. They often provide more soundings and show more rocks than the modern digital versions. Bound together with detailed notes on tides, local conditions, obstacles to navigation and safe anchorages, they make an ideal sailor's companion on voyages within the Hebrides. For more than a century, countless boats of every kind have enjoyed safe cruising in the west of Scotland thanks to this collective contribution. What had been risky to navigate, except by a few seasoned veterans, was now open to all. The CCC hadn't just inherited a cruising common; it had done much to create one.

Another reason for using the earlier edition was that it allowed me to follow in my father's footsteps. He had highlighted critical bits in the text wherever he had sailed. It was as if he were beside me when I planned a passage, pointing out the hazards to be aware of and adding his own observations. It would have been good to have my grandfather's notes too but that copy was handed in to the Navy at the outbreak of war, when his motor yacht, *Tarka*, was requisitioned to service a number of Balloon Barrage Vessels moored in the Clyde.

The last time I'd been into Ardinamir was as a boy on *Primrose*. Irene McLachlin had been in residence and was usually on hand to bellow instructions from the shore at any yacht straying off course. On this occasion, I would have to manage without her. Looking at the sketch chart, I didn't think the entry would present too much difficulty, provided I waited for the tide to fill the pool. Once inside, there was room for several boats to anchor between the muddy shallows lying to the north and south of the bay. The only potential hazard was a narrow rockbound channel in the northwest corner, which the tide swept through like a millrace. I motored up close to the entrance and waited for the tide to cover the bottom of the outer beacon. Once it was underwater, I pushed *Molio* gently into the entrance, hoping to avoid *Primrose*'s fate all those years ago when she had stuck at the narrowest point, despite Irene's bellows.

Molio coasted over the bar with the motor in neutral and slipped into the deeper water of the inner pool. So far so good. It was smaller than I'd remembered but, as there were no other cruising boats, I didn't anticipate a problem with anchoring. On looking around for a good spot, I soon found there were mooring buoys all over the place including seven or eight covering the best area. Two of these held small craft but the rest were unused. I manoeuvred in amongst them. Most were old, hardly afloat, and of doubtful strength. I circled over the deep part of the pool and back towards the entrance. It looked as if there was a possible gap for an anchor in the north of the pool, in between shallow mud on one side and a tidal stream leading to the overflow channel in the northwest corner. I motored slowly over the vacant gap, slipped into neutral, and pushed the tiller hard over to bring *Molio* round in a complete circle for anchoring. She was slow to turn, strayed too far north, and touched bottom – once, twice, on the third touch she jammed firmly in the mud. Feeling a right muggins, I tried astern but she was stuck solid. At least Irene wasn't there to give me a bollocking.

With the help of the sketch map, I worked out where *Molio* was stuck and saw that she would have to be dragged sideways to reach deep water. I tied two twelve-metre jibsheets together and secured one end to the new kedge anchor, a Rocna, which was the latest version of the well-known plough anchor. Then I tied the bitter end to the Samson post, rowed the anchor out in the dinghy and chucked it over the side. Back on *Molio*, I braced my feet and pulled in on the rode. The Rocna gripped well. Molio shifted, then moved slowly out into the centre of the pool. Soon she was floating again. On the next attempt, I manoeuvred *Molio* into position without incident and dropped the main anchor in three fathoms, putting out ten fathoms of chain, and made fast. Satisfied that we weren't dragging, I brought a beer up from below, popped it open, and sat back. A heron was fishing just twenty yards away. It could have been a lot worse.

The wind picked up in the evening so I went out in the dingy to see how *Molio* was lying. She was pulling hard on her chain, stretching it bar-taut in the gusts. Her stern was well out into the centre of the bay, almost touching a faded pink mooring buoy, and only yards from the tidal stream. I went below and found an anti-snubbing line. Back on deck, I attached the hook at one end to the anchor chain above the water and tied the other end to the Samson Post, leaving about fifteen feet free. Then I eased out some more anchor chain until the nylon line was taking the weight of the boat, and re-secured it. The nylon would stop the boat jerking the anchor chain and snapping the anchor out of the mud. Satisfied, I went below and crawled into my bunk. It was a warm evening and I unzipped the bag.

I awoke with surprise: a cold drop of liquid had landed right on that sensitive spot on your side – the tickly bit which lies a couple of inches above the waistline. It took me a second or two to work out what was going on. Then I registered the drumming rain on the deck and the hum of wind in the rigging. I thought of moving across to the dry side of my bunk and dropping back to sleep, but first checked the clock with my torch. It was 1 a.m. Something didn't feel quite right. I decided to inspect the boat and clambered out of my bag. I pulled on a waterproof jacket and grabbed the spotlight before climbing up the ladder to the cockpit.

Sweeping the light round the boat, I made out the faded mooring buoy that had lain alongside, only now it was thirty feet in front of *Molio*'s bow. I swept the powerful beam round to the stern. *Molio* was in the centre of the tidal stream race. With powerful gusts above and tide below, both pulling in the same direction, she was dragging her anchor and slipping back even as I looked. At this rate we would be in the shallow, fast-flowing part of the channel in a couple of minutes. Once there she might keel over and fill. I needed to act fast. My mind was still groggy from sleep. If I started the engine and then went up to the foredeck to lift the anchor I would almost certainly lose control of the boat whilst working at the bow. The safer option would be to motor over to the mooring buoy, dragging the anchor with me, and grab it. The problem was that I might foul *Molio*'s anchor on the ground tackle of the mooring. It wasn't the time for perfection. I pulled out the boathook and laid it on the deck then leapt below to start the engine. It roared into life. I switched on the deck lights, which lit up the boat and surrounding water, grateful for all my earlier work on *Molio*'s electrics. Back in the cockpit, I relocated the mooring buoy with the spotlight and motored slowly towards it.

The powerful deck lights created a theatre of light as we moved through the surrounding darkness. When the pink buoy was alongside the cockpit I could see there was a yellow pick-up buoy attached which was half submerged. I hooked it up. Taking care to pass it outside the main shrouds but inside the whisker shrouds, I brought it forward to the bows and hauled in. A chain loop came up on the rope, which I slipped over the Samson post. Back in the cockpit, I used the spotlight to line up a couple of markers on the shore before going below to make some tea. After thirty minutes I checked the markers again. There was no change in their bearing. We hadn't budged.

I lay awake for most of the night listening to the rain. Small drops driven by the gusts rattled against the coamings; in the lulls, heavier drops fell from the furled mainsail and smacked onto the coachroof. Inside the occasional drip pinged into a saucepan. Eventually the first grey light of morning showed through the portholes and I slept for a couple of hours. The sound of an engine roused me and I clambered on deck to watch a small creel boat make its way towards the entrance. I waved to the skipper, who veered over towards *Molio*. He told me that the mooring belonged to a large yacht but was seldom used. Reassured, I went below and lit the grill to make toast for breakfast. The rain eased during the morning and, as it did, the wind moderated. I decided to haul up the anchor as the mooring was clearly sufficient on its own. I brought in a couple of fathoms but that was all I could manage, even with the winch to help. *Molio*'s anchor must have snarled the mooring. I let out a bit of slack and tried motoring hard astern but we were held tight. Rather than make the situation worse, I switched off the engine and rowed ashore, hoping that one of Irene McLachlin's family might still be in residence at the farm. Sadly, Ardinamir House was lying empty. It was the same story next door.

Back on *Molio*, I rang some friends living on Easdale Island who recommended a local water-based business and gave me the number. I called and left a message. They rang back forty minutes later to report that 'Graham was on his way'. Before long I spotted a RIB with two figures coming down Seil Sound from the north. It slowed for the bar into Ardinamir Bay and then sped over to *Molio*. Graham was already in his diving suit. He was a big chap from the North Country, tough-looking, with long grey hair heaped over his shoulders. He got straight to business.

"I'll go down, take a look."

On went blue fins, weight belt, regulator, nitrox cylinder, mask and pressure valve. His partner, Wendy, helped where and when she was needed. He was ready in a couple of minutes and fell back over the side of the rib with a determined lunge. For a few seconds he floated on the surface, checking his gear, then swam over to the anchor chain and dived. Bubbles took the place of his disappearing fins.

Keeping one eye on the bubbles, I turned to Wendy who was tying back a shock of sun-bleached hair.

"Are you a diver too?"

"In the tropics." she smiled. "I only dive here if I can put my elbow in the water and not notice the temperature."

"And we know how often that happens."

Her laugh lit up her soft, almost weathered, features. She seemed the perfect diver's buddy – warm, quick-witted, responsible. She started to tell me about Graham.

"I never met such a clever man. I don't mean academically but in all kinds of other ways. He can build anything, or fix it when broken. When we met, he was troubleshooting computers for an insurance company but never getting more than three hours sleep. So he found a job with the lighthouse people, sorting their generators and batteries. It just seemed so easy for him. Diving is his hobby." As she talked I noticed big bubble explosions going round and round the pink

Slow-boating in Molio is one of my greatest joys.

Primrose, our family Falmouth Quay Punt, anchored off Ormidale Lodge in 1958.

We boys on holiday aboard Primrose in the Firth of Clyde – one for all and all for one.

Neil Stronach and his daughter Sonia check out Molio in Crosshaven just before I concluded the deal to buy her.

Relaxing aboard Molio despite the failure of my first attempted passage to Scotland.

Stephen Hall drying out clothes in Kilmore Harbour. With Stephen aboard we were going to mak *it north, one way or another!*

Charging across the North Channel to Scotland with Ailsa Craig, aka Paddy's Milestone, just off the bow.

"Imperceptibly, the two boats moved closer until they touched, creating a circle of thin ripples that spread outwards."

First summer cruise: feral ponies living free on the Holy Isle under the watchful eye of Lame Yeshe.

Entrance to St Molio's cave with nature's garland of woodbine.

Riding lamp lit at Sanda Island: "The lamp glowed softly in the twilight like a guardian sea-faerie on watch in the rigging".

Pilot cutters racing at Crinan Classic Boat Festival.

Stormbound in Plockton: "When the rain arrived it came hard and fast, bouncing off the surface of the sea, raising a white mist which enveloped the bay turning yachts into ghost ships".

Taking advantage of a break in the weather to get ashore in the dinghy.

Second summer cruise: the 8 metre Truant silhouetted by the setting sun points out tomorrow's passage through the Gulf of Corryvreckan.

I descended below the sea mist that was cloaking the high moorland plateau of Canna.

A basking shark nosed up to Molio.

From time to time I transcribed handwritten cruising log and odd notes to digital form.

Water lilies in a lochan on Benbecula, like a living painting by Monet.

Salmon leaping within fish farm pens in Loch Uiskevagh.

Departing the Outer Hebrides in a freshening breeze.

Leaving the land behind.

"Hirta appeared behind its own veil... I had no difficulty in understanding why it was a spiritual haven of the Gaels."

The Mistress Stone − "what if my sweetheart was in the balance and a lifetime with the woman of my dreams? Would I have dared then?"

Looking west from Hirta into the vast Atlantic Ocean.

St Kilda - freedom to breath, to shout, to sing, almost to fly.

Walking down Village Street with a feeling that I was trespassing .

I found perfect shelter in Poll an Tighmhail, the pool of the tax house, at the southeastern corner of Harris.

buoy. Wendy noticed them too. "I see you've been doing quite a bit of knitting."

"Yea, crocheting all night," I replied, distracted by the sight of the yellow pick-up buoy bobbing under the water and then up again. Might it be a distress call? Wendy didn't look the least perturbed but my imagination was getting the better of me. What if Graham was stuck in a tangle of rope and chain? Wendy must have noticed my worried glances.

"See all the small bubbles," she pointed to the rising ring of tiny spheres. "There's a leak in his gear."

After a while, the big and little bubbles started coming in our direction and then Graham surfaced next to the rib. He lay on his front for a minute. Wendy didn't seem alarmed. Then he unfastened his heavy gear, which Wendy hauled on board. Making a lunge, he porpoised over the edge of the rib and on to the floor. He breathed deeply for a while. Even Wendy was a little concerned and asked if he was okay. He nodded and then looked up to me. "I got your anchor, carried it round two lots of chain that didn't belong to you, several times. I've put all the chain and your anchor beneath your boat."

It was a master class in understatement. *Molio*'s three-eighths thick chain weighs a ton. "Will you come aboard for tea," I asked, "or something stronger?"

"No thanks I want to go diving this afternoon – it's my day off. But I'll take a quick look below."

He climbed onto *Molio* while I rang his office and made a donation to the local community fund.

"She's a lovely old boat right enough."

"Seventy this year. Needs a bit more TLC as you can see, but she's a wonderful boat to live aboard."

He nodded. "You only get one crack at it. So you want to live." For the first time I saw him smile. It was a long, slow smile, the kind that comes when a man lives by his own code and is well satisfied. "You know, I'm lucky. I had the best trainers. They taught me engineering and then they taught me diving. It's that simple. Once you have skill, you have self-respect. No-one can stop you then."

I nodded this time, smiling at his words. He really had it sorted.

"I'll help you get the anchor in," he volunteered and, without waiting for me, went up to the bow and hauled in the chain by hand. "That's you ready to go." He climbed back into the rib and with a wave they were off, heading for the Garvellachs and adventure, and in the evening, I was quite sure, there would be lobster and scallops on the menu.

It was an exciting lifestyle that spoke to me. Perhaps Kyla was right about adventure, that it was just an escape, but compared to the cocoon of office life it felt like the real thing. Why should I give it up? If she wanted a quiet life of dull uniformity then no doubt she also wanted a contented husband who sat at home. Maybe she would try to change me. I shook my head. Good luck to her.

I checked the ship's clock and saw that I'd already missed my chance of leaving the pool at high tide. I resigned myself to spending another day in Ardinamir. At least it would give me a chance to explore. Later in the afternoon I rowed ashore and climbed along to Torsa Beag, 'Thor's little island'. It blocked off the northern side of the anchorage, leaving only the millrace running down one side. With a stretch of the imagination it could be viewed as Thor's hammer rammed in between two larger islands, big Torsa and Luing, so as to stem the flow of the tide. *Molio* looked the picture of innocence, resting peacefully in the landlocked pool. I could see the shallows and exact spot where I'd anchored. In retrospect it was a poor choice as *Molio*'s stern had been too close to the tidal race. It had only taken a combination of ebbing tide and gusting wind to take her stern into the middle of it. There wasn't much grip for the anchor in the soft mud. The outcome was inevitable. It was one more lesson in coastal boating to store away.

As I rowed back to *Molio*, I noticed that the tide had turned again and water was now flowing back down the millrace and into the pool. It gave me an idea. A little later I rowed over to the edge of Thor's hammer. As I approached, I kept within the still water to one side of the tidal stream until I was up beside the rocks and only yards from the mouth of the river that was now flooding full tilt into the pool. With a few strokes of the oars, I powered the dinghy through some kelp and into the torrent. Water surged against the Avon, rippling its rubber sides and sending us hurtling downstream. Looking down at the dark water I appeared to be motionless, held within the embrace of upwelling mushrooms, yet a glance to my right revealed mooring buoys tearing past in flashes of pink and red. I lay back and looked up. An overarching canopy of hazels went rushing past as if I were lying back on a horse on a glorious, giddying gallop. I laughed with glee! Shoals of little fish jumped beside me as we whooshed into the middle of the darkening pool. From there, a few strokes with the oars took me to *Molio* and I could begin again. I put my back into rowing and soon regained my starting point at the lip of the torrent. This was the best bit. I waited like the skier about to push out on to the slope and then lunged into the stream. This time I challenged the river, sprint-rowing against it with all my might. For just a moment I almost held up and then I lost it, and we were off on the roller coaster again with the little fish for company. On the third ride, I rowed hard again but this time with the tide. We dashed under the hazels at awesome speed. There was something about the free ride that kept me chortling and guffawing with laughter. I couldn't get enough of it. A family of Canada Geese landed on the pool and joined in the fun with their honking. An oyster catcher flew overhead shouting out "kleep-a-kleep" rights to its territory. Back and back again I went, just as we had done as boys on *Primrose* in what felt like another lifetime but one that linked in some strange way to this one. Eventually I decided on one last ride for old time's sake before gliding back to *Molio* in the twilight.

As I lowered the oars from the cockpit into *Molio*'s main cabin, I heard a strange squeak-snort from the tidal race and looked back. There was something in the water. Was it a little head staring at me? Or maybe just a half-sunken dinghy buoy? I fetched my binoculars and looked again. Nothing. Still there had been something. Resting my arms on the winch platform, I trained the binoculars on the tidal race and then moved them to the right to the kelp bed. There it was – a little head. As I watched, the head was replaced by a rolling back, followed by the hook of a tail as the otter dived into the millrace. That furry fellow was enjoying the exact same game as I had, only his would have a fishy ending. I smiled to myself and sighed. Kyla would have loved to see him. Unbidden, her voice came to me then, from that first night on *Molio* when she had sung Robert Burns's beautiful love song. I crooned it softly in the night.

Had we never lov'd sae kindly,
Had we never lov'd sae blindly,
Never met – or never parted –
We had ne'er been broken-hearted.

Chapter 12

Stormbound

The good folk of Plockton had laid out moorings for use by visiting boats without charge. May their hearths be filled with peat and their tumblers never short of a dram. I picked up the last free one with gratitude, aware that another gale was heading in our direction. Strong winds were becoming a regular feature of the summer. Poseidon was in a temper: stirring up storms in the Gulf of Mexico and flinging them in a long curve across the Atlantic. No doubt his mates on Mount Olympus were sitting round the bar watching to see whom they knocked down. Fortunately, the Hebrides are full of sheltered anchorages and I'd spent the last few days dodging in and out of them, on my way north. My brother Robin would be arriving in a couple of days' time on the train from Inverness. With luck the weather would improve and we could cross the Minch to the Outer Hebrides; he'd been boning up on navigation and on possible landfalls. From there it only required a few days of settled weather for a passage to St Kilda.

The wind was not yet up to gale force but, even so, I was surprised to see a modern yacht motoring out of the bay while raising its mainsail. Competent crews will go out in heavy weather, partly to test themselves and partly, I suspected, to make each day of their yacht charter count. It's a business that fits with today's fast lifestyle. The boat is picked up on Sunday, fully fitted out and ready to go, and dropped off the following Friday or Saturday. As often as not, the crew eat dinner ashore and may even sleep ashore. The latest yachts are equipped with impressive aids: networked GPS navigation systems, radar, bow-thrusters, powered anchor windlasses, and in-mast reefing that requires just a push of a button from the cockpit to shorten sail. The combination of technology and training has raised overall seaworthiness. I took my woolly hat off to this adventurous crew.

A ray of sun found its way through the clouds, picking out the fleet of dancing boats. People had been arriving in Plockton Harbour in every kind of boat from kayaks to ocean-going yachts to take shelter from the oncoming storm. By and large the skippers were decisive, knew their capabilities, and were independently minded. One of the things I enjoyed when boating was being surrounded by free spirits. Boats draw that out of you. They demand that you make decisions and carry them through. There is no time for consultation when beating off a lee shore. The decision to tack must be made at the right moment and then followed by immediate action. It builds judgement, skill and self-reliance.

Many of the dancing fleet shared the same stubby lines as the departing vessel. They had been fashioned with computer software to combine sailing power with comfort below decks. The macho nature of the designs extended to their names: *K-Vector III*, *Synergie*, *Shogun*, *Stormer* and *Playtime*. It was as if the boats themselves had become assertive and masculine, as a reflection of modern society. By contrast, the graceful lines of the older yachts in the Hebrides meld with their element as do the streamlined bodies of pelagic fish or the soaring wings of oceanic birds. Their grace and charm was mirrored in poetic names such as *Moonbeam*, *Pippa* and *Sceptre* or in the names of water birds like *Cygnette*, *Ibis* and *Petrel* or much loved flowers, *Heather*, *Iris* and *Primrose*. Sometimes the names spring from myth and legend like *Gawaine*, *Gemini* and *Sea Witch*, and sometimes they hint at the affection of the owners for their shapely craft, as in *Ayrshire Lass*, *Black Bess*, *Irene*, *Mi'Lady*, *Nellie*, and *Prudence*.

Next but one to *Molio* was an elegant wooden schooner of about forty-five feet, with fine lines, white topsides and smart mahogany doghouse. I could just make out her name, *An Gèadh Glas*, 'the grey goose'. She sat low in the water like *Molio* but I guessed from her rigging she was of greater age. I admired her fine lines as I drank my coffee. There is something about wood that lends personality to a boat. It has practical advantages of course, being strong, supple and durable. If cared for in the right way it endures for decades, even centuries. It can be worked into almost any shape, revealing endless varieties of grain and texture which bestow great beauty. Wood insulates from the heat and cold, and it sounds harmonious. There's none of the metallic clanking, clacking or clonking that emanates from modern yachts but instead a thrumming, tapping and thudding, which falls softly on the ear. The harmony we find in wood is a clue, I believe, to the deeper reason why humans value it. For countless millennia our ancestors lived in trees. Even after we had evolved the capacity to walk, the curved fingers and strong arms of the early bipedal hominines reveal their close association with trees. At night they climbed into the safety of the branches, lay down in leafy beds and were rocked asleep. The love of trees and the love of wood lie deep within us. Because of that, a wooden boat is more than just a boat. It is part of the primeval forest, the ancestral home, and the sailor's hammock is the leafy nest that sways in the canopy. At least two of *Molio*'s former owners lived on her permanently.

A chirrup from my mobile alerted me to an incoming email. It was from Kyla, her third since Sanda Island. The first had accused me of trying to shanghai her aboard *Molio*. It was light-hearted but I had ignored it. The next had been about rock art, something we were both interested in. I had ignored that one too. This message was different.

If love is passionate and intense it is controlling and destructive with no room for manoeuvre. I can't spell that! Healthy love is a sidling up in friendship and trust. It involves calm!! In other words you need to bloody calm down and actually feel the ground under your feet!!

What I'm saying is that friendship is bigger than romance or passion. It involves feeling and looking around. I fear you are in a 'never look back' mode always out challenging the next horizon. I want you to stop and look around. Learn to question yourself. So you can just be sometimes.

You know I didn't mean all those things I said on Sanda. Maybe it's just not possible for us to find a calm place to speak from. Hmmm I stick to my instincts though. I think you neeeeeeeeed to calm down and round out. You are expecting tooo much from excitement and adventure. I am so slow and careful, why would you like me if not that I was causing you to slow down?

Instead of slowing down and trying to understand her message, I focussed on the last sentence. If she thought jumping ship was being 'slow and careful' then she needed her head examined. The unavoidable fact in this case was that she had gone off with Bermuda Shorts. There was no explanation of that fact here, and little sign of real contrition. Suppose we did get back together, how could I trust her not to flip again? What was to stop her going off with some other man on the next occasion? Unless she mastered her emotions I could never trust her with my heart. Even if she managed that there was another matter to consider. I really needed someone who believed in my dreams. Did Kyla believe in them? Did she want my kind of freedom?

I rowed ashore and walked over to Rubha Mòr peninsula. The path wound through damp woodland with moss and ferns and out over heather bound crags, which revealed artists' views across Loch Carron. It was a good place to think. As I walked, the sun came out and I felt at peace once more. In one dell, I glimpsed the grey-blue loch through a blue-green canopy of Scots Pine. Gusts sent dark crescents racing over the surface. In the distance, the mountain tops were swathed in heavy cloud. I followed the path down to a secluded shingle beach, shielded from the body of the loch by a wooded islet some fifty yards offshore. The air was filled with the smell of bracken. I took off my boots and socks and tested the water. In a moment I'd stripped off and plunged in. I swam out to the islet and back again, going fast to warm up, before lying back to float and watch the clouds racing past above. Sun and storm. It was the way of the west.

A large rock with a flat surface looked like the perfect place to dry out. I splashed back to the shingle beach, found my phone and climbed up. Maybe Kyla was right that I expected a lot from adventure but that was how I worked. I needed that time on my own with my wits fully stretched to think things out. That was when I was most in touch with myself. It was when I knew who I was and where I was headed. There was just enough reception. I sat down naked and keyed a reply.

If I was Rabbie, you were my red red rose. But you've chosen another and you should keep to your path.

I hesitated and then added:

Give my regards to Bermuda Shorts.

I chuckled at that. The truth was that I didn't need her confusion in my life. I wanted someone who believed in me without question, someone whose passion matched mine, who would stay with me in rough and smooth waters. Someone like Cori. With the decision made, I pulled on my clothes and walked back through the woods with more of a lift in my stride.

On the way out to *Molio*, I was hailed from the old schooner, *An Gèadh Glas*. I rowed over and was greeted by the owner.

"Are you from the other wooden boat?" she asked. "Would you like to come aboard for some tea?"

I climbed the step ladder with a word of thanks and stepped down into the cockpit where I was appraised by the cool gaze of a genteel 'Miss Marple', who was combining roles that evening, as owner and hostess.

"My name is Emily and this is the ship's skipper, Chas." She introduced me to a tall white-haired gentleman coming out of the dog cabin, whose own combination of ease and unassuming dignity reminded me of Alistair Cooke, the BBC's former *Letter from America* correspondent. I introduced myself and we discussed the impending gale for a few seconds before Emily took me below to look at the accommodation.

"What a beautiful boat!" I exclaimed, admiring the customised fittings and noticing the absence of the wooden boat smell – a musty, mildewy tang that I was battling to combat in *Molio*.

"She was built in 1894 by Camper and Nicholson and we've owned her for forty years." Emily said proudly as she ushered me into the saloon. It was as dark as *Molio*'s, despite the long glass skylight above. I sat back against an embroidered cushion and admired two small paintings hung on the mahogany panelling. Chas came through with a tray, and set out the tea on a polished table with high fiddles. Emily poured from the teapot into china cups. "Are you sailing on your own?"

"I am at the moment. My first mate jumped ship at the Mull of Kintyre." I didn't elaborate and she didn't enquire further.

"There were three of us. We cruised in the Hebrides or to more distant waters every summer. After my husband died, I couldn't give up this beautiful boat. Chas does all the work now. He's in his nineties you know, but he navigates, manages the sailing, cooks and does the maintenance work. Un homme à tout faire. He'll give you a tour if you like."

We talked on for a few minutes about some of her voyages and then I went aft to seek out Chas. He was in the doghouse organising some charts. I admired the mahogany coamings glowing nut brown. Every edge had been rounded. Chas put the charts to one side and showed me the GPS navigation equipment and switch panel. There was no sign of corrosion, no damp, not a spot of rust.

"How do you keep her so dry?" I asked.

"Ah, come on deck and I'll show you." He fished about in a drawer and brought a few bits and pieces with him. We stepped outside where Chas knelt down carefully on the teak planks. "This," he said, brandishing a plastic bottle with a long nozzle, "is the magic ingredient – Captain Tolley's Creeping Crack Cure." I managed to suppress a laugh at the name but he ignored my look and began to demonstrate its usefulness. "Look, you put a few drops along a suspect seam." I watched as the first drop of milky liquid fell on to the deck, just at the border between teak plank and rubber caulking. "It works by capillary action. If it disappears, then you have a leak." He continued testing the seams but they were all tight. "When you find a suspect area you investigate with this." He held up craft knife and probed a short distance into the edge of the black caulking with the razor sharp blade. "You cut out the suspect piece. Scrape clean the exposed wood and refill. Once you get the hang of it, you can keep the boat completely tight."

I looked along the deck. The planks of teak were ribbed – worn down in the middle by decades of scrubbing leaving the edges a quarter of an inch higher. The forty-foot length of rubber seam that sat between each pair of planks bore no resemblance to the ruler straight seams proudly displayed in yachting magazines. They reminded me instead of the sand rivers that meander through African bush – as viewed from the vantage of a light aircraft. In a tight gorge the rubberised river was narrow, but out on the plains it spread out. In one section it bulged to the left and in the next to the right. Each bulge, each bend, was the handiwork of Chas as he tested, probed and repaired leaks. He had been looking after this boat for four decades and each dark river spoke of his devotion. On our side of the boat there were fifteen rivers.

Chas took me up to the foredeck showing me, in passing, the galvanised shrouds painted in pitch. At the deck they connected to bottle screws that he'd dressed in leather coats to avoid sharp edges. Sails were neatly furled along the booms within white covers; the skylights had matching white covers to give protection from leaks in a downpour. We descended into the fo'c'sle. It was another work of art. The ship's ropes were neatly coiled and hung to port and starboard. It kept them tidy, ready to hand, and yet out of the way. Even the kedge anchor was suspended and lashed to one side. A small wooden hatch in the deck opened to allow the anchor chain to pass through and down a green leather apron to the chain locker on the floor. Everywhere I looked I could see the handiwork of Chas, master mariner and caretaker of *An Gèadh Glas*.

"Where did you learn to sail?" I asked, back in the doghouse.

"I learnt to sail my father's boat. One year he asked me to take her down to Spain for the summer. After that I used to ferry her about for the family. Actually I was wondering if you learnt in a similar way."

"Just around the west coast here in our family boat. Actually my brother is joining me tomorrow and we were hoping to cross the Minch."

Chas raised an eyebrow. "How long does he have?"

"Not long. What do you think of the forecast?"

"You know, the Hebrides will still be here next year. May and June are your best chance for settled weather."

I nodded but made no comment. It seemed overly cautious advice. We made our way on to the deck and Emily came up to see me off in the dinghy. As I rowed the short distance over to *Molio*, I reflected on her unconventional life. She and her late husband had crafted a wholeness and sweetness from their devotion to this boat. *An Gèadh Glas* was the love child of a happy ménage. Like her namesake, the wild goose, she now journeyed with consummate ease across the summer horizons, bringing grace and charm wherever she alighted. And how did Chas fit in? Back on *Molio*, I put some new potatoes on the stove and poured myself a glass of wine. The more I thought about, it the more I realised that he was the key to their lifestyle. He'd devoted all his life to cruising yachts and most of it to looking after *An Gèadh Glas*. Here he was at ninety, still doing it. It wasn't escapism for him. It wasn't even adventure. He knew what he wanted in life, excelled at it, and in the process looked after both boat and boat-family.

I drained my glass and poured another. Retrieving the mobile from my pack, I called Cori. She picked up right away.

"Hello Cori, it's Martyn."

"Hello sailor man, what you doing?"

"Right now I'm drinking red wine on *Molio* and thinking about you."

"Uh-huh, I'm drinking Dark Island brew and thinking about a new song."

"I hope that's about us." There was a pause, long enough for me to think I had overstepped the mark.

"Got to go, sailor man."

There was the sound of a kiss and the phone went dead.

In the morning, I took my tea up to the cockpit to look about. The wind had risen in the night and was now gusting to force six from the southeast, driving white horses across the bay. Fortunately, *Molio*'s mooring was in the most sheltered part, over towards the Duncraig shore. It was doubly fortunate that there was a tiny railway station right next to the mooring. I rang my brother and suggested he get off the train at Duncraig rather than Plockton. No sooner had I replaced the mobile on its perch above the chart table than my oldest brother Greer called.

"How's it going on *Molio*?" It was good to hear his cheery voice.

"I'm on a mooring in Plockton and waiting for Rob to arrive."

"You've heard about the next storm? It's going to be a strong one. There's an even heavier one coming behind it."

"It's a pity. We'll just have to wait and see. Are you on *Pippa*?"

"We're on board at the moment, in Ardfern, but we're going home for a few days to let it blow out."

With the wind set to increase, it made sense to have the outboard ready for action. *Molio* had a two horsepower Yamaha which is kept fixed to the stern rail. They don't come much smaller but it still delivers the power of four Olympic oarsmen. That kind of muscle might come in very handy. I drained last season's petrol into an empty can, made up some fresh two stroke mix and topped up. After finishing, I put on wet-weather gear, emptied the dinghy of rainwater and mounted the Yamaha on the stern. It started with the second pull and I motored over to the shore.

Rob stepped off the train with a cheery smile, a grip with spare clothes, and a carrier bag of fresh provisions; all ready to look out for his younger brother as he had done on countless occasions when we were boys. I noticed that his rufous beard was whitening in places, but it was as thick as ever and only slightly marred his resemblance to the Emperor Claudius. Uncannily, he shared a mild limp and a penchant for law with the Emperor, but hadn't so far shown any inclination to conquer the British...

"How's *Molio*?" he asked as we walked down the path to the shore.

"She's in good shape and, what's more, she's dry as a bone inside."

"Oh well done. I won't have to wear these waterproofs below decks then?" He was already suited up in bright red waterproofs. "How's the weather looking?"

"It eased off a bit this afternoon."

"I've brought the CalMac timetable for ferries to the Outer Hebrides. If there's a window in the weather I can get a ferry from

Harris or North Uist to Skye and the coach from there to Edinburgh."

"Greer says there's a severe gale on its way."

"Typical," Rob laughed. "In that case, I have a new card game to teach you."

As we pushed off the dinghy, I thought his red sailing gear contrasted rather well with my own yellow and white. The outboard started with one pull and we powered over to *Molio*. After stowing Rob's things below I made some tea while Rob found a deck of cards and taught me to play Switch. It reminded me of the countless games we used to play when stormbound on *Primrose* – Monopoly, Cribbage, L'Attaque, Dover Patrol, Tri-Tactics, Chess, Solitaire, Patience and so on.

Next morning it was calm, but there was a heavy layer of cloud and a stormy feeling in the air. Rob tapped the barometer.

"It's dropped six points overnight," he reported.

"That doesn't sound good."

"Lovely barometer though. Just like the one on *Primrose*."

On the radio, the farmer's forecast mentioned a large low-pressure area sitting south of Iceland. It was stationery and dragging moist air rapidly over the west of Scotland – we should expect gales and rain for a further five days. The boats in Plockton Harbour looked a bit apprehensive as they bobbed about in the unnatural calm. We decided to spend the day on board and chatted away about old times. A bunch of seagulls came round the boat. It looked to me as though they were starving; perhaps they had no food because the fishing boats were tied up. We chucked them some bread which they ate ravenously. The sky grew darker and darker.

When the rain arrived it came hard and fast, bouncing off the surface of the seas and raising a white mist which enveloped the bay turning yachts into ghost ships. Rainwater was coming through the deck seams in the fo'c'sle, but in the cabin the boat was dry. We peered out of the portholes at the spectral fleet. After a few minutes the rain grew in ferocity. The roll of tenor drums pounding the deck hardened into the crashing flam of snares as bigger drops crashed into the boat. We went up to the cockpit, keeping under the sprayhood. Visibility had shrunk to fifty yards, isolating each boat in its own private storm. Rain missiles were tearing holes in the water, pitting the surface where they struck, each dark crater surrounded by a splash of white. As I stared at the waterscape, lost in a dwam, a cormorant surfaced next to the boat with an eel, which it shook and tossed until finally it had the head going down its gullet. No wonder they were named 'sea ravens'. And then, almost like a tap being turned off, the rain stopped. The clink of slack rigging could be heard across the bay as boats rocked uneasily.

I wondered what the other crews were thinking. We were a bit like a crowd of theatre goers in the foyer during the interval of a gripping drama – bemused, not quite there and not quite here. A dark squall raced across the bay, shaking the boats like a shark with its prey, leaving streaks of white in its wake. Yachts heeled, jibbed at their moorings, and swung wildly. Lying low in the water, *Molio* also heeled to the blast before turning to face it, comfortable in her element. It was followed by another. Soon the squalls were frequent, hammering the sheltered bay and setting the motorboats spinning on their moorings. I heard wailing in the distance and then spotted a squall coming along the hillside, setting the pine trees rippling. As it came closer, we could see a black curtain beneath it. When the screaming heebie-jeebies hit, even *Molio* was spun around by the weight of the wind. Rain shot past horizontally. The neighbouring motorboat was knocked so far back on its haunches that it pulled the heavy mooring buoy clean out of the water. Sun followed the rain.

Rob read a passage from *Primrose*'s log from 1957 when the family and dogs were stormbound in Oban. My mother, who has a poetic nature, was getting a bit fed up.

The wind's like a shower of old witches; screaming and shouting till they're done with their dirty work and then sitting back mumbling and muttering only to start bellyaching again, and working up to fresh mischiefs.

"It wasn't really Mum's cup of tea being on a boat," I said.

"No, but she always had complete confidence in Dad, even in a gale.

It wasn't just that Dad did things properly. He looked after the gear and kept his boats in great shape. More than that, he had an instinct for sailing; he knew exactly what his boat could do."

"Do you remember the time that he and cousin Isobel were storm-bound in Loch Fyne?" I asked. "They were on *Pippa* with nothing but mackerel to eat. Isobel had to get back to London for a high level meeting but there was no let-up in the gale. Dad decided they could do it. They set off heavily reefed and ran down to Fairlie on the backs of big seas. Isobel remembers they had cans of beer tucked between their legs and time to crack some jokes. It was dicey coming into the moorings packed with other boats under those conditions. He told Isobel he would only make one pass and if they failed he would beat across to the lee of Cumbrae Island for the night. Somehow she got the mooring buoy. They secured the boat and were blown ashore in the Avon dinghy without any gear or personal items. Isobel said she was never worried about her safety with Dad."

Rob was engrossed in the story, reliving the stormy passage, log-book closed on his lap. "I didn't hear about that escapade," he replied with a shake of his head, "but I can tell you another one." Without pausing he recounted the time that he and Dad had been sailing *Pippa* up north in the summer of 1970 but the time had come to start heading south. Coming from Arisaig they sailed down the west coast of Mull, passing close to the Dutchman's Cap, knowing that a westerly gale was imminent. Dad had decided to head for Bunessan and by the time they arrived they were reefed down and sailing on their ear. They dropped the hook inside Eilean Ban (White Island) but the seas were coming into the loch and *Pippa* was pitching up and down like a bucking bronco. A local chap on the shore caught their attention and waved them further west. Dad got the engine going and Rob had the task of pulling the anchor up on to the heaving deck. Even with the engine's help the chain was bar taut in the waves. He wound a loop of chain round the Samson post as *Pippa* went into a trough and let the boat do the hauling for him as the bows rose, quickly taking in the slack and readying for the next trough. He managed the job and they battered their way west into a sheltered spot indicated by the local. On getting ashore they scrambled out of the dinghy which somehow blew up into the air and landed on their backs, but they made it to the pub where Dad bought their guide a drink. Three days later they awoke to calm conditions. Hoisting sail they drifted over to Martyr's Bay and dropped the anchor into a blue-green sea over a patch of white sand. The corncrakes were rasping in the field as Dad took Rob to see the Abbey where the morning sunshine streamed through the windows onto the old wooden pews. It was the peace and calm of Iona after the storm that stayed in his memory, that and his complete confidence in Dad.

As the afternoon wore on it felt as if we were sitting in the centre of a giant painting depicting a stormy seascape. It might have been by Turner. Only our transcendent Turner was working with real life as his canvas. The clouds scudded across the sky, the squalls darkened the bay, the boats jerked and spun, and the cormorants went fishing. One enterprising gull scavenged at the base of the motorboat's mooring buoy when it lifted clean out the water.

It was calmer next morning and the forecast indicated a few hours respite. We could head north to Gairloch but it would be risky given the distance. The alternative would be to go south, taking advantage of the shelter in Loch Alsh, and anchor behind Isle Ornsay on Skye. It would give Rob a chance to take the helm and from there he could pick up a bus to the mainland. As for my voyage, I could either sail north after the next gale passing through the Inner Sound between Skye and the mainland, before turning west across the Minch to Harris in the Outer Hebrides, or else head south down the Sound of Sleat to pass Skye on its mountainous southern side before crossing the Sea of the Hebrides to South Uist. Either way, I would be in striking range of St Kilda.

We hauled in the dinghy, deflated it and strapped it down over the fo'c'sle hatch before setting off. Rob donned his red weather gear and grinned encouragement as he took the helm. It gave me a chance to relax and look around. Heavy skies hung above the dark mountains enfolding Loch Alsh. Paler mists descended the glens and fanned out over the leaden waters which appeared to part in order to let *Molio* through. Lulled by the shelter, we discussed the possibility of continuing to Arisaig with its convenient train station. Coming through Kyle Rhea on the ebb, we smacked into a brisk, southerly breeze. The powerful tide setting against the wind had kicked up a vicious sea. *Molio* heaved up and smashed down on the steep waves. Sheets of spray drenched the cockpit. Another yacht turned back. We clawed up the Sound of Sleat making barely three knots on the engine. Crockery crashed in the cupboards. We wedged ourselves in to keep from sliding about as *Molio* lurched one way and then the next. The lighthouse on Isle Ornsay slowly increased in size on our starboard bow but finally we could turn in behind the islet's shelter. Gusts were racing down the short stretch of shallows. We found a visitor's mooring and made fast. Divesting ourselves of wet weather gear, Rob set about cooking spaghetti bolognaise whilst I dipped *Molio*'s bilges. The mysterious leak had increased again.

In the night I listened to the wild orchestra. Laughing wavelets rushed along *Molio*'s side making musical chords, 'de-re-ling', 'de-re-ling', 'chu-ker-ting'. The heavy rigging moaned and the lighter lines tapped excitedly against the mast. Eventually, I fell into an uneasy sleep. As there was no sign of a second break in the weather, Rob decided he might as well go back a day early and hopefully return later in the summer for some sailing. We inflated the dinghy and mounted the outboard in her stern bracket, then motored up the bay to the pier. We walked over to the main road and managed to hitch a ride for Rob with a passing motorist. He waved goodbye and gave me a big thumbs up. We hadn't managed to hoist sails once but it hadn't dampened his spirits. I turned around and trudged back to Ornsay feeling a bit blue.

At the pier I watched as a heavy black fishing boat with a massive mast approached. I took a rope thrown to me by the bearded skipper and tied it to a bollard. They winched the vessel alongside the pier wall with thick warps, and let her settle on the mud in the ebbing tide. It turned out that *Molio* was on their mooring but the bearded skipper wasn't perturbed.

"Och no matter, we will just sit here on the mud whilst we go about our business."

"Thanks very much." I really meant it. Although they shared the mooring with visitors, he was quite within his rights to ask me to move.

"How strong is your mooring by the way?"

"Och that one. I laid it with two-hundred-pound anchors. You're not going anywhere tonight."

My smile widened. "That's good to know. And will you stay here long?"

"We're off across the Minch tomorrow."

"What?" I faltered. "You know the latest forecast is force 10?"

"Och, its fine."

I shook my head. These guys must go out in all weathers. I looked over their boat once more. There was a name etched on her bow that was hard to make out – *Fifie of Sand*.

"I can see you're not a sailing Fifie."

"We came after that. She was built in 1934."

She was strong all right, probably built as a seine netter. But these guys must be Vikings even to think of going out. I felt sure it would be a mistake. "That's a full storm coming. Why chance going out?" I might as well have saved my breath.

"Och it's fine," he added one last time before heading up the road. It seemed everything was "Och it's fine" with this skipper.

Back on *Molio* I washed some dishes and fidgeted with bits and pieces but, without Rob, it wasn't much fun. I decided to go back ashore for a drink in the Ornsay Hotel.

Inside the public bar an open log fire crackled away and a dozen folk were sitting about chatting. There were several rows of whisky bottles, all fine malts, behind the counter. I stripped down to shirt and jeans and ordered a plate of langoustines to go with a glass of house white. While waiting, I met some people off another boat and we discussed the grim forecast. Sailing had come to a complete halt. A young teenager arrived in black jacket and jeans, with black hair down his shoulders, and a black piping box under his arm. He placed it on a stool and chatted with some friends. He seemed to be off in his own world, like a west coast version of Orlando Bloom when playing the Elvin prince in Lord of the Rings. Eventually, he opened the box and took out a set of silver-mounted ebony pipes. He warmed up his fingering on the chanter for a few seconds before launching into a slow air – The Mist Covered Mountains of Morvern. It is a haunting melody and was one of my father's favourites. His next number was a fast reel which was played finger perfect, but he stopped unexpectedly, and came over to check that nobody minded his playing. Reassured, he struck up again. After a short break, he pulled out a fiddle and soon had us tapping along.

It was a great evening of music which cheered me up no end. The wind powered the dinghy back to *Molio*. I sat in the cockpit for a few minutes to see how she was doing. Short waves from the Sound of Sleat were coming round the Isle of Ornsay against the wind, causing her to rock back and forth in the lop. By 22:00 stronger gusts were rushing down the bay from the hotel, mustering up three-foot waves in the short reach. Other boats were rocking up and down like fairground rides. Even *Molio* dipped and heeled in the squalls. The wind kept strengthening. Down below the cabin was draughty and cold. At 11 p.m. I went up on deck to check the mooring and had difficulty walking to the bow. *Molio* was pulling back on the warp like a horse attempting to bolt while attached by a strong tether. If she'd been pulling like that on her anchor, I would have stayed up all night on anchor watch. As it was, I retired to bed. Even with the reassurance of a thirty-ton mooring, I didn't sleep well. In the morning, the gale was still raging and I was tempted just to stay in my bunk. But in the end I got up and busied myself with various tasks about the boat. I was cold and tired. My mind had slowed down and I found it easy to forget what I was doing. The only way to cope was to complete one thing at a time. After a while I found I had to write down what that thing was or I'd forget it.

By the fourth morning the big depression off Iceland finally filled up and the wind calmed down. At last it was possible to continue with my voyage. The question was which way – north to try again for the Outer Hebrides or south towards home waters. It had been a stormy summer. A new gale was already halfway across the Atlantic and would be arriving in a few days. We were well into July and the best time for a passage to St Kilda had passed. Was it worth continuing? I didn't want to make the wrong decision. I heated up some milk and made a large mug of boat latte, then thought about it some more.

I wasn't up there at Isle Ornsay just to prove my sailing prowess; I was trying to find greater joy in living back home. I was looking for a way to unshackle myself from other people's expectation and build personal freedom into the fabric of daily life. It didn't make sense to be clawing my way north with each break in the gales. It wasn't supposed to be an endurance test. Would it not be better to return next summer? I could set off earlier in the year when there was a better chance of good weather and sail with a song in my heart rather than gritted teeth and dogged mantra. I decided on south. You have to know when to fold, at least that's what I told myself. I raised the main, let loose the yankee and dropped the mooring. As I sailed out the anchorage I nodded my thanks to the black fishing boat still parked on the mud by the pier. Someone had managed to instil a bit of common sense in them after all. Rounding Isle Ornsay I jibed *Molio* onto the opposite tack and headed south down the Sound of Sleat.

Chapter 13

Wild Mountain Thyme

Passing between Arisaig and Eigg, I fell into a kind of reverie. Wind and sea, islands and tide, this was my world now and it was woven right through me. I no longer needed to think. *Molio* carried me down the coast, taking me round Ardnamurchan and through the Sound of Mull. Towards evening, we crossed the Firth of Lorn under sail and picked up a mooring at the Oban Yacht Club. As I was heating up a tin of beans my mobile rang. It was Neil calling from Ireland.

"Now Martyn, have you got that woman there to keep you warm?"

"Huh. I've nothing here but a bottle."

"That Scotch stuff? Jeannie Mac but it's a rough time you've been having. So what happened to yer one?"

"She jumped ship – a few weeks back."

"Now why would she be doing a thing like that?"

"Christ knows, Neil. She blew up in my face and then joined a young fellow in another boat. Someone she didn't even know."

"That's a weird one all right. And has she not been in touch?"

Neil's voice was slow and thoughtful, so much so that I found myself thinking about Kyla differently.

"She's sent messages but anyone that fickle is bad news. I'm done with her."

"Sure that's bad news all right. And is she still with this guy?"

"Aye she is." I told Neil about a text I'd received from her sister.

"And would that be her younger sister by any chance?"

"She texted that Kyla was seeing him."

"And you believed her now?"

"Well why wouldn't I? Wouldn't you?"

"I might, and then again I might not. Kid sisters can't always be relied upon you know."

I paused to absorb that one. "Is there something you're not telling me, Neil?"

"Just you think about it, Martyn. She's a good girl at heart that Kyla of yours. And she's been through it all right. She may need you now more than ever."

Could Kyla have been in touch with Neil, I wondered. It was possible, but Neil hadn't been there on Sanda. He hadn't seen her abrupt change of heart or her icy dismissal of our plans. I moved the conversation onto other matters.

Pouring myself a large dram I sat back on *Molio*'s faded cushions and thought back over the conversation. It was true about sisters. They can be best friends but they can also be rivals. Perhaps she'd fed me a line. Was Kyla's outburst on Sanda some kind of panic attack – more connected with her past than the present? It was confusing. I'd rather be with someone who knew what they wanted all the time. I checked the ship's clock and decided it wasn't too late to call Cori. Now there was a woman, a rough and tumble girl with bags of energy. She wouldn't be phased by a bit of sea air. What's more, she would love to go cruising on *Molio*. She might even compose a sailing song.

"Hello Cori, it's Martyn."

"Hello sailor man. Have you been misbehaving?"

"Fat chance, I've been stormbound at Isle Ornsay."

"You should have told me. I could have come over."

"I'll be down at Crinan in a couple of days' time. I'm planning to go through the canal on Saturday. I could use a hand, if you can get down."

"You can't manage all on your little ownsome?"

"What I meant," I laughed, "is it would be lovely to have you on board to make tea and be bossed about."

"Huh!" she snorted and I could imagine her mischievous grin. "I'll see what's possible."

Next morning, I was off early, beating down the Firth of Lorn under full sail in order to catch the ebb tide past Fladda and reach the tidal door of Dorus Mor before it closed. It was perfect sailing weather in sheltered seas. The sun danced in the wavelets, gulls swept past our stern, two porpoises rolled in play. *Molio*'s bow cleaved the waters which swept past her beam in arching waves. She staggered in the gusts and burrowed down deeper. One sunlit isle after another was left behind in her foaming wake. I checked the clock as I gybed *Molio* round Craignish Point and began running up the loch. I was looking forward to spending the evening with Greer and Carie who were back on board *Pippa* in Ardfern and preparing for their own cruise. I'd given them my ETA as I left Oban, so making the passage on time was a matter of family honour. The yankee, main and mizzen swelled in the gusts thrusting *Molio* forward. I set the wind vane steering and walked up to the bow to feel *Molio* at full stretch, yankee shuddering, foam hissing, cleaving the loch in two. Halfway down Eileen Mhic Chrion, the long island that shelters Ardfern, I went aft to drop the mizzen and take off speed. As I passed the black rock that lies outside the narrow entrance to Ardfern Marina I let out the yankee sheet and hauled in on the furling line. I struggled with it but it was jammed solid. Looking along the port side I could see that half a dozen loops had slipped off the furling drum. *Molio* was more than halfway across the opening and going like a train. If I tried coming up into the wind I risked running aground. I would have to miss the entrance and make for the head of the sea loch. At that moment a RIB came charging out. It was Greer. He waved and sped over.

"Greer," I shouted. "The furling gear has jammed."

"Standby and I'll come aboard." He powered alongside *Molio*, matching her speed. We were doing seven knots as we raced past the next little island and sped towards the shallows. He passed me the painter which I made fast on a short line to the cockpit. Then he killed the engine and leapt aboard. "You're bang on time!" he said with a laugh.

I laughed too. Big brothers can be wonderful. "You have the helm," I shouted as he stepped into the cockpit. "Look out for the shallows." I raced forward. The yankee was cracking and exploding as it alternately filled and spilled. The sheets were whipping about the fore-deck ready to clobber the unwary in the face. Better control this demon first, I thought, and signalled to Greer. He pulled in the starboard sheet. The yankee settled. I glanced at the water as Greer gybed *Molio*. The bottom wasn't that far away. Now we were tearing towards the eastern shore. I pulled the furling line through all the little fairleads on the deck, coiled it neatly, climbed out on the bowsprit, and passed the coil round and round the forestay until the line fell directly from the drum. Back on deck, I shouted at Greer to loosen the sheet. I pulled on the furling line and the sail rolled in easily. I made a mental note to keep tension on the line at all times. It could cost me a sail if I didn't.

"She handles like a dream," said Greer as I returned to the cockpit. "Heavier than *Pippa*, but I can see why you're taken with her."

"Thanks Greer, that was mighty good sailing."

"That's a nice bit of heather on *Molio*'s pulpit," he remarked, ignoring my praise, "just to show where you've been."

I looked at the sprig of purple ling in the bows. It was a bonny sight when set against the blue water and green hills.

"Aye, round Ardnamurchan. But it's nothing by today's standards."

"Not everyone in here," he nodded at the marina, "could sail an old wooden boat on this coast."

"But it's *Molio* that looks after me," I laughed.

Greer went ahead in the RIB to prepare Pippa *VII*, a powerful Beneteau, that was moored at the head of the main pontoon. As I came alongside, Carie was at the bow looking tanned and fit in a striped sailing top, with sunglasses perched in her hair, waiting to take *Molio*'s bow line. Greer had some fenders over the side and took *Molio*'s stern line. Soon we were moored snugly alongside. *Molio* was a bit awestruck by this suave new companion who towered above her. In no time, Carie had me sitting at the table on *Pippa*'s aft deck with a chilled beer in hand. A little later I was taken on a guided tour. The opulence in comparison to *Molio* was seductive. Walk-in showers with hot water, real beds, lounge area with TV, three-burner stove, microwave, fridge and so on. It was the difference between a suite in a grand hotel and a pioneer's shack. Greer showed me *Pippa*'s navigation equipment, including the library of electronic charts that could take her anywhere.

"The first time I started using these instruments," admitted Greer, "I spent so much time looking at the screen I sailed straight onto a rock."

I laughed, partly at the story and partly with joy at his honesty. We all hit rocks at one time or another. The boss of one of the charter companies told me that he refused to put plotters in the cockpit of his yachts because they distracted the skippers and the boats were constantly hitting rocks. Although I carried a handheld GPS device on *Molio*, I preferred to use paper charts, and usually kept the current one in the cockpit inside a clear vinyl case so that I could keep an eye on my position.

To my mind physical charts offer some unique advantages. They provide a wide horizon of information about the surrounding lands and ocean floor. In using them, you position yourself within the seascape by checking prominent hills, islands, points of land, rocks and navigation buoys, or by consulting depth soundings, and then by seeking correspondence with the chart. Often it takes just a glance, sometimes much study, but in the process you build a mental awareness of your surroundings. In *Primrose*'s day you might take this hands-on approach to navigation a step further by using your artistic skills to improve on the standard charts.

I stepped across the gap between *Pippa* and *Molio* to find *Primrose*'s old logbook with a description of this kind of thing. Leafing through the pages I found the entry and read it out loud to Greer and Carie.

12th August 1958

Primrose anchored next to 'Islay', a varnished Bermudian cutter in Tarbert with Dr Mackay and son. (They showed me their charts.) They had more or less quartered the admiralty charts and posted them onto stiff cardboard; they were stowed in a large wooden box. Land was shaded in coloured pencil, or water colour, also sand bars etc, making everything handy and clear. They had plain postcards in tin boxes on which they had pasted art paper. On these they had painted water colours of various entrances to small difficult anchorages and passages, like Cuan Sound, Tinker's Hole etc etc. They are beautifully done and most helpful.

Greer nodded at the memory. "Beautiful, surely, but you have to admit that finding your way into a difficult anchorage with the rain lashing down is far easier with satellite navigation – no matter how good an artist you are."

"It's a whole lot less stressful too," added Carie.

"True," I agreed, wondering if I was at risk of becoming a tiresome curmudgeon. "I suppose it's not so much the technology that I take issue with, but the way we use it. It's so easy to take a backseat."

"Does that matter?" asked Carie. "Getting there safely is the most important thing."

"I remember one time when Rob and I were sailing in *Pippa III*. We were making for Tiree and it was getting late. The rain came on and a sea fog just rose up all around us. Visibility was soon down to a hundred yards – and that was before the invention of GPS."

"So how did you manage?" asked Carie, poking me in the ribs.

"It was dodgy," I conceded. "We plotted a compass course to Gunna Sound at the north end and then closed slowly with the shore. When the depth reduced to ten fathoms we turned northeast and used the echo sounder to follow along the ten fathom contour. We listened out for a bell on the buoy at the east end of the Sound. Then Rob checked the direction of the radio beacon on Hyskeir Light and found we had overshot the buoy, so we reversed direction and this time found it. In the end we made it into shelter using the chart and the soundings."

"But today you would use the GPS?" asked Greer.

"Definitely I would, but I've never forgotten that evening. Every sense was straining, eyes, ears and even noses, to keep us safe. The reason I'm uneasy with electronic navigation is because of the hidden price to pay, you end up cutting yourself off from the natural world. If you connect satellite navigation to an autohelm and link it to a servo-assisted sailing kit, you end up with an automated yacht. All you have to do is choose the destination. At what point does it cease to be sailing?"

"Come on boys," said Carie. "You can finish this conversation over dinner." She and Greer had invited me for a meal at the Galley of Lorne. After a week of storms, I was down to absolute basics – baked beans, sardines and Carnation milk. So this was one invitation I had no intention of refusing.

In the morning, Greer helped me turn *Molio* around in the marina so she was facing back out and then gave me a shove off. With a wave I took *Molio* through the narrow entrance and set off down Loch Craignish. About an hour later I was in the sea lock at Crinan. Once up in the basin, I moored *Molio* against a low-lying bank with the help of Clarissa, one of the canal staff. I switched off the engine and swung *Molio*'s bowsprit over the grass to make adjustments to the furling drum. As I worked there was a commotion from across the basin. A dirty trawler was revving its engine, black smoke pouring out of its exhaust. The skipper was arguing with one of the lock keepers. "We effing came in last night," I heard him say. I noticed Clarissa walking over to the trawler. She was a senior lock keeper and not the type to take any non-sense. "You've been here a week," she declared loudly. There was more arguing and a lot of scowling. But Clarissa was a tough cookie and the trawlermen knew it. Eventually, cash changed hands. In defiance, the skipper let rip with some heavy rock music through a PA system mounted on the wheelhouse. Nobody made a fuss. After a minute or two, the music was turned down, and then switched off. It was another small victory for the harbourmaster and his staff.

I went below to get on with the next job. The starter switch had become unreliable and Greer had suggested that I clean the contacts of the large battery isolator switch. I was down by the chart table working on the contacts with emery cloth, when Clarissa came on board.

"Are you moving soon?" she called down.

"Midday," I replied.

"I need to move your boat across to the other side. We're bringing in a large motorboat that will sit here."

It seemed an unnecessary hassle, given the space on the far side, where a couple of fishing boats were already moored. "My engine isn't operational at the moment," I called up. "But I can move if you give me a hand with the ropes."

"Okay," she said, talking to someone on her walkie-talkie, then turning back to me, "Can you be quick?" She lifted the stern-warp off the iron ring on the shore and passed me the free end. Then she walked over to the next ring to free off the bow warp, which released *Molio* completely.

"Make sure you grab the stern rail," I called as she threw me the end. *Molio*'s bow drifted away from the basin wall as the breeze caught her. Clarissa walked back to the stern and held onto the rail casually, slowly walking along the bank as the boat drifted in the wind. I hastily coiled up the bow line, making it ready to pass to her from *Molio*'s other side, as the bow came further round. She was still talking into the walkie-talkie and not paying attention. I came aft quickly.

"I have to go," she called. "Can you manage?"

I jumped ashore, and grabbed the end of the mizzen boom, the only extremity still reachable from the bank. Clarissa disappeared at a trot. *Molio*'s bow had now swung out into the middle of the basin, and the stern was trying to move across the open water at the entrance to an old sea lock, immediately to my side. I was teetering at the corner of the cement wall. *Molio* is a heavy boat with a mind of her own. If she wanted to go, there wasn't much I could do to stop her. I realised that I'd have to go with her. I leapt for the stern, grabbed the guardrail and scrambled aboard. On the other side of the basin, the dirty trawler had left her dock and was heading towards the sea lock which had opened to receive her. As she passed in front of *Molio*, she picked up speed. A fisherman on the bow shouted at the man in the wheelhouse: "Watch the effing gate!" He glanced down at me and beamed. "It'sh the brandy," he slurred holding up a large mug of Irish coffee. "He canna stop her noo." Right enough, the bow crunched into the side of the lock scraping off three feet of paint. The fisherman chortled. I heard a mechanical clunk and saw the boat's large propeller begin to thrash the water as she went hard astern. Gathering way in reverse, her stern slipped safely past *Molio* but then her bow began swinging out into the basin, on a direct collision course.

I shouted to the man on the bow, "I've no engine."

He swivelled round, facing the bridge, "Steer her straight, yer bastard" he yelled. It was all happening in slow motion. The bow was picking up speed as it swung out into the basin. *Molio* continued to drift into its path. I began to run forward, making ready to fend off, hoping not to injure myself.

"Throw me a rope!"

I looked back. It was Cori. In one swift movement, I picked the coils of the stern warp off the deck and hurled them. The end landed on the edge of the basin. She was onto it like a cat, snatched it up and ran towards the nearest post. I secured my end to the furthest aft cleat, but there wasn't enough line for Cori. She turned to face me, dug both feet into the turf, wound the rope round her arms and leant right back, legs like ramrods, as flat to the ground as the crew of a racing dinghy on a trapeze. The warp came up bar tight. *Molio* stopped. The Fishing boat's heavy bow whooshed past inches from the bowsprit. The fisherman yelled at the bridge, "Stop yer bastard." And *Molio* began moving gently across the basin back to our new berth.

"Thanks," I called. She smiled that cheeky grin of hers, "I'm always rescuing you, Martyn."

"Mmm, you should hang about then and it wouldn't be necessary."

She looked me straight in the eye, "Have I earned my cup of coffee?"

An hour later, we began working *Molio* down the canal. Cori had helped several boats through before and knew the ropes. She ran on ahead to prepare the next lock for *Molio*. I steered the boat in and threw her the mooring lines. Then she closed the gate and let in water from the far side to raise *Molio* another step. The sun blazed down. It was fun working with her. She put all her effort into each job, turning the heavy iron handle that opened and closed cills in the lock doors, heaving the massive gates open and throwing down the ropes. She tied her hair up with a sweat-band but, even so, beads of perspiration ran down her temples. Damp patches appeared on her white tank top. Guys on boats coming in the other direction couldn't take their eyes off her. When we got to a longer stretch she came aboard, standing immediately in front of me. No perfume, just a healthy woman. Her body next to mine. I wanted to put my arms around her but hesitated. Something was about to happen, but a crowd of questions intruded.

The next lock showed up as we rounded a bend. I steered *Molio* towards the pontoon in front. Cori jumped ashore and ran up to the gate; leaning against it, she walked it open. I nudged *Molio* in and she shouted for the ropes. That done, she went back to close the gate behind *Molio*, and from there forward again, to open the cill on the front gate. She walked out on the little platform just as a car skidded to a halt on the gravel track running alongside. A man opened the door and strode over to the lock gate. He shouted something at Cori who ignored him and began to open the cill. He walked up to her, still shouting, but I couldn't make out his words above the roar of water tumbling off the leaking walls and surging under *Molio*. I hauled in on the bow rope to keep the bows from being caught by the current. Cori shouted something back at the man and turned her back. He reached her side, body tense, still shouting and put his arms on her shoulders forcing her round to face him. That was it. I secured the rope and ran aft to the ladder in the wall. As I started to climb, I looked over my shoulder. He had grabbed the back of Cori's head and was kissing her hard. I saw that she wasn't struggling. And then to my amazement she returned the kiss, leaning back, her arms encircling his neck, kissing with ardour, letting it linger. The man glanced once at me and then strode back to his car and drove off fast. Cori finished opening the cill. When the boat was up at the top level she walked over.

"I have to leave, Martyn." She seemed a bit lost.

I handed over her jacket. "I'll ask a friend to give me a hand."

She nodded and walked slowly along the path to the next lock where one of the white canal vans was parked. I watched her talking to the lock keeper. They drove off together towards Crinan.

I didn't feel angry. I didn't feel upset. I felt slightly sick, as if I had just stopped myself jumping out of an aircraft without a parachute. I'd been swept up in a tide of passion and almost carried away by it. Passion of love, passion for life, passion for freedom: if you'd asked me an hour before, I'd have said it was everything. But I'd have been wrong. Passion on its own isn't enough, not when it is blind, not when it ignores common sense, not when it brings havoc and worse. Is that what Kyla had meant? Love needs to be built on something stronger. What did she call it? A sidling up in friendship and trust. Christ, how right that felt.

The lock keeper returned a few minutes later and helped me down a couple of locks to Cairnbaan. I moored there and made myself some tea. Greer had given me the number of a retired lock keeper. I rang Hugh. He could meet me in an hour at the end of the next long stretch of canal. I finished my tea and cast off, going slow and enjoying the sensation of gliding through the wooded countryside of Argyll. There was something almost dreamlike about it. Lilies filled the wide bends. Branches from rowans and hazels hung from the banks. A mallard quacked loudly and took off, leaving its wake spreading across the still water. A couple of cyclists on the tow path waved as *Molio* swept under arches of oak and maple. We passed a mauve-pink bank of rosebay willowherb – one more artist's painting brought to life.

I began to hum a favourite song, and then I remembered the words.

> *O the summertime is comin'*
> *And the trees are sweetly blooming*
> *And the wild mountain thyme*
> *Grows around the blooming heather*
> *Will you go, Lassie go?*
>
> *And we'll all go together*
> *To pluck wild mountain thyme*
> *All around the blooming heather*
> *Will ye go, Lassie go?*

When Kyla sang it, you were there beside her pulling thyme on the hillside. A feeling of contentment took root and a smile spread slowly across my face. We'd be back next summer, *Molio* and I. There'd be wind in her sails and ideas a-leaping, and should Poseidon take a break from his games, even a short one, we'd be ready to make it all the way.

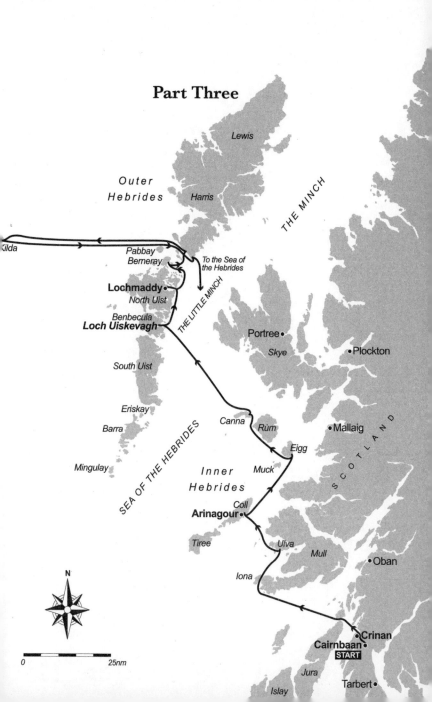

Part Three

Lewis

*Outer
Hebrides*

Harris

THE MINCH

St Kilda

Pabbay
Berneray

*To the Sea of
the Hebrides*

Lochmaddy
North Uist

THE LITTLE MINCH

Portree•

•Plockton

Skye

Benbecula
Loch Uiskevagh

South Uist

Eriskay

Barra

Canna   Rùm

•Mallaig

Mingulay

Eigg

Muck

*Inner
Hebrides*

SEA OF THE HEBRIDES

Coll

Arinagour•

Tiree

Ulva

Mull

•Oban

SCOTLAND

Iona

N

•**Crinan**
Cairnbaan•
START

Jura

0   25nm

Islay   Tarbert•

Chapter 14

Cup and Ring

"Are you the owner of the green ketch at Cairnbaan?"

How I hated those early morning phone calls. This one had come as I was having coffee and toast for breakfast. "Yes," I replied wondering what disaster it might herald. We had been having strong southwesterly winds but *Molio* wasn't on a mooring. She wasn't even in the water. It was January and she was in the boatyard at Cairnbaan sitting on a steel cradle under the cover of a green canvas tarpaulin.

"You know she's been blown over then?"

"What!"

"Aye, this morning. I was shaving and looking out at the boats. There was a fearsome gust. It came o'er the hill behind the boats, screaming like a banshee. We've had nothing like it this winter. It shook our slates I can tell you. Anyway, I looked up and she was gone. I work for the canal, like, so I got your number from Ewan."

I mumbled my thanks even as I began thinking about what to do. There was no need for a frantic rush this time. *Molio* wasn't adrift or lying on the beach being pummelled by waves. Adam would be in touch soon. I better take a look at the boat insurance.

It was not long before the phone rang again. "Adam here. Do you want the good news or the bad?"

"Good, and make it as good as possible if you don't mind."

"She is repairable."

There was a pause as I digested this. "Better give me the bad then."

"She was hit sideways-on by a freak gust. She's so heavy she flattened the cradle. She ended up at an angle of about twenty-five

211

degrees lying alongside the canal bank."

"Is there any danger of her slipping in?"

"I thought of that. She's awfully close but her main weight is on the flat. She should be fine for a few days."

"How bad is the damage?"

"There's quite a few planks will need replacing. A couple of frames are cracked. I need to look carefully at the others. There's a load of diesel spilt from the starboard tank. It's a right mess."

"Okay, thanks Adam. Can you make doubly sure she can't slip further? I'll talk to the insurance people now but, no matter what they say, can you make sure she's safe?"

"I've already put chocks under her to prevent any movement. I'll get back over there this morning to clean out the diesel."

I wanted to drive over and see her right away but I was on a tight deadline to finish a report. I'd been working in Uganda on the threats to wildlife from oil extraction in Lake Albert. It never occurred to me that I might be the cause of wetland pollution myself. My report was due and I would be returning to Africa the following week. I just didn't have time for boat problems. I rang the insurance people. They said they'd had several boats blown over. Some were insurance right-offs. The first thing to do was to arrange three estimates for repair work. I turned on my office computer to look for possible yards. There was an email from Barry waiting in my inbox.

I am forwarding this e-mail about a prospective buyer in Switzerland. I realise it is unlikely that you will be interested, yet I know circumstances can change unexpectedly – for all of us. He contacted me twelve years ago wanting to buy when my sailing partner and I were selling *Molio*, but in the end we didn't sell and I bought my partner's share instead. The Swiss guy particularly wants a pre-war Shepherd-design boat. Well, he just called again to see if she was still for sale!

Hope you had a fine cruise in the Hebrides last summer.

Regards, Barry

'Circumstances can change unexpectedly,' I nodded to myself. Even if this was a cosmic joke, there was a kernel of truth in it. Barry's email was tempting. *Molio* had become a never-ending source of worry, and a never-ending recipient of restoration work. Despite months of effort and all the money I could scrape together over the past two years, the list of work needing doing was as long as ever. She still had a potentially serious leak below the waterline; the decks still let in rainwater. She needed rewiring, new rigging, new boom, ideally a new cockpit, and lots more TLC on the deck and coamings with teak oil, a back-to-the-wood paint job on the hull and complete refurbishment below. Which brought me back to cost. She was an expensive lady to keep. With one phone call I could do a deal with this Swiss guy, hand over the boat and release myself from the whole complicated business of keeping her afloat. It would mean I could pay off my bank loan, replace the ancient wreck of a car in my driveway, which was becoming a liability and, frankly, an embarrassment, and free myself from immediate financial worries. Did I want to keep *Molio*? I couldn't believe I was even asking that question. I'd better go and have a look. I rang the embassy in Kampala, and arranged a three-day postponement on my next mission.

Two days later, I set off in my old estate car heading for Cairnbaan. Now that the trees had lost their leaves, I could enjoy views across the quiet waters of Loch Lomond to the dark hills and clinging mists where history lay brooding. As I drove through the glens and over the passes with their patches of snow, I felt my cares beginning to leave me under the soothing caress of the West Highlands. I loved this part of the country. It was why I kept *Molio* there. Why couldn't I organise my life to move west too?

Approaching Cairnbaan, I caught a glimpse of *Molio* on the far side of the canal. She was a forlorn sight, canted over with the rain running down her side, like a wrecked ship caught on an inland reef. I parked the car and walked over. Adam had built two stacks of massive timbers to prevent her sliding into the canal. The crumpled girders of the cradle were still digging into her side. Their sharp edges had broken through the hull, gouging out chunks of wood below the waterline. Several planks had been completely destroyed. I had to face reality. Voyaging in *Molio* was proving fruitless; every mishap was another drain on my bank balance. I was in debt and now I was without a dream. It was past time to sell the boat. I ran my hands down her side to where the wood was stove in. "Sorry old girl," I said. My fingers moved on to touch the splintered edges of her tired planks, "What happened to you?"

I thought about our journey from the south of Ireland and the joy of arriving in the Clyde, and then again our journey to Skye the previous summer. She had been my passport to adventure. I was always more myself when off in the wilds, living from hand to mouth whilst tracking down some intriguing mystery. It was why I'd been drawn to the remote parts of Africa, why I'd travelled the forests of Borneo, and why I'd gone sailing as a boy in the Hebrides with my father. The mystery might be mundane, like where to camp, when best to fish, or how to figure out what wildlife was in the area, or it might be a deeper question that engaged me over many years of study. It was a return to the ancestral way, the old way, when the hunter followed a spoor with senses alert, body taught, and soul fully engaged with that of his quarry and the greater spiritual realities beyond. I had found that I knew myself best when out in the wilds. I knew who I was and what I stood for.

I took a step back from *Molio* and examined her again. The damage wasn't pleasant to look at but it was localised. It looked as though the girders had crumpled slowly, preventing a catastrophic fall. Adam could repair her right enough and I knew he would do a perfect job. Standing in the rain, I reflected on how unsettled my life was. It could be a trial at times but it had been better since finding *Molio*. I couldn't abandon her now. I felt the strength of my resolve growing. I would see to it that she was repaired to the highest standard; that she deserved. In return she might take me to the Outer Hebrides when the summer arrived and, if the weather held, out beyond their sheltering arms to the wide Atlantic Ocean and to St Kilda. I patted her again. "That's settled old girl."

Half an hour later Adam arrived in his 4x4, followed by the local crane. We talked over the repairs that were needed. I asked him to undertake some additional work – new floor and locker hatches for the cockpit, enlarged chain locker in the fo'c'sle, trotter boxes as extensions at the foot of each bunk, so that six-footers could stretch out, and one more investigation of the leak below the waterline. If he could complete the work by mid-May, I planned to take her on a long cruise.

What a change a few months can make. On my return to Cairnbaan, the alders, maples and birches were in leaf, the rhododendrons were bursting into flower and the primroses lit up the canal banks. *Molio* was upright and held in place by twelve sturdy timbers. Her winter tarpaulin had been folded up and put away, damaged planks removed, new ones fashioned from pitch pine and fitted seamlessly. Inside, Mike had made a beautiful job of the chain locker and trotter boxes.

Kyla rang as I was donning my overhauls, wanting to hear all about the boat and my plans. We were close again in a 'friends at long distance' kind of way. To my surprise she wanted to join me again on *Molio*. The teacher she'd been covering had returned to her class leaving Kyla without a job. I didn't discuss dates or waste time in speculation, just told her how pretty the spring was in Scotland. I set up a small ladder and began scraping off loose paint. I planned to patch prime the bare wood, filling some of the seams and uneven surfaces, then roll on antifouling below the waterline and brush two or three coats of Epifanes enamel on to the topsides. It would take about ten days, allowing for some rain. Behind me, the owner of *Truant* was well advanced with his own preparations. His paintwork was immaculate.

By the time the big crane arrived from Glasgow, *Molio* was looking her best yet. It picked her up like a toy, lifting her high above the other boats before lowering her carefully into the canal. The mainmast and mizzen followed and were lowered carefully through the deck and onto their resting blocks. *Truant* was plonked down next to her and rafted alongside. I spent the rest of the day adjusting and securing the rigging. Next morning I got to work early, attaching the main and mizzen booms and bending on sails. By afternoon I was ready to test the engine. I checked oil levels in the engine and gearbox and started her up. I let the engine run for a few minutes while chatting to some of the other owners. There was a yell from the bank. A tall woman with dark curly hair was staring down at us. She shouted again but I couldn't make out the words. She strode down the gangplank and came along the pontoon. Her shoulders and arms came in tattooed bulges and a six-pack stomach was visible between black crop top and cargo pants. She looked to me like Xena, the Warrior Princess. She reached *Molio* and stopped to shout at us.

"When are yer gone in the water?"

The broad Scots dialect came as a surprise. She stared without blinking, as if daring someone to give the wrong answer. She could put any of us under the turf, I reckoned. There was silence as we considered her question, not exactly sure what she wanted, but realising its importance. Eventually someone spoke up.

"Not for a while." She dismissed this with a scowl.

"I'll be going next week," I offered. She didn't even look at me.

The owner of *Truant* had been considering her question more carefully: "When did we get craned in?" he asked her.

"Aye," she responded. "When was it?"

"Yesterday," he replied.

"Huh!" her shoulders heaved with this corroboration. "Ma window wiz broken." She glanced across to the motor launch moored further along the bank, then turned back to us, glowering. "Did yon Adam move her?" She glanced up the road to where he lived.

The owner of *Truant* winced. He was a friend of Adam. "Yes, but it was the safest place for the crane to put its legs down. He had to move her."

Xena was livid, "I've told him no' to touch ma boat. Right, I'll get Paterson onto him."

At the mention of this name, a murmur ran up and down the assembled boaters. Ewan Paterson ruled the Crinan Canal with a fist of iron. Fees and duties proliferated, and the unfortunate sailor who dodged any one of his dues faced a heavy fine from the magistrate. The ultimate sanction that Ewan held over our heads like the sword of Damocles was to remove our boat from the water and impound it. Most of the sailors I knew would rather jump off a bridge than lose their boat. To the little party of sailors looking up at Xena now, a boat was not a plaything or a floating caravan, it was our passport to the lonely lochs and far-flung isles of the Hebrides; it was the key to a door that opened upon the communal world of sailing. It represented all that was right in our lives. We protested feebly: "Adam was careful"; "He only moved her a few yards along the bank"; "It was an accident". But it didn't mollify her. We couldn't tell her that somebody's mast still strapped along the deck had knocked through her boat's window. It was a long way to the nearest hospital. Xena turned abruptly and stomped off towards her boat. A short while later I noticed she was photographing it from every angle. The owner of *Truant* walked over to the hotel to ring Adam and warn him of the approaching Tsunami.

Driving back to North Berwick a day later, I was well satisfied. *Molio* was ready for cruising in her new livery – tan sails and teak deck on the top, a hull of Devon green which reflected in the ripples around her, and a bottom antifouling of Moroccan leather. Nostalgically elegant, she sat amongst the rushes and water lilies like a painting on a vintage biscuit tin. The next week was spent on final preparations. I purchased a large notebook with plain paper which would double as a logbook and sketching pad, and ordered a detailed Admiralty chart of the Sound of Harris. My brother, Rob, promised to keep an eye on the house and water the tomatoes. He would come to help if I needed extra crew at any stage. On the morning of departure, I gathered up a collection of old jerseys, jeans, cotton shirts and woollen socks and stuffed them into one of *Molio*'s duffle bags. A duvet, extra sleeping bag and pillows went into another bag. All that remained was to collect Kyla from the station. I checked my watch. It was time to go.

The glasshouse architecture of Edinburgh's Waverley Station cast a shaded Victorian light over the main concourse, which was thronged with milling passengers. It would provide the perfect backdrop for one of David Shepherd's paintings of steam engines brooding in the sidings. It also added a frisson of anticipation to my impending meeting with Kyla. I found the platform for the King's Cross train and tried to contain myself. Right on time the wedge-nosed locomotive came into view, swished past and glided to a halt. Its robotic doors opened and people started to crowd onto the platform. I had a moment's panic.

Would I recognise her? I steadied myself. The moment I spotted the autumnal locks my fears were forgotten. I waved above the heads of the throng. She moved to one side, untypically shy, hair tumbling over a sea-green jacket. This time I noticed she had a suitcase in tow. Pushing my way up to her, I held out my arms and lifted her high into the air.

"Higher please," she said.

I laughed and lowered her down. "You are looking gorgeous Kyla. I love the jacket."

She rummaged in her case, "I have some leeks for you from the school garden." She looked up in time to see the forced smile on my face and burst out laughing. She hadn't forgotten my dislike of leeks after all. She took my arm as we walked and started telling me about the pond they'd made in the nature club.

"Any joy on the job front," I asked as we reached the car.

"The head asked if I would take a permanent job at the start of the year."

"And what did you say?"

"I said I'd like to try. It will be part time but it means I can continue with my therapy."

I looked at her. There'd been more than a hint of steel in that reply. Something was changing.

We drove out of Edinburgh and along the motorway to Glasgow, immersed in conversation about *Molio*, sailing and possible places to visit. We planned to set off the next day, heading through the canal in a northwesterly direction towards Crinan.

Molio was sitting at the pontoon, just as I'd left her. We pulled up next to the gangplank and began stowing our gear on board. It was a warm evening but still too early in the year for midges – a rare combination in Argyll. Kyla went for a walk along the towpath while I finished adjusting the shrouds and stays. She arrived back at the boat looking carefree and happy and we walked over to the Cairnbaan Hotel on the other side of the canal. The bar was modelled on an old country inn with wood panelling along the sides and a large stuffed trout on the wall. We ordered a bucket of Loch Etive mussels and a bottle of Chablis.

There was still enough light following dinner for us to see our way to the canal bank. With the tips of the pine trees stilled and the stars lighting the heavens, I turned to face Kyla. I brushed back a curl of auburn hair from her eye, letting my hand linger on her cheek.

She took my hand, "Come on, I want to show you a ring."

I followed her down a narrow alley behind the hotel and up a rough footpath that wound through some pinewoods, to the top of a small hill. She climbed a fence and walked out across the open moorland. Looking back, I could see lights twinkling like stars in the distance. The galaxy of Lochgilphead was nearest; further out in space the galaxy of Ardrishaig marked the entrance to Loch Gilp. An owl hooted from the wood.

"That's strange," Kyla said, "I know it's somewhere near here."

We climbed a second fence, and arrived at a flat stone where some ancient rocks had broken through the moss.

"Do you have your torch?"

I searched in my pack and found a small Maglite. Kyla took it and shone the pencil beam over the stone.

"Not here."

I followed her higher up the hill. The ground grew marshy and I could feel the water coming through my shoes. "Here, I think." The beam lit up some grassy tussocks and came to rest on another stone with the flattened curve of a whale's back. The surface was worn smooth from long exposure to the elements. She shone the torch towards the far end.

"Oh precious little chap." Kyla bent down to examine a tiny frog. "And just look at what he's showing us." I squidged my way round the side of the rock and knelt down beside her. Torchlight played across the mottled mushroom skin, but the little frog sat still. In amongst the plants its camouflage would be perfect, but here it was silhouetted boldly against the bare rock. "Do you see?" whispered Kyla. And then I saw it. The frog was crouching on the lip of a faint ring set into the naked stone. In fact, a double ring; for within one was another and within that a distinct cup-like depression. Beyond the cup and rings was a second set and beyond that a third. Kyla stood up and widened the focus of the torch revealing ring upon ring, and in amongst them were single cups with no adornment. It was as if Queequeg himself had been there to tattoo the whale's back. I stepped back. I didn't know what the cup and ring marks meant but they weren't the scratching of an idle hand.

"I've seen something like this in Africa. Cups left by Bushman hunters in a rock shelter. They used them to make fire."

"This is the time of Beltane," said Kyla. "The Celtic festival of fire and fertility."

I knelt back down again and looked at the marks. "Maybe these cups were used to light fire as well... with a dry stick and tinder."

"By drilling with a bow?"

"Like the hunter gatherers today, only using a stone cup instead of a fire stick. If that's right," I was warming to my theme, "they would need to find a larger stick as the cup grew larger. Eventually a new cup would be started. I've seen pictures of fire sticks with rows of cups just like that."

"Every family must have had a fire in those days and kept it burning all night."

"That's what the mobile Bushmen do today. They don't even have permanent huts, let alone brick houses. Their fire is their home and they carry their fire with them. What they have is fire-homes."

"These rings are the community round the fire." I could tell Kyla was deeply moved by this thought. For her the community was almost sacred.

"It reminds me of the ring round the campfire that is stamped into the desert sands by Bushman dancers."

"The sacred spark... fire and love," added Kyla, as much to herself as to me.

"How do you mean?"

"When the stick twirls in the cup, it creates the spark that ignites fire. When maleness encounters femaleness, it also creates a 'spark' that brings new life. Fire and love; and look these rings are the extending family."

"When you say it like that," I swallowed, feeling butterflies alighting in my tummy, "it feels right."

"These associations would be stronger back then. They would be felt and understood without all the thinking we do. The tradition would pass on from one generation to the next. Even today girls jump over the Beltane fires to procure good husbands."

"Up on these hills, they had fire beacons didn't they? Imagine that. Great torches in the night."

"And each a community," said Kyla. "Linked to its sisters by firelight."

In the morning, I started *Molio*'s engine and left it to idle whilst unfastening the springs and making ready with the bow and stern lines. Hugh arrived at nine and prepared the first lock. With his expertise we made good progress over the low hills of Knapdale and arrived in Crinan Basin shortly before midday. We moored next to a small café with a wonderful smell of freshly brewed coffee and newly baked bread. But rather than picking up those aromas, *Molio*'s cabin smelt of diesel fumes. I took up the floorboards and eventually tracked the source to a leak in the engine manifold. It was small but it would only get larger. I looked up the telephone number of a welding expert that Adam had recommended. He promised to come over right away.

Kyla went off to explore round the basin. Not long afterwards a tall gangly man in his late thirties arrived with a bouncing gait and mop of wiry hair, looking a bit like an Afghan Hound pup. "Hi, I'm Magnus," he grinned. "So what's the problem?"

I beamed back, liking his easy style. "Come and have a look."

I started the engine and Magnus took his time to feel round all the possible places where fumes might be leaking. Satisfied, he turned to me: "It's the stainless connector at the manifold there. They go every couple of years. We could order a new one from Lombardini, which would take a few days." I winced. Or, I can whip this off and do a temporary repair that will last you through the season. I can make you up a better one in the autumn. You'll get four years out of my part." He smiled again.

"That would be great, on both counts." I replied.

"I used to live on a boat all the time," he confided. "In fact this is the first time I've lived in a house."

"How do you like it?"

"I've got my own workshop with all my kit – climbing, kitesurfing, welding. It's great to have the space." He seemed happy enough but I suspected the extra room was more by way of compensation than celebration.

"Where's your boat now?" I asked.

"I sold her. No regrets. I built her in Cape Town – thirty-two foot, all steel and gaff-rigged. I lived on her in the Caribbean. Worked the off season, welding stainless mostly, and went south in the Hurricane season to kayak and laze about in South America. I was in Rio mostly. But I also did a spot of boat delivery."

"That bareboat delivery stuff must have its moments: what with all the problems the owners haven't told you about." I tried not to think about *Molio*'s leak. Barry hadn't been very forthcoming about it.

"Blown out sails, crappy maintenance... yeah, that kind of thing. Only time I came off a boat was on a delivery run – from Cape Town to Rio with two French crew. It was one hell of a sail. Thirty miles out from Cape Town I was freeing the boom, which had got wedged against the chimney of the diesel heater, when it swung clear and took me with it. I was in the bloody Atlantic with all my gear on – wellies, thermals, oil skins, huge fisherman's jersey, the lot. It was pulling me under."

"Didn't you have a harness?" I asked.

"No harness. But the Frenchies came after me. One of them rigged three reefing lines under the boom and let it right out, trailing the ropes beneath. They snared me on the first pass. I pulled myself into the boom. I was built like an ox in those days, muscles on muscles, but with 300 kg of water in my kit, it was impossible to get on the boat. I just held on and they got me out. I was twenty-two and those guys saved me."

Magnus unfastened the stainless steel exhaust fitting and showed me how it had thinned and cracked. "I'll take this back to my place and patch it up. Be back this afternoon."

I walked round the basin to see if I could spot Kyla, and found her in the café chatting to the manageress about the more interesting features of the Celtic male. I left them to it and wandered over to the sea lock, where *Truant*'s owner, Lachlan, was talking to one of his charter party. A trawler was approaching from the Sound of Jura. One of the crew shimmied up the derrick in the stern and began doing pull-ups followed by dips. He wore a short-sleeved grey smock over black neoprene trousers and looked more like a fitness instructor than a fisherman. As the boat pulled into the lock, I noticed a row of fish boxes stacked along the sides.

"Look at that; those boys have got razor shells."

Truant's owner looked down and nodded, "They'll be sold alive in China within twenty-four hours."

The guy in the stern jumped off the boat, vaulted over the arm of the lock gate, and began to guide a refrigerator van as it reversed into position. The other crew started winching the boxes of razor shells onto the side of the lock. The shells were tied in packets, about ten to the packet and fifty packets to the box, looking like so many bundles of dynamite sticks.

"Any idea how they catch them?" I asked, knowing how quickly the razor shell will dive down its long burrow when disturbed.

"They drag electrodes slowly across the sand behind the boat. They're a bit like welding rods. When a strong current is applied, the razor shells pop up out of their burrows. One of the boys follows behind in his scuba gear and picks them up. When they're finished they mark off the area using GPS coordinates on an electronic map so they won't waste their time going back."

"That's hi-tech fishing all right. Can't imagine it will last long. Razor shells grow slowly." I looked at another box that was being winched off the deck. More dynamite sticks. Except these were living sticks and some would be twenty years old − living clams dressed in seven-inch shells of butterscotch and cream, part of the richness of our sandy shores. I turned back to Lachlan, "I suppose they pay a fortune for them in China."

"And they don't even taste good: they're tough and unpleasant. I can understand the demand for scallops which are gorgeous with white wine. Everybody wants them. In the eighties a box of scallops went for seventy pounds on the pier, and the boats were bringing in two hundred boxes a day.

"How about today? Are they still catching them?"

"It took ten years to finish them. There's not a single fishing boat harvesting scallops now." He looked despondent. "First they fished out the herring, then the lobsters, then the prawns, then the clams and now these. We only seem to overfish."

"What is wrong with us?" I shook my head. "As a boy we sometimes fished up clams using our dinghy and an oar blade. Great big fat ones. Now I'm getting the same feeling that I have when walking in the African bush knowing there are no black rhino to look out for. A big chunk of colour and excitement has gone out of the African bush. It's the same here: no clams, no cod, no giant cockles."

"I don't blame these lads," said *Truant*'s owner, watching them stack boxes in the van. "They are up from Glasgow and just making the most of it. It's the ones higher up who need to sort it out."

"With our wild fish stocks so depleted, the industry is no match for fish farming. But we could easily do better. Give local fishermen ownership of their patch and we would soon have sustainable local fisheries."

"Would that really do it? These guys are very competitive."

"They've never had exclusive rights to their own loch or sound or stretch of coast. Not now and not even a hundred years ago. They've never had a resource to care for and protect. It's what I've learnt in Africa. Give people their resource rights and it changes everything. If government forgot about setting quotas for the maximum catch and focussed instead on setting up local fisheries, you would see a change. Fishermen would begin to work together to look after the seas out of self-interest. I bet they'd rebuild their old communities too. It's not difficult to implement. Why can't we do it?"

"We're all in this together." Lachlan swept his arms around him. "When I bought mahogany to repair *Truant*, I agonised about it for weeks. I wanted to keep the boat true to her classic origins but also protect the big trees in the rainforest. In the end we sourced timber that was produced sustainably."

The last of the boxes was stacked into the van. The doors were closed and it drove off. The fishing boat reversed out the lock, turned and headed out to sea.

"That's stealth for you," I remarked. "Into port, unload and out, all within half-an-hour and miles from anywhere."

"Maybe see you in the islands?" said Lachlan.

I nodded, "Good sailing."

Back at *Molio*, I found Kyla with two young boys in tow. They had glasses of water in their hands and were watching her with wide eyes as she chopped up apple, orange, dried apricots and kiwi fruit as a snack.

"It's feeding time at the zoo," said Kyla eyeing me up, "and I've got some for you to chase away that frown."

I let go the fishing thoughts and showed the kids the fo'c'sle. They were soon having a wild time, rushing down the companionway and popping out the fo'c'sle hatch. Children seem to love discovering secret ways; so much so that I wonder if it isn't part of our genetic make-up. Imagine our ancestors migrating steadily across a continent, perhaps in the wake of retreating ice, camping for a few weeks or even months before moving on. The discovery of a new cave or passageway by playful children could be of real importance. After the children had left, Kyla made tea, producing fresh milk from the café and scones filled with butter and honey.

Two gents shuffled along the edge of the basin inspecting the boats. On reaching *Molio* they looked at her and murmured, then murmured and looked again. Eventually one of them walked over and nodded: "You've got a project for the summer I see." I masked my irritation. He was not to know that I'd been working on *Molio* for two years or that I'd laboured for a fortnight this spring, scraping, filling and painting the hull. Just as the eye is irresistibly drawn to a blemish on someone's face so, it seems, it is attracted by the algae stain on the side of *Molio*'s cockpit, the cracked deck caulking in the bow, the patched sail, the worn canvas covering of the gas cylinder in the stern, and the last rusted shackle at the foot of the mainmast. I had begun to doubt that I would ever be free of the wise nod and its kindred comment, 'You've got a project there'.

Kyla poured me more tea and told me off for being touchy. "That old boy has a point. *Molio*'s wood looks dry and unloved. You should feed it with teak oil; it will bring out her real colour." She was good at seeing things from the other's point of view.

Magnus Woolf arrived an hour later and showed me his repair. He'd welded a piece of stainless steel over the thin section of the connector piece as neatly as any patch sewn by a seamstress. It didn't take him long to attach it, and once he was done, I started up the engine. Even at high revs there wasn't the slightest sign of a leak from the connector. I switched off and refitted the cockpit floor hatch. "That is immensely satisfying," I said to Magnus.

"Right," he replied. "That will cost you a glass of wine."

I poured three glasses of Spanish white, which I'd bought at the hotel. Magnus took a large gulp and picked up the bottle for a closer look. "Galicia, ah, there's a beautiful country."

Kyla came up to the cockpit, having changed into a cocoa brown tank top and frayed denim shorts and eyed Magnus from behind her Titian locks. She decided he was okay. "What's so beautiful about it?" she asked.

"The beaches are perfect. They all have the blue flag. They're spotless even when surrounded by industry." Magnus was evidently used to beautiful women. He wasn't mesmerised. He didn't show off.

"How do they do that," asked Kyla, "when even our remote beaches are covered in plastic."

"The fish farmers are the ones who want to keep the place perfect. The young ones put pressure on the local government to tidy up and look after the place."

"Fish farms don't give a toss about the environment," I butted in.

"The shellfish farmers in Galicia are determined to keep the coastline pristine," said Magnus. "Over here, it's another matter. Take Loch Gilp where I live. If you dig for lugworms in the bay, you find black mud just below the surface. It smells rotten. It's because of the sewage. It's the council that doesn't give a toss."

Kyla wrinkled her nose. "I don't know. I think the councils would clean up the beaches if they could afford to."

"Councils support fish farms because they provide jobs," I pointed out. "Yet, nothing is done to recover wild fish which would also provide jobs."

"There's not much the councils can do about overfishing without help from government," said Magnus. "But if we had oyster farms in Loch Gilp, the council would be forced to act. They'd clean up the bay."

"You really think the farms can clean up the bay?" asked Kyla.

"Yes I do. The new generation of fish farmers want a clean environment. Last year I helped fit canvas screens underneath the feeding stations in some of the new fish cages. The feed is coated in antibiotics and pesticides; the screens prevent it falling to the sea bottom and polluting the marine life. These days the operators watch the salmon feeding from the shore via a video link. When the fish have had enough, they switch off the feeder to prevent excess food escaping. It's good for business and it's better for the environment."

"Too bad the farms aren't even Scottish then," I grumbled, unsure whether to accept this new image of green-minded fish farms.

"I'm like you," said Magnus who seemed to understand what was troubling me. "I hate to see fish penned up, but the operators don't like to cause harm either. They just want a decent job."

I heard a plop and looked over *Molio*'s side barely in time to see a blur of chestnut fur. A chain of large bubbles came towards *Molio* and passed under her stern. Magnus reacted instantly, jumping from the deck to the bank. Kyla and I were on his tail following the bubbles as they ran along the narrow gap between the boats and the side of the canal basin. They kept under the fenders where the shadows lay thickest. Eventually we lost them near gate 2.

"What do you think, otter or mink?" asked Magnus.

"More likely wild mink," I replied.

"Clever fellow coming in amongst the boats," said Kyla.

"What wouldn't you do for a yummy sea trout?" I laughed.

Magnus gathered up his tools and prepared to head on home, "You've got my number. If you get stuck – anywhere – give us a shout."

We had one more visitor at around five o'clock. I was topping up *Molio*'s diesel tanks, a delicate task requiring the steady control of a stream of oily liquid into a wobbly funnel, when some bloke walked up.

"Will you be going out today?"

I didn't recognise him at first and replied testily: "No, I've got a lot of work on here." "Okay," he replied. "You know you only have one week free of charge in the canal after launch?" It was a rhetorical question. "You've been here two weeks now." He didn't attempt to hide the note of triumph in his voice. I looked up and recognised the spiky hair, military moustache and sideboards of Ewan Paterson, the much-feared canal chief.

I could hear the cash register going, Ker Klonk, Ker Klonk. "Ah well," I replied straightening up, giving myself a second to recover and another to fish about for a likely riposte. "It's been a difficult year what with *Molio* being blown over in your new boat park. I just don't know if I can trust keeping my boat here." I could see the barb sink home. "But in any case, I should be ready to leave in the morning."

The professional mask quickly repositioned itself. "The boat park is not managed by British Waterways," he replied. "You need to discuss the matter with the new manager. I shall inform my staff that you will be leaving in the morning." With a curt nod, he walked off to check on the other boats.

We had some soup followed by fresh scones, cheese and a second glass of Galician white. It was a warm evening and, as it grew dark, the first midges of the summer came out with a mean hunger. We went below. Kyla lit the oil lamp above the galley whilst I put mosquito meshes into the portholes, shut the fore and aft hatches and closed the companionway doors leading to the cockpit. It didn't stop the blighters.

Chapter 15

Wolf Island

By the time the canal staff showed up for duty next morning, *Molio* was ready for sea. The burgee and ensign had been hoisted, sail covers removed, charts and binoculars placed in the cockpit, the engine was ticking over and the mooring springs released. Lachlan came by with a gift of fresh rolls and the morning's newspaper; he cast off the bow and stern lines and wished us bon voyage. We motored into the sea lock where Clarissa was waiting for us. After making fast, I stepped ashore and accompanied her to the canal office where she began to fill out a receipt. I pulled out my wallet to pay.

"There's no charge," she said.

"Are you sure?"

"Yes," she replied with a smile. "Ewan told me himself."

A few minutes later, the massive sea gate swung open. With a burst of power from the engine, *Molio* picked up speed and surged out of the dark lock into the sparkling ocean. Kyla fetched in the fenders while I studied the charts and tide tables one more time. We passed through the tidal door of Dorus Moor at slack water, and this time I allowed the gathering flood tide to pull *Molio* towards the Gulf of Corryvreckan. We entered the passage between the high hills of Scarba and Jura one hour after slack water, passing three porpoises and heading towards a line of white water which marked the heart of the cauldron. *Molio* bucked a bit in the tidal upwelling. As we approached, I studied the whirlpool through binoculars. Under these ideal conditions it was little more than the back eddy of a large river. We entered the turbulence still under power and pushed through with only a tail swing to show for it. Emerging on the western side of the gulf, the island-clad seas and far horizons of the Hebrides lay before us, basking in the late spring sunshine.

I showed Kyla the different islands on the chart before going below to check the batteries were charging. Satisfied, I put the kettle on for coffee. While waiting for it, I retrieved a smaller scale chart to plot a course from Corryvreckan to Rubh Ardalnish, a point of land that lies about two miles inside the south-western tip of Mull. My aim was to close with Mull at this point and then navigate westwards, inside the Torran Rocks, a loose clustering of dangerous rocks that have gained notoriety for wrecking yachts and larger craft. Later in the morning, as we entered this inner passage from the east, I was concerned to see three modern sloops motoring from the west and heading straight towards the rocks. I was halfway to reaching for the VHF to warn them, when I realised they were using a narrow middle fairway that passes through the centre of the rocks. They came on at six knots, apparently fearless of the swell breaking off hidden reefs all about them. This, I realised, was the liberation that satellite navigation can bring.

It was impressive but, like the Crosshaven dogs, I preferred to stick to my old ways. We moved in close under the towering cliffs of Mull until well past the last of the Torran Rocks, then came out from shore to clear the shoals off Erraid and entered the Sound of Iona. Kyla reduced speed as we cleared the last hazard. I went up on deck and hoisted the mainsail to take advantage of a light breeze that had arrived from the northwest. I let the yankee fly and took the helm. With the engine off, there was only the chuckle of our bow wave blending in with the sounds of the sea as we drifted towards Iona.

It could have been a perfect moment embracing so many contrasts: cruises of my youth and those today, skills versus instincts of sailing, the humdrum of life aboard as opposed to the deeper currents of Celtic monasticism and, of course, man and woman. But other things were nagging at my thoughts. Kyla was happy now but how long would it last? Beyond that, I was concerned with the lack of progress in my journey to St Kilda, not so much the voyage itself as its underlying purpose. When on the track of some unsolved mystery, whether as a scientist or in day to day matters, the answer usually begins to build in my mind, emerging bit by bit like a painting. It may take days or weeks or months, but that is how it happens. Not this time. I was looking for the keys to personal freedom because I needed to make the right decisions in my life. I'd been on their trail for years. I still hoped to find them on St Kilda but all of a sudden the spoor had gone cold.

As we closed with Iona, the shallow blue-green waters of Martyr's Bay surrounded us. I told Kyla about the Clyde puffers that used to service the islands. "Dad and Mum were anchored right here in our family Folkboat, *Pippa*. They were enjoying a calm sunny morning just like today, thinking about a run ashore, when a puffer arrived from the south and steamed up beside them. It went on past and just kept going until it grounded on the sandy bottom. Nothing happened for a while. There was no sign of life on deck. Slowly the tide receded, exposing more and more of the boat's rust red bottom, until finally she was sitting high and dry on the sand. There was still no sign of life, only a wisp of smoke from her black-tipped funnel. Eventually, a figure emerged from a door under the bridge and lowered a ladder to the ground. A horse-drawn cart came down the beach from the island and made its way out to the boat with a couple of men and a dog. They loaded up with coal and went back to the island, coming back for several more loads. The ladder went back up. There were no further signs of life. The tide slowly returned. In the evening the puffer floated off the sand and steamed back the way it had come."

Kyla listened gravely. "How different it sounds."

I nodded, looking down the Sound of Iona and breathing deeply: "Like an old stone wall, there was plenty of space for living in amongst the stones."

Molio ghosted north. In the afternoon, we passed the Abbey on Iona standing like a beacon against prejudice and superstition, as it had done since St Columba established it in the sixth century and St Molio visited as a young man. Laying off half a point to the east, we continued our passage, making now for Ulva and the shelter of Cragaig Bay. We arrived in the evening, anchoring close inshore next to a stone-built cottage, the only building in the bay that had a roof. All around the bracken-clad slopes were the ruins of other cottages, part of a village that had once nestled on the south-facing slopes. I imagined the villagers must have enjoyed the warmth of the sun and the protection offered by the numerous low-lying skerries that took the brunt of the Atlantic swell. Anchored nearby was a blue ketch which had its engines running.

Waking early, I watched idly from my bunk as a golden disc of light appeared on the varnished mast and began to descend gently from the coach roof above my head to the floor below. It was the size of a cantaloupe melon – a golden melon that danced on the pinewood mast. Suddenly it contracted into a tiny disk and sprung on to the end of my bunk where my toes peeped out from under the duvet; it wobbled there for a few seconds before moving along the varnished lockers on one side of the bunk, passing my knees and middle to take up station next to my face. It stopped there and wobbled for a few more seconds in a languid, liquidly kind of way and then reversed direction, moving back along the bunk, jumping on to the mast and disappearing into the fo'c'sle. On cue, another disc popped into view by my face. It had a faint line running across the middle. That was the giveaway. The sun, streaming through the portholes, was casting golden discs into *Molio*'s dark cabin, bringing Ulvan Tinkerbells to life. As *Molio* turned and rocked in the williwaws coming down from the hill above the village they wobbled about the cabin, casting a magic spell wherever they landed – and, for the rational-minded, the shadow of *Molio*'s safety line strung between the stanchions on deck.

I scrambled out of my sleeping bag, pulled on my jeans and put the kettle on. Kyla was still out for the count with nothing visible except the tangled red mane of a kelpie. I went up to the cockpit with a mug of tea to admire the anchorage. Mist lay on the hills above the silent village. A tern was fishing in the lagoon, its cry mingling with the lapping of wavelets. As I watched the blue ketch hoisted sail, pulled in her anchor and came gliding past. Peace descended. A few minutes later, Kyla joined me in the cockpit looking relaxed and happy. A favourite poem of my parents sprang to mind, which celebrated the peace that steels up softly on a small boat in a quiet highland bay:

The lark's on the wing;
The snail's on the thorn;
God's in His heaven –
All's right with the world!

Fortified by porridge and toast, we decided to go ashore. Kyla took her pencils and sketchpad. I checked my pockets before clambering into the dinghy – Swiss Army knife, biro and pocket notebook. It felt good to leave behind my standard town kit – wallet, loose change, house keys and mobile phone. We pulled the dinghy up the shingle by the empty cottage and set off to explore Cragaig. It had been a typical Scottish clachan where land was leased jointly by a number of tenants from the landowner, providing the community with a common for their shared agriculture. The thatched cottages were located on the best farmland at the foot of the hill; livestock were grazed further up.

There was little left of the other cottages, just the remains of stone walls that barely rose above the bracken. Each cottage appeared to have a haul-out beach at the head of a nearby inlet running into the sea. We sat down in the bracken next to one. The lush green turf surrounding the rocky inlet was splashed with clumps of yellow irises. The beach was littered with large stones, but the cottar had cleared a small channel so that his fishing boat, probably a simple open rowing boat, could be hauled up to the high-tide mark on mud and shingle. There was a low causeway of stones about forty or fifty feet long running across the channel. It looked as though it would act as a breakwater to reduce wave action at high tide, and protect the boat from being bashed about. The haul-out beach was well preserved as if awaiting the boat's return.

"Martyn, look!" Kyla tugged at my sleeve.

I followed the direction of her outstretched finger and saw a mink coming down a tiny stream and into the gut. Its fur was dark and streaked, its tail shorter than an otter's and the face more pointed. It crossed over the little causeway where it was mobbed by a pair of stonechats and then disappeared into some larger rocks.

A raven flew above, croaking to its mate. The old village was warm and peaceful.

I stood up and offered a hand to Kyla, "Shall we carry on?"

"Do you feel the atmosphere here?" she asked without taking my hand.

I nodded. "Shall we go?"

"You go on. I want to do some sketching."

Leaving Kyla, I walked round the side of the inlet where I stumbled on a tiny ruin with thick walls. Climbing one of the walls to get a better view, I placed my hand on a large flat stone which rocked, making a heavy ringing sound. I thought about the man who had placed it there with skill and strength, centuries before, perhaps with pride and even love for his new home. What would he think now if he could see these ruins, and the empty village? I thought I knew. When the Bushmen of the Kalahari were cleared from their homes by powerful men that controlled a nation, they moved into urban ghettoes where the women ended up as prostitutes and the men as drunks. When one group was shown an old film of their desert home, they sat and wailed. How many Ulvans had wailed for their lost way of life?

I walked on, trying to free my mind of ghosts. English bluebells were flowering under the bracken, and cherry-pink orchids stood in the marshes, almost tropical in their luxuriance. At the far end of the bay I reached a small burn tumbling down Glen Glass. Looking upstream, I saw what looked like a ruined watermill. Closer inspection revealed a millstone for grinding corn lying in the centre of the walled building and further up the remains of a dam and lade for channelling a stream of water. There must have been a prosperous community here at one time. The sheltered waters yielded fish, shellfish and kelp; the fertile soils of the south-facing slopes produced vegetables and cereals; the mill provided wheat flour to make bread for the community and for selling on to Mull; the hill offered grazing. Yet, despite this healthy economy, the boats had gone, the millwheel was still and the village lay in ruins. Was it the victim of the clearances or was it, as others have argued, a self-inflicted wound? Writing in their classic, *Highlands and Islands*, Fraser Darling and Morton Boyd speculate on the quiet failure of the populations of small Hebridean islands to husband their available natural resources once the population began to exceed the carrying capacity of the land.

I found Kyla back at the first cottage, sitting on the grass next to some bracken with a cloth wrap lying open to reveal artists' pencils of every Hebridean colour. She was sketching bluebells that were nodding with their weight of blooms under the green roof of bracken fronds. She closed the sketchbook as I arrived, and placed it in her leather satchel. She smiled a greeting but I could see she was preoccupied with her own thoughts. Rather than interrupt her reflections I busied myself with carrying the dinghy down to the water's edge and then rowed her out to *Molio*. In the afternoon, I stretched out on the bridge deck to read about the Hebrides. Kyla worked below, polishing the brass oil lamp. Later she made us omelettes with salad, and then retired to her bunk with a book. Later still, I made her some herbal tea with wild mint from the hill, poured myself a dram and took it with the ship's logbook up to the cockpit.

I had begun to piece together an account of that time of economic turmoil on Ulva and the heartache that ensued. It is a story that unfolded all across the Highlands and Islands in the eighteenth and nineteenth centuries. It has often been told. In retelling it one more time I want to show that those events are not confined to some distant, or even not-so-distant, past but intimately linked to changes taking place in our own time. What the history of Ulva reveals is how a new economic order can force a wedge between people and their land, tearing away personal freedoms, fomenting injustice, and ultimately pitting government against its own people.

It has been suggested that Ulva abounded in wolves and that the name comes from *Ulf eyr* meaning 'island of wolves'. Certainly, during the period of Norse control over the Hebrides in the eleventh to thirteenth centuries, wolves were numerous on the mainland of Scotland: they were notorious as killers and scavengers. Kyla reminded me that the old burial grounds in the Highlands were often on islands that were wolf-free. So wolves might be taking us down the wrong track altogether. It is also possible that Ulva was named after a Viking chieftain called 'Ulfr'. Whatever the reason for its name, the island is about the size of Richmond Park and tucked into the coastline of the much larger Isle of Mull. It is covered with rough pasture and has craggy hills rising to a thousand feet.

We can get an inkling of the scale of the tragedy that unfolded from a bald account of the numbers of people on Ulva. Census records give 266 people in 1764, rising to 604 in 1837, before falling rapidly to 203 in 1851 and to 53 in 1881. The population continued to decline with only 16 islanders recorded in 2001.

The chief at the first census was Lachlan MacQuarrie, the last of a long line of land-owning chiefs stretching back to the Norse period. At that time, the area around Cragaig included large oak trees as well as birch and hazels as did much of the West Highlands. It must have been richly beautiful. The villagers depended entirely on their livestock, grain and vegetables as there were no fishing boats in 1764. At the beginning of summer, the people set off to the higher ground with their flocks to occupy the shieling huts next to the best upland pastures, where they lived until August. They then moved back to the low grounds to rest the hill pastures and attend to the crops. This ancient way of life came to an end when the old chief was forced to sell the island that his family had possessed for nine hundred years, to pay off debts, no doubt incurred in the bright lights of Edinburgh and London.

Ulva changed hands several times in rapid succession until it was bought, in 1785, by Colin Macdonald, who was a wealthy man with an interest in the burgeoning kelp industry. A period of prosperity followed. By 1800 every family on Ulva owned at least one boat and the island produced enough potatoes for export. Colin's son Ranald, popularly known as 'Staffa', took over the island on his father's death and continued to invest in the property. On his visit to Ulva in 1810, Sir Walter Scott noted that Staffa had managed the kelp beds carefully. For four months in summer, kelp and wrack were cut from the rocky shores at low tide, dried, and then burnt in stone-lined pits. The yield of ash, rich in soda and potash, was sent to Glasgow and Liverpool factories for use in glass and soap making. There was in fact a close relationship between the price per ton of kelp paid by manufacturers in Glasgow and Liverpool, and the number of people living on Ulva. In this way, Staffa had trebled his income and doubled the number of people on the island, bucking the trend of emigration already beginning elsewhere in the Hebrides. It was still a source of Highland pride at the time to have many tenants living on your estate. Another of Staffa's visitors, Sir John Carr, admired the attention that his host lavished on his tenants. '*Their food consisted of mutton, lamb and beef, of which they consumed a great deal; fish, of which they had upwards of 20 different species within a few hundred yards of the shore; geese, ducks, hens and chickens. Many tenants not only provided their families with butter and cheese, but had a surplus to dispose of. Each had also a garden where cabbages, turnips and potatoes were grown.*' Their bread was made from home grown barley and oatmeal, which was ground in watermills like the one at Cragaig. The island even had a bakery and four shops. By and large, the tenants lived the good life and apparently were 'distractedly fond' of their landowner. This chimed with the picture in my mind's eye of a prosperous and happy community as I walked amongst the cottages and their haul-out beaches.

Behind Staffa's fine show of open-handed hospitality were unfavourable economic realities. The old shieling custom of grazing livestock on the high ground had been abandoned in favour of the cash earned from producing kelp ash. By 1810, the price of kelp had peaked and was in decline. Staffa could no longer conceal his shaky finances and was forced to convey his estates into the hands of trustees who took possession in 1817. The island passed eventually to one of the island's own, Lieutenant-Colonel Charles Macquarie. His investment was ill-timed as the market for kelp ash soon collapsed entirely. On his death in 1835 his trustees sold Ulva, together with some land on Mull, to Francis William Clark, a Morayshire businessman, for £29,000.

Like his immediate predecessors, Clark saw himself in the role of an 'improving landlord'. He learnt to speak Gaelic and took steps to increase the efficiency and profitability of the island's agriculture. The farms on the island were divided and fenced with stone dykes. Draining, clearing of stones, and liming with shell sand went forward with Clark's encouragement. Potatoes were sold in the neighbouring parishes and a ready market for barley was found at the Tobermory distillery. Clark wasn't making money from kelp, but kept hoping for a return to profitability. Then in 1843, just as the islanders' future seemed assured once more, their industry was shattered by a final blow from which the community never recovered. The potato harvest was devastated by blight in the years from 1846 to 1848, robbing the islanders of their staple food supply. The crofters were barely able to maintain themselves and the estate had no surplus funds. The Rev. William Fraser, writing from his Ulva manse towards the end of 1846, described the state of most of his parishioners as 'miserable beyond description. I give you it as my candid opinion, that there will be many deaths here soon unless something be done immediately'. It was at this point that Clark's allegiance to business overcame his allegiance to his tenants.

Clark reasoned that the most advantageous use of land on Ulva was in the rearing of sheep and black cattle, and that the distress of the people was best served by emigration 'under proper regulations'. As the crofters were occupying land that had passed from father to son for generations, many were opposed to leaving. Some of these families were moved on to smaller farms and then, at a later date, to a house with barely sufficient grass for more than a cow or two, and then to nothing at all. When they would not clear off altogether, Clark's factor and men set fire to the thatch. The families were not even given time to collect their possessions, and their livestock was seized. One case tells of a sick woman living with her daughter in one of the houses that Clark wished to pull down. He had the roof taken down, all except the portion directly above her sickbed. Another case tells of a poor woman taking water from the well. When Clark came along, she ran away terrified, leaving behind her kettle, which Clark smashed into pieces. Thus it was that, in five years, the population dwindled from over 600 to approximately 200. All across the Highlands, when the bad times came, the landowners demanded rents, and when these couldn't be paid they burnt down their tenants' houses in front of the families.

It is easy to feel the injustice of those days, but no matter how dark an episode in history, it may still contain a nugget of unused gold for those that sift through the rubble that remains. The nineteenth-century clearance of the cottars made room for a new economy that was based on the new breeds of hill sheep, like the Cheviot whose long dense fleece was ideal for tweeds. Instead of clearing the land for themselves, why didn't the Highland landowners assist their tenants in a new form of farming based on the Cheviot? This proposal was made in 1795 by Sir John Sinclair, a highly regarded landowner, economist and Member of Parliament, but it fell on deaf ears and was not implemented even on his own estate in Caithness. Part of the tragedy of the clearances was the missed opportunity to rebuild the Highland economy on the strong demand for tweed and a new communal enterprise by tenant farmers.

The possibility of a new communal enterprise, or *positive communal response* as historian TC Smout called it, is I believe the golden nugget left over from that dark episode of our history. Can Scotland even today find a communal way of using her natural resources which rivals or even betters the productivity of the private landowner and which could become the foundation for a fairer society? For inspiration we need look no further than Ulva and her three illustrious sons of tenant families: Neil Livingstone, the father of David Livingstone; Major-General Lachlan Macquarie, Governor of New South Wales and Father of Australia; and his brother Lieutenant-Colonel Charles Macquarie, who eventually purchased the Ulva estate in 1825 to become laird himself. With talent like that, what problem of the estate could not have been overcome had the tenants been given a share in governance of island resources? It is a lesson from the empty clachans of Ulva: people freed from the tyranny of land ownership will stand up and show their worth.

I glanced up at the clock. It was midnight. Kyla was fast asleep on her bunk. I went up to the cockpit and used the last of the light in the northern sky to check my landmarks. *Molio* hadn't shifted. I poured myself another dram. There was time for one more thought about the history of Ulva. Unlikely though it might seem at first glance, there was a connection between the ruined cottages of Cragaig and today's mooring business at Crinan. They represent the first and last acts of enclosure in Scotland. The enclosure of Ulva's land created a thriving estate but destroyed communal life. In Crinan the development orchestrated by Crown Estate creates a thriving business but destroys an ancient traditional anchorage. Do we really want to create a coastal network of mediaeval fiefdoms in which every minor manager demands tribute for the right of boats to seek shelter?

It is not just the harbours. The common waters of our coastline are also being enclosed to create privately-owned fish farms, which are moored in almost every loch and inlet. The justification of the Crown Estate is similar to that offered by Parliament two hundred years ago. Back then, enclosure was supported for the benefit that they assumed would follow 'for all society from the emergence of a capitalist class which improves the land'. Today's enclosures are justified for the benefits they bring to an entrepreneur class which can 'improve' the coastal waters. Unpleasant though it may be to state, the commissioners of the Crown Estate are stealing the commons and turning them over to the moneyed classes. In the words of a seventeenth century protest chant against English enclosure of common land:

> *The law demands that we atone*
> *When we take things we do not own*
> *But leaves the lords and ladies fine*
> *Who take things that are yours and mine*

Does it have to be this way? One of the finest hours in recent Scottish history was the passing of the right to roam bill, which confirmed in legislation the ancient tradition of universal access to all lands of Scotland. Here, as nowhere else, the government of this proud and much-loved nation has shown its respect for the common man and woman. We might extend that notion to the ancient tradition of universal access to all sea passages and sea lochs including the right to anchor without charge in natural harbours and coastal havens. Can we not learn from the past? Or must we turn over our coastal resources to private management for the narrow benefit of a small number of sea lairds?

Kyla laid a mug of tea next to me.

"Morning skipper." She squeezed round the table and sat down on my bunk.

I grunted a reply feeling a bit thick-headed.

"Did you see any ghosts?" She asked.

I mumbled something about the emptiness of Cragaig. She lay down beside me, shoving me over towards the lockers.

"Last night I could smell the thatch burning."

I twisted round to look at her. She looked strained and I saw that her right eyelid was dragging. I stroked her forehead.

"Didn't you sleep last night?"

She took my hand in hers. "I'm going to try and sleep now."

I lay there for a while before crawling over Kyla to take a look at the day. It was warm with a faint breeze and hazy sunshine. A williwaw whistled across the bay and then quietness descended again.

It occurred to me that I hadn't heard or seen a single sheep. Yet they were the trigger for all the troubles we'd been brooding on. I went back below to make some porridge, which I carried up to the bridge deck with some charts. The atmosphere here was getting to both of us. It was surely time to move on. An hour later I upped anchor and motored slowly down the narrow channel through the skerries. Outside there was a long swell coming in from the southwest. *Molio* rose and fell easily. I hoisted sail and set off to the west, passing inside Little Colonsay. Once clear of Gometra we met a shorter sea coming in from the northwest, which combined with the long swell to make an uneasy motion. What little wind there was now headed us. I turned on the engine again and *Molio* bucked and lurched as we ploughed along at six knots.

North of the Tresnish Isles there were no boats to be seen, just an endless lumpy sea, a mottled infinity of living grey and silver pieces. The big swell kicked up *Molio*'s counter and pushed her into a roll, the smaller sea coming at her bow made her jib and start in endless repetition. I remembered sailing with my father in seas like this. Unlike me, he would never use the engine and the day would go on forever as we rocked and bounced along. My brothers and I marked off one painful mile after another along the horizon of some distant hill.

But for him, shoogling all day on a lumpy sea was a grand release, an escape from the heavy responsibility of his work and an open door to the mythic world of the imagination. The sea is our most primal world. It has been here from the dawn of humankind, and it will continue to be here for our children and grandchildren and on and on down through the ages until all of us are gone, and the Earth may breathe a sigh of relief.

Somewhere out in that silvery-grey expanse, on passage to the Isle of Coll, I accepted that Kyla wasn't ready for a long Hebridean voyage. She was like a seabird with a broken wing that needed to heal before it could soar once more above the ocean swell. I on the other hand was ready, and so was my boat.

Chapter 16

Isle of The Great Women

Approaching Loch nan Eathar, the 'loch of small open fishing boats' on Coll, I reduced speed before bringing *Molio* up the west channel to the village of Arinagour, which nestled at the head of the loch between a grand old pier and a grey stone church. Along the shore a band of exposed kelp, the same dark gold as heather honey, framed the Hebridean waters that were glowing in the translucent greens and blues of a tropical sea. Slowing to a standstill, I went up to the bow and dropped anchor in a green patch, midway between the pier and a stone perch. As I did, a large Atlantic seal hauled itself onto a nearby rock, grunting with the effort – or was it with the satisfaction of scratching an itch? Kyla was keen to go ashore for fresh food and took off in the dinghy with a shopping list. I stayed to work on the decks, hoping to close off a couple of new leaks before rain arrived. I dug out my bottle of Captain Tolley's Creeping Crack Cure and used Chas's technique to test about twenty suspect wooden plugs that sat above the bronze deck fastenings. I popped out the dodgy ones and applied gluey primer with the last half-inch paint brush in *Molio*'s store. It smelt like the dope we used for making wings of model aircraft at school. Once it was dry, I began filling the holes with sealant. It wasn't elegant but comfort took precedence over looks.

Kyla came back full of beans but not much shopping. "Look what I have for you," she cried brandishing a used half-inch brush. "The shopkeeper gave me his own and says he is expecting more on tomorrow's ferry. I also found you this." She held up a tin of Spotted Dick pudding.

"Ah," I grinned. "Now that is real food."

She gave me a friendly shove. "Not much fresh though. This is all I could find." She showed me what was in her bag: a handful of cherry tomatoes, four ripe bananas and a soft yellow pepper. She took down *Molio*'s new fridge – a cool box which we ran when the engine was on. It contained some carrots with yellowing tops and furry white roots, a soft cucumber, and half a dozen potatoes sprouting white shoots.

"How about dinner tonight at the Coll Hotel?" I suggested.

Kyla looked seriously anxious: "I've nothing to wear."

"You don't have to wear anything. I mean you do, but you don't need anything special."

She laughed, "Okay, I'm going to clean up the fridge and then I shall have a sponge bath."

In the evening, we rowed over to the steps at the pier. Kyla sat in the stern, wearing dark glasses, a white V-neck which inevitably drew the eye downwards and a dark green waistcoat that lit up the falling tangles of red hair. She was dressed to kill.

"You're dangerous," I said.

"Mmm," she smiled.

"Guys here get island fever you know."

"Row harder," she commanded.

Over at the hotel it was still early enough to be quiet. The lounge bar had a great view over the loch and I could see *Molio* holding her position nicely, but there was a touristy atmosphere about the room, a kind of whispered conformity. The pub at the back had no window, but was the local watering hole. I decided that *Molio*'s anchor was dug in fine. We chose the pub and ordered some bottled ale at the bar. Kyla asked what seafood was on the menu and a guy at the counter pitched in with a suggestion that she try the scallops. It turned out he was a diver and had brought them in that morning. I noticed, with mild alarm, that he was wearing Bermuda shorts. I looked more closely. Dark haired, with a day's worth of bristles, he could have come straight off a fashion catalogue.

The guy next to him, on the other hand, didn't look so fit – a bit puffy round the jowl and with a stressed look in the eyes. He had shaved his head, making it harder to judge his age, but I guessed in his early forties. He looked the friendlier of the two, so I struck up conversation with him, making some aimless comment about a big old seal in the bay. He turned out to be the RSPB warden. We were soon conversing about corncrakes, puffins and skylarks, and the precise meaning of natural habitat. Kyla talked to catalogue-man. Judging from the odd fragment overheard, it was mainly about RIBs and diving. When the scallops arrived on a bed of locally grown lettuce and spring onions, she took my arm and dragged me over to a small table. It was good to see that her appetite had returned. Boats do that to people. I thought again about my instinct that she wasn't yet ready for a long sea voyage. Could I have been wrong?

"Do you think we could sail to Eigg from here?" Kyla asked, as she put down her fork.

"It's on the way. It's about twenty, maybe twenty-five, miles from here."

"You remember Rob and Ellie? You met them at the party in Edinburgh."

"Oh them," I said in mock surprise. "They were quite normal."

"They've moved to Eigg and turned the big house into a sustainable Earth centre. Could we visit them?"

"Forecast is okay, west or northwesterly breeze and a slight sea. We can leave in the morning."

Kyla was picking up, I thought. Maybe it would work out after all.

The bewitching call of a cuckoo woke me at six the next morning. There had been one calling at Ulva and another at Cairnbaan. I lay there listening to the call for some time, conscious of Kyla breathing beside me. Eventually I swung out of my bunk and went up on deck to welcome the day. A couple of hours later, we upped anchor and sailed away from the 'loch of small fishing boats', running with a nor'westerly breeze. Gybing at the entrance to catch the northerly flood, *Molio* took off on a close reach.

The breeze died away as we closed with the land a few hours later. Towering above us, the Sgùrr of Eigg impressed its primal authority over two more puny mariners. I dropped the mainsail and edged in through the reefs of the northern entrance just as the rain came on. With the tide now high, it was difficult to locate all of the reefs shown on the chart; added to that, it had started to ebb so that we needed to keep up speed to prevent *Molio* being carried over rocks. I was edgy. My eyes jumped from chart to the passage ahead, to echo sounder, to GPS and back again. We came through the first set of perches without difficulty and there, immediately in front, were two more perches marking the passage into a sheltered inner pool. Its wide expanses looked inviting. Beyond the perches a large blue ketch swung on a mooring, to one side of it a white sloop was tied to the harbour wall. I relaxed and applied more throttle to take *Molio* between the second set of perches where the tide was now flowing against us like a river. It seemed shallow between the perches but I assumed it was a bar at the entrance, and that the pool would deepen immediately. We began to sweep round in a circle in preparation for anchoring on the seaward side of the blue ketch. I was forty yards in when I had my first doubts. It was no deeper inside the pool than at the entrance; in fact it was far too shallow. I pushed the helm hard over to bring *Molio* in towards the pier. As we began to turn, Molio suddenly slowed to a standstill. We were on the mud. I thrust the engine into reverse and revved hard; nothing happened, just a cloud of churning muddy water at the stern.

I glanced at Kyla who didn't seem to think anything was amiss. "I may need you to take a rope over to that pier in the dinghy," I said. She looked at me in consternation.

I noticed a man standing in the cockpit of the white boat which was now about forty feet away. "How much depth do you have?" I shouted.

"Just a minute," he replied and disappeared below. Time passed. What could he be doing? Eventually he reappeared. "Four feet," he yelled. I couldn't believe it – they were the larger boat and *Molio* draws five and a half feet. In any case how could there be less water next to a pier? At that moment the skipper came up from below and assessed the situation immediately. "We have a lifting keel," he called out. That confirmed it, we were in trouble.

I turned to Kyla. "Forget the dinghy." I thought hard. The tide was rushing out of the entrance and rapidly emptying the inner pool. *Molio* had already taken a list to port. We had a minute or two at best. If we failed to free ourselves now, we would have to wait for the incoming tide next morning. As the water drained away, *Molio* would lie further and further over on her side, until the mainmast came up against the pier and eventually broke. It would then be a struggle to prevent the incoming tide from flooding over the cockpit coamings and down into the cabin. It was critical we got out. I untied the mainsheet from its cleat on the aft deck and pushed the boom out to port until it was a couple of feet beyond *Molio*'s side, then refastened.

Kyla was staring at me intently, well aware now that this wasn't part of the anchoring plan. I forced myself to be calm before speaking. "We have one chance. I want you to put all your weight onto the end of the boom. Lean right out. Tipping *Molio* to one side will put an angle on her keel which will lift it an inch or two above the mud." She went out immediately, almost falling into the water. I pushed the engine into forward gear and gave maximum throttle. It roared with power. Then I added my weight to Kyla's. The screw churned in the water throwing mud into a great plume astern. We didn't budge. I threw myself even further on to the boom. *Molio* swivelled a few inches in the port direction. She was facing the pier now. I heaved myself against the boom to rock her. "With me," I yelled. Kyla heaved in time. *Molio* moved a fraction, swivelled again, then moved a few inches more, then a foot, and then a yard grinding immediately to a halt, then another yard, and she was turning again towards the entrance, then two yards. I leapt for the tiller to hold her direction. Again we lurched forward and this time the power of her Lombardini diesel, the equivalent of 96 Olympic oarsmen, bulldozed her from the muddy bed. *Molio* gathered way, bumped, gathered way, bumped harder. She was a strong boat. I left the throttle fully open. Again we gathered way and by this time we were travelling at four knots and approaching the perches.

Kyla put her hand on mine at the tiller, "Not too fast, Martyn."

She was right, I flicked the engine into neutral as the tide took us out between the perches to deep water. Looking back I saw the crew of the white yacht dancing a victory jig on the bow, the skipper's arms punching the air. They knew how close it had been. I waved at them and turned back to the chart. We headed straight for the centre of the main channel.

"Those Eigg guys," I shouted to Kyla, "they're just wreckers. Like your Mum's Cornish ancestors." Adrenaline was running high.

"Like your Mum's Cornish ancestors," she laughed.

"Those big yachts," I said, "who would have thought they were mud crawlers?"

"They must be from down south."

"What did he say about the depth: 'Just going down below to check, back in five minutes'?"

"Back in ten more like!"

"Those big women of Eigg were after a salvage job," I said, remembering its other name, Eilean nam Ban Móra, Island of the Big Women.

"They wanted to strip poor *Molio* bare."

"But with one bound, *Molio* was free." This time we both laughed.

"And what a victory dance they gave us," recalled Kyla, her eyes glowing.

We turned south towards the old pier, savouring the joy of unrestrained movement. Once past the pier, we anchored in three and a half fathoms, out of the way of the current and in the shelter of Eilean Chathastail, 'Castle Island'. I dug in the anchor with reverse gear on the engine before going below and pouring two drams. Kyla shook her head so I knocked them both back.

"I was just thinking back there: where will we sleep tonight?" she smiled at me.

"I was going to sleep on the side cupboards, so I'd be ready to face the incoming tide."

"It doesn't bear thinking about."

"No," I sighed, coming back to earth. "Truth is, Kyla, that chart was clear. It was my stupid fault."

She came close, "But you weren't helped by those perches."

We awoke to light rain and a forecast of strong northerlies. I made some hot porridge with raisins mixed in, but Kyla wasn't hungry. We set off in the dinghy and rowed round the point by the old pier, finding a concrete slip on the far side where we beached the Avon. We continued to explore on foot, walking past the ferry terminal and along a track that led round the landward side of the inner pool. The tide was now tracking in across the mudflats and had almost reached the blue ketch, which was standing high and dry on twin bilge keels. The white yacht was also clear of the water, leaning against the pier with its bow pitched forward. We were thankful to have escaped. The sun came out as we walked back to the pier and found Eigg's one and only café. Inside it had the same atmosphere as a friendly truckers' stop: warm, wooden floor, utilitarian tables and chairs, smell of bacon, mugs of tea, and the sounds of chatter mixed with plates being washed. The only difference was the view. On the far side, huge windows looked out over the southern bay to where *Molio* was dancing on the sparkling water. Out past the shelter of Eilean Chathastail, white horses were charging in from the west and beyond the seas were the far hills of Ardnamurchan. I ordered a bacon roll and tea. Kyla asked for filtered coffee. While we were waiting, I put my camera battery on charge making the most of Eigg's alternative energy ring.

A little later, we went to look at the gift shop. As I was looking about, Kyla fell into conversation with Ann, the lady in charge. If there is such a thing as naturally attractive, then she was it. Large eyes, soft mouth and thoughtful brow; her face seemed to reflect not her age so much as her manner; at once outgoing, self-conscious and above all, serene. She wore a jolly blue sailor's smock and smiled happily at Kyla who was now chatting with her about the community buy-out.

It had been a momentous turning point in the island's history. Like Ulva, Eigg has had its share of good and bad lairds. The most recent couple were celebrities, reluctant to give out leases to the island families, most probably because it would have affected the commercial value of the estate. Without secure leases, the islanders were unable to access improvement grants from the local authority. The lairds used these and other feudal powers to restrict enterprise and development, no doubt with the advice of their lawyers. Nevertheless, a core of islanders hung on and Eigg even began to attract newcomers, who valued the communal lifestyle. With an overwhelming sense of solidarity and a vision for a radically different future, the Isle of Eigg Trust was established in 1994, with the aim of buying the island. Buoyed up by their shared determination, the imagination of the islanders started to unchain. They began to learn new skills – web campaigning, IT, fundraising, institutional strengthening, public relations and the politics of landownership in Scotland. In the end they did it. On 12th June 1997 the Trust bought Eigg and the islanders were liberated from centuries of dependency. For evermore it will be Independence Day on Eigg, the day they won back control of their land and natural resources. Since then, the islanders have picked up a raft of new expertise – communitybased development, governance by participation, business management, administration, accountancy, negotiation, building renovation, construction, property management, lease revision, environmental restoration, alternative energy, tourism and forestry. They have been growing their freedom.

"Yet even today," said Ann, "some of the islanders say they were more comfortable with a laird 'that they can tug their lock to' than with incomers and their democracy. They don't go to the open meetings. They say they can't cope with the clever speaking."

"I've been to many community meetings that were taken over by a few charismatic people," agreed Kyla.

"Still, mostly we are happy enough and pleased with the new electricity."

"We need to learn from you," observed Kyla warming to one of her passions. "There is so much to do on the mainland with recycling and cutting down on waste."

"Och, we just must be aware," said Ann. She pronounced 'ah-ware' with a high note for the 'ah' and a low note for the 'ware' which was drawn out and soft, like music. "Now on the subject of waste not, want not, will you both be sharing a piece of homemade cake with me?"

To my amazement, Kyla accepted the slice offered and took a huge mouthful. After the fruitcake we set off up the hill to find Rob and Ellie who had established their Green Earth Centre in the laird's house. We found it down a driveway filled with rhododendrons, palms, eucalyptus, flame trees and other exotic plants. Its stone-carved balcony and almond-washed walls looked more like a colonial villa than a Highland lodge. As we came near, a little boy with long hair came running round the house and grabbed Kyla by the hand. "Have you come to stay?" he pleaded.

Kyla laughed, "Maybe," she said. "Take me to your leader."

The back of the house was rigged for alternative energy: solar water-heating panels connected to a lagged outdoor tank while the glassed-in veranda offered passive heating through open windows into the house. The back door stood open. Next to it, two older boys were arguing. A woman with glossy black hair and wide smiling eyes came out as we approached. "Kyla," she gasped and held up her arms. The girls hugged.

Disengaging, Ellie looked over at me, "We met at Paul's party. I remember now. I hope you can stay?"

"Nice little shack you have here," I said eying up the seven bedroom mansion.

"Bit cramped but we manage," she laughed. "Come and meet Rob." She led us through the hallway towards the sound of hammering. A man in saggy overalls was standing on a step ladder, demolishing the plaster. The first impression was purely of ginger hair: a thick mop almost obscured his eyes, a moustache drooped over his lip, a beard over his chin and a pony tail hung over his neck. "Kyla, good to see you," he called. He came down the ladder, shook the plaster off his overalls and strode over to give her a huge hug. She was doing pretty well on the hugging front I thought.

Ellie began to organise the household, shooing the children outside and suggesting to Rob that he show me the Centre while she and Kyla had a chat.

Rob took me round the house, pointing out the dry rot and the extent of his renovation work which he was doing single-handedly. In one room a floor had been cut out and in another the window frames were being rebuilt.

"My main winter work is renovation. Ellie does the vegetable gardening and I do the timber work. In the summer, I help her with teaching courses on sustainable living except when I'm away on the Greenpeace boat."

Out back he showed me his new toy, a wood-mizer for cutting timber from trees blown down on the island.

"It feels as if I'm back in the 70s," I volunteered, soaking in the atmosphere. "You have magic here!"

Ellie found us chatting outside half an hour later, and told me that Kyla wanted to see me. We walked back to the house. I felt apprehensive.

She was reading to the three boys who were staring up at her goggle-eyed. She looked relaxed and happy. As I came in, she closed the book. "That's all for now." There was a chorus of groans. She stood up and took me outside to walk in the gardens. We stopped at a gnarled Scots Pine.

"It's my favourite tree." She laid her cheek against the red flakes of bark and looked up into the crown as if seeking strength from it. "I can't stay with you, Martyn."

It wasn't a surprise but even so the words hit me like hammer blows.

"We are not right together." She placed her hand on my mouth to stop me speaking. "I can't heal in your presence. Don't you see? I get caught up in your passion." She looked at me despairingly seeing the confusion in my eyes, and sighed. "You're lost on some kind of hero quest. Whilst I... Well, I need to rest. I need to slow down... with the earth under my feet. I can help here with the gardening and cooking. More than anything, Martyn, I need my friends, my community. Can't you understand that?" She trailed off staring into nowhere. She rallied once more, "You've carried me a long way Martyn; now I need to walk myself."

I looked at her tired shoulders and strained eyes, knowing her mind was made up. It was the mind of Kyla this time, not some angry goddess. Part of me knew she was right but still I wasn't ready to accept it.

"We can work at it. I'll calm down, tootle about. You'll see."

"No Martyn. I don't need your help for this. I have to find my own way."

"I won't get in your way. I'll just be the guy who fixes things."

She put her hand on my chest and looked into my eyes. "Don't you see, your presence just prevents me from getting better. We can never be right for each other."

"How can you say that?" I answered angrily.

For a moment, she stared at my face, as if searching for something. "It is better if I stay here. I can help at the Centre and I'll have time to mend." She looked up and smiled and it seemed that there might just be a chance for the two of us. She came close and kissed me quickly on the lips. "Take care out there on the sea."

"Don't you want your things?"

"That's all I need," she glanced at the satchel. "Ellie will look after me."

"I can get your bag?"

"Go. Please go."

Turning to leave, I gazed one last time at Kyla. Her eyes were vacant. She looked at the end of her tether. I walked along the drive and down the hill towards the pier, hardly aware of my surroundings. *Molio* was exactly where I'd left her, sitting deep in the choppy waters, tugging at her anchor, making a picture out of the empty cove. She had become the one constant companion in my life. I watched her for a while, until somebody put their face almost into mine. It was Ann from the shop.

"Is Kyla not with you?" I looked into her calm grey eyes. I shook my head not trusting myself to speak.

She seemed to understand, "It will be good for her on Eigg. Don't worry. You'll see."

I nodded and walked down the slip to the dinghy. Once on board *Molio*, I gathered Kyla's clothes and other bits and pieces and packed them into her overnight bag. I pushed the bag into a bin liner tying it tight to keep out the moisture, and wedged it carefully with her sleeping bag in the small trotter box at the end of her bunk. Why was I having so much difficulty in letting her go? I paused for a moment. I had wanted her as my companion for many reasons but most of all because she opened an inner door. In her presence, the spiritual side of my existence was always open, always close – the intimate awarenesses of

253

people and wild creatures, the unexpected connections and the purpose that gave me direction. It was magical but it turned out to be a one-way crossing. She didn't want my way, the way of the open road and endless horizon, the test of skill and the quest for truth. It seemed to frighten her. I took a long breath and let it out slowly, letting go of the upset, letting go of Kyla. *Molio* rocked on the tide, nudging and cajoling me. I breathed again even more deeply, reconnecting with myself. As I remembered the purpose of my journey, I felt the energy returning. I knew what I was doing. I knew where I was going. If anything, it had become even more important that I find my own brand of freedom. I lifted the cushions on my bunk and pulled out a chart marked Sea of the Hebrides.

Chapter 17

Battle of Dreams

Motoring out of the anchorage and past the old pier, I noticed that the inner pool had filled up. The two yachts were afloat and the twin perches opened once again on what appeared to be a perfect land-locked anchorage. Yesterday, the big women of Eigg had nearly claimed a prize, and now they had reset their trap for the next unwary sailor. I turned my back. Once through the skerries I brought *Molio* round to bear south. A breeze caught the mainsail and we were off. Soon there was nothing else in my world but the hiss of foam, the great Sgùrr above, and the open sea beyond. I gybed round the bottom of Eilean Chathastail and headed west between Eigg and Muck, tightening the sheets as I cleared the sound, to make for the western side of Rum. I could just make out the lower wedge of Canna beyond. As I closed with Rum an hour or two later, the northerly breeze stiffened and the seas became steeper. *Molio* began kicking up sheets of spray which had me ducking behind the dodger at regular intervals. The hard sailing lifted my mood. The sun shone out of a cloudless sky picking out a host of daisy-white horses charging in amongst thistle-blue seas as if determined to delight me, while the towering hills on either side of Glen Harris on Rum soon sent my spirits soaring with the eagles. Three islands, Eigg, Rum and Canna, lay across the Sea of the Hebrides like so many stepping stones. Collectively they were called Na h-Eileanan Tarsainn, 'islands that traverse the sea', by the Gaels who no doubt stopped for rest and replenishment as they rowed their galleys from Morar on the mainland across to South Uist or Eriskay in the Outer Hebrides. Canna, 'the porpoise isle', lay furthest into the stream and had the best anchorage.

I made towards A' Bhrideanach, the western point of Rum. A loose translation of the name is 'St Bride's nose' which seems a fitting description for such a prominent point jutting into the Sea of the Hebrides or 'St Bride's Sea'. Passing A' Bhrideanach, I sheeted in tight and made towards Sanday Island, the southern companion of Canna, tacking east into the Sound of Canna but losing some ground in the process. Eventually, I switched on the engine to sneak north against the wind and round the eastern side of the island. My father would have disapproved. It was growing dark as I entered Canna Harbour. I counted ten other boats spread out across the anchorage, but found room inside them, with eight feet of water expected at low tide. It was just enough for comfort. I dropped anchor and tidied up on deck, fan-folding the mainsail and securing it with ties.

In the morning I was up early to look around. A black guillemot, smallest of all the auks, was bobbing to one side of the cockpit, dipping her bill and shaking her head in mild anxiety at my sudden appearance. After a while, she settled down and started diving for food. I could clearly see the white wing patches flashing as she flew down. For some reason, it reminded me of the white tail-flash of the impala that I studied in the Zambezi Valley. When the female impala bolts for cover, her tail flashes as an invitation for companions to follow. Perhaps the flashing wing of the guillemot helped the young bird to follow its diving parent and learn how to find food. I watched the trail of tiny bubbles coming towards *Molio*, disappearing, only to reappear on the other side. When she surfaced, there was a flatfish flapping in her beak; she shook it about before swallowing it for breakfast.

After my own plain breakfast of toast, I dug out some hiking boots and rowed ashore, beaching the dinghy just below Canna House. There was a sign at the gate saying 'garden open', so I climbed the steps and walked down the fuchsia tunnel. Reaching the other end, I found myself in the centre of the front garden. All about were secluded walks, lawns and borders; directly in front lay the laird's house, a handsome mongrel of Scottish stone and Tuscan design. It was gifted to the National Trust for Scotland in 1981 but annoyingly it was closed to visitors. I walked round to the back of the house, where there was a large vegetable and fruit garden, and admired the rows of radishes, onions, lettuces and potatoes. Each row was marked with a stick painted white at the top with black lettering – carrots, green beans, and so on. There were neat pathways edged by wooden boards and a potting shed complete with a pair of sagging leather boots. It reminded me of an illustration in Beatrix Potter's Tale of Peter Rabbit. I had seen a few of his wild cousins in the hills above. I didn't find Peter there but I found the gardener, Mr McGregor. He was stooping from a great height to tend the vegetable bed, as calm and considered in his size 12 boots as the island sanctuary around him.

"It's amazing what you can grow in the West Highlands," I said, looking around at the fruit trees.

"We have pretty much everything," he agreed, "apples, pears, cherries, plums. There's a grape vine over in the corner. Our main problem at the moment is drought – the island is running low on water."

"Are you winning with the rabbits?" I asked.

He rested an arm on the hoe, "I use that netting," he indicated the two-foot-high mesh running round the beds, "but it is a constant struggle."

"Plenty of food for the eagles and buzzards then."

"The rabbits are everywhere. They burrow under the ancient ruins and they stop the woodlands from regenerating."

"Have you thought about introducing some polecats? I bet they would solve your problem and you'd be conserving a native species into the bargain."

"We've been eating rabbit pie," he laughed. "That helps. It's coming out of our ears. Go down to the restaurant tonight and you'll see what I mean."

"Does Margaret Fay Shaw still visit?" I asked, referring to the much-loved wife of the last laird.

"She passed away a few years ago, aged 101. We could have used her wisdom now to solve the impasse between Trust and islanders."

I asked why there was an impasse, but Mr McGregor just shook his head. I left him to battle with the ground elder and walked down the track heading west along the edge of the sea, before climbing up the hill to the central part of the island. In every direction were vast blue-grey seascapes, giving the island a feeling of remoteness. I checked a couple of times for mobile reception without joy. Continuing north across the dry moss bogs and stony ridges, I eventually found what I was looking for. At the foot of a grassy slope lay a jumbled arrow of pale rocks, the largest barely moveable except by the strongest man. They were set in the rough shape of a Viking boat, which pointed northwards, as if ready to journey down the long reach of sea lying between the hills of South Uist on the western horizon and the Isle of Skye in the east. It was indeed a Viking burial cairn, known locally as the King of Norway's Grave. Its significance for the buried chieftain came immediately from the setting. From the distant hills of North Uist, the Shiant Isles that lie further north in the centre of the stormy Minch would be visible, and from those islands there was direct passage to Cape Wrath, the 'turning point' of the Norsemen and the most north-westerly point of the British mainland. Once there, it was a day's passage to Orkney, and the same to Shetland where the scent of Norwegian pines might carry on an easterly wind. It was the Viking equivalent of the M1 motorway, a voyage this king must have known well. Buried in his boat, with his sword and helmet by his side, he was prepared for his last voyage home.

The ninth-century Vikings found all they needed on the porpoise island: fertile soils for vegetables, grains and pastureland, woodland for timber, and fish aplenty in the surrounding waters. The seas around Britain have been denuded for so long that we forget how prolific they once were. A visit in 1787 by the British Fisheries Society found cod, mullet and ling to be so numerous off Canna that they hooked fish as fast as they could throw out their lines. One ling weighed forty-four pounds and measured five and a half feet. The islanders made good use of their local fishing bank and also hunted basking sharks for their oil-rich livers and seals for their oil-rich blubber. Recognising the unique combination of a perfect natural harbour and sea banks teeming with fish, the Society recommended establishing a fishery on Canna, but then couldn't agree a price with the principal farmer who saw the fishery, with its better paid work, as a threat to his labour force.

I walked back up the hill, traversing row upon row of lazy-beds, which spread from the fertile lowlands up into the hill country. It was a sign of just how much pressure there had been on the land, as the population on Canna built up in the eighteenth and nineteenth centuries, reaching over four hundred in 1815. When the kelp industry collapsed, the island faced a crisis. As on Ulva, commercial considerations came to the fore and the same heavy-handed solutions were imposed. On Canna they were used to justify the clearance of 200 tenants. The chief architects of the 1851 Canna Clearance were both Highlanders, and one was closely connected to the island. It is hard to rationalise such harsh behaviour by local men.

Some have condemned the Highland landowners and others blamed the financiers for the clearances. If there is a meaningful lesson to be drawn from this appalling episode, it is surely the one elucidated by John Lorne Campbell, the last laird of Canna and renowned Gaelic scholar. *'What is so highly objectionable about the Highland Clearances,'* he wrote, *'is the complete lack of security of tenure for small tenants...'* Three words – *security of tenure* – this is the nub of the matter. The tenants had no legal claim to their land, or to any improvements they made to their land, or even to their homes. They had no long-term rights to their grazing either. The same stranglehold applies across much of the Highlands and Islands today.

John Campbell sought to rectify the past by giving Gaelic culture a living and vibrant future on Canna. Not having any children, he feared that after he and his wife died the island would pass into the hands of an absentee landlord, and become another rich man's plaything. He solved the problem by leaving the island, his Gaelic library, and an endowment that contributed to the island's running costs, to the National Trust for Scotland. In other words, he passed his dream, an Olympic torch for Gaeldom, to the most trustworthy body he could think of.

Reliving the past is an easy thing to do when walking on Canna. I shall blame John Campbell for laying a pattern of thought all over his Hebridean isle as he pondered on the signs of past occupation which cover the landscape. Everywhere I looked were mounds, graves, duns, circles, banks, walls and freestanding crosses, and everywhere I went there opened up new vistas of the surrounding seas. Given this heritage, it would perhaps have been surprising if Canna had not become an island of dreams. Campbell had got me thinking about his dream of Gaelic communities working their common resources. I wanted to walk with him and talk about the Hebridean commons. I keep coming back to them – those natural resources of our country, the forests, woods, pastures, moors, organic soils, fresh water lochs, rivers and springs, useful plants, fungi, wildlife and fish which make up our natural heritage. There's a good reason for my preoccupation. Natural resources have become the focal points of struggle in society, not just in Scotland, but throughout the world. They are the battlegrounds on which those that aspire to live freely collide with forces intent on exercising absolute control. The future governance of our commons, I believe, is where the future of freedom will be decided for the majority of people on Earth. In Scotland, politics, power and property have walked hand in hand for centuries: astoundingly, more than half of Scotland today is owned by just five hundred people. Consequently the majority of our natural resources are still providing silver and gold to a tiny privileged minority.

At the top of the hill I enjoyed panoramic views of the Hebrides. To the west lay the Outer Hebrides, stretching in a long protective line that broke the power of the Atlantic swell; to north and south were the islands of the Inner Hebrides; and to the east lay the mainland. All these islands, these seas, and these long, indented coastlines, were once a kingdom ruled by the Lord of the Isles. His people expelled the Vikings without any need for assistance from the mainland Scottish Crown. The people of the Hebrides – St Bride's People or Brigid's people – had their own Gaelic language, their own customs and developed their own careful way of using the resources of their realm. They used the shieling pastures and fishing banks as common resources and by all accounts acted fairly in apportioning shares. Once apportioned, the idea that one man might prosper by encroaching on the shares of his neighbours was considered highly offensive and improper.

At that time the land belonged to the chief of the clan, and was divided by him amongst his family and clan members. He was the father of his people and he originated from the same stock as them. His land was their land. His cattle were their cattle. Their quarrels were his quarrels. He helped them when they were in need, settled disputes and protected them and their cattle against enemies. The clan, or *clann* in Gaelic, means children, and has its origins in deeply-rooted Gaelic traditions of kindness. The people were governed by a patriarchal rather than a feudal system. In time of war, which was most of the time, the chief led the clan in battle and his clansmen followed. Even the humblest belonged with his chief and shared a pride in his clan that is scarcely conceivable today. Such was the way of the Highlands and Islands at the dawn of the sixteenth century. What followed after the demise of the Lordship of the Isles in 1493 is important to understand, as it still divides the nation.

What happened, what shocked the culture and changed society, was the implanting of class discrimination into Highland society where before there was none. To understand how this came about we need just a little more history. In the sixteenth century, Lowland Scotland was converging with England and diverging from traditional Highland culture. Then, in 1603, came the union of the English and Scottish crowns. The Gaelic language, formally spoken fluently by the Lowland Kings, became known as 'Erse' or Irish, implying that it was a foreign tongue. The Scottish Parliament decided that 'Erse' was the principal cause of Highlander resistance. Through negotiation with a number of Highland nobles, it enacted the Statutes of Iona in 1609, which required clan chiefs to send their heirs to Lowland Scotland to be educated in English-speaking Protestant schools.

These events fomented a class difference between English-speaking Highland landowners and their Gaelic tenants that has remained with us, in essence, to this day. The chiefs became lairds – owners of Highland estates who retained only symbolic chieftainship. Their children assimilated the culture of the landed gentry in England and began to look down on their own Gaelic culture. As for the clansmen, the reforms, the outlawing of Highland dress including the kilt, and the systematic eradication of their language and religion left a shattered people that were scattered over the Highland glens and Hebridean islands; yet still they defended their traditional rights and values. These rights included their common use of the land and its resources. But without the laird's blessing, or legal entitlement from government, they lacked the *security of tenure* necessary for developing their land.

In the present day the Highlands and Islands are still owned and managed by a few hundred lairds, although many of the old chiefs from ancient families have sold up to millionaires and billionaires from other countries. The incomers have even less understanding of traditional values. Meanwhile along the coast, ownership of the marine resources of the seafloor has passed to the Crown Estate, while inshore and offshore fishing rights fall to the Scottish Government in Edinburgh and the European Commission in Brussels. All these bodies are remote from the West Highlander, yet impose their authority with little understanding of their Gaelic heritage and their communal and conservative traditions.

As a people, the Gaels have been denounced as barbarous, ignorant and rebellious by James VI and his Court in the seventeenth century; as idle and incapable by English and Scottish gentry in the nineteenth century; and today as backward-looking and unenterprising by the new entrepreneurs. No doubt they will continue to be disparaged by future generations unless control of their natural resources is returned to them. Having been denied ownership for four hundred years, the Gaels have become alienated from authority. They have become alienated from their own natural resources. The charismatic wildlife, the deer, the salmon and the grouse, which should have been quintessential common resources to be cherished and used sustainably by the community, are viewed instead as playthings of the laird.

As John Campbell observed, community ownership and control of land in the Highlands is fundamental to its economic development. Only when local users of bountiful resources – such as fisheries, forests, fresh water and wildlife – take a substantial part in decisions over management can sustainable harvesting take hold. Only when users have a personal stake do they begin to monitor other users and take steps to ensure their compliance. Only with *security of tenure* do sustainable practices flourish. Without ownership and control it will be much harder to retain a population in the remoter parts of Scotland, more so one based on traditional Gaelic values. Campbell dreamt of a prosperous Highlands and Islands in which communities worked and safeguarded their own commons. Is that such an unreasonable dream?

A wet fog hung over the harbour next morning, obscuring all but the near shore. Even Canna House was invisible behind a grey curtain. I counted seventeen boats in the murk besides *Molio*, each with a skipper wondering what to do. I was content to sit and wait, smug in the knowledge that I had no deadlines and my bunk was dry. A little later, three yachts motored out relying on their satellite navigation systems. I could see skippers on some of the remaining boats anxiously scanning the mist, hoping to detect an improving trend. I considered the prospects for making a passage across the Minch to South Uist. To begin with, it would be a day spent in fog and perpetual drizzle, with strong tides but light winds. There would be plenty of scope for the mind to play tricks for there would be nothing substantial to see until it was too late to avoid. My radar reflector was at home and, although I had a collapsible backup on board, it would not prevent collision with an inattentive freighter. The other problem would be making landfall. My handheld GPS unit should be sufficient for that, especially in combination with the echo sounder, but I didn't like being dependent on electronic aids. As I was thinking, a foghorn sounded a deep drawn-out note which ended in an eerie echo. It reminded those of us still anchored in the harbour of the many dangers at sea.

It was difficult to work out where the sound was actually coming from. I looked at the Sailing Directions. There was no foghorn on Canna or on Sanday. Surely there couldn't be a ship passing between Canna and Mull? I pulled out an Admiralty chart. The nearest large lighthouse was on the low lying islet of Hyskeir about eight miles to the southwest. It would have a foghorn and, in windless fogbound conditions, the sound could easily travel to our harbour. It sounded plausible except for one thing. Sadly, and with little meaningful discussion, all foghorns in Scotland had been decommissioned. I didn't know what to make of it but I knew that I wasn't going anywhere that day. As if in confirmation, the automatic bilge pump clicked on. It had become more frequent since *Molio*'s grounding on Eigg.

Rather than sit about in the gloom I decided to row across to Sanday and visit the old Catholic Church, one of the few landmarks still visible. Back on *Molio* the fog lifted a fraction at midday and I decided on another expedition to Canna, this time to find the monastery of the holy women. The remains of this settlement lie at the foot of high cliffs on a grassy ledge which juts out above the sea. It is one of a handful of early Christian sites which are dotted about the Hebrides, mostly in remote locations. It was supposed to be accessible by foot from the cliff top, but one of the visitors that I'd met at the Catholic Church had found it necessary to use a rope. I walked west along the same shore route as the day before, continuing this time to the deserted remains of Tarbert village. There I climbed over heather-covered hills to approach the cliffs from the top. As I climbed, the sea-mist thickened and the visibility decreased to less than half a mile. A few broken fence posts marked the edge of the cliff where I could hear the sea crashing one hundred and fifty feet below. I checked the time. It was already five o'clock. I continued making my way westward keeping close to the cliff edge. The path took me up a number of rises as the cliffs grew higher. Soon the mist was so thick I could barely distinguish the black rocks and white spume at their feet. I walked slowly on. Visibility reduced further to forty yards as the thick vapour drenched my clothes. Then it was down to thirty yards. I could just make out my immediate surroundings but there was no clue as to where the sun might be. I approached the cliff edge again. All was silent save for the sound of distant waves. White clouds brushed past. More silence. Nothing but the edge and the void. It was mesmerising. I took a step closer. There was just me and a silent universe, waiting. The sea sighed below. I took another step. At my feet a movement, a piercing eye, a great hooked bill. A golden eagle launched itself into space, dipping and then catching itself up with the first beat of its wings. Three more slow beats – woomph, woomph, woomph – took it out from the cliff, neither gaining nor losing height but flying straight as an arrow into the fog. A few more beats and the mist began to enfold it, seeming to open up before and close round behind. The eagle never faltered or veered. Just the great beats, the purpose, and then it was gone. I stood as if held – for how long I'm not sure. About me the mist stirred in a hypnotic invitation. Then, down below, I heard the distant sound of surf once more. I turned abruptly and stepped back to the path. Taking out my compass, I hurried back inland towards the harbour.

The fog was thinner at sea level and I was able to make my way out to *Molio* in the dinghy. I changed into dry clothes before rowing ashore for a hot meal in the Gille Brighde, or 'oystercatcher', café. With much ingenuity, a kitchen, bar counter and six wooden tables had been squeezed into a whitewashed cottage just next to Canna House. It was full of sailors waiting out the fog, but one table was still free. I took off my waterproofs and sat down. The chef, who doubled as waiter, came over and introduced himself as Frans. He struck me as a larger version of Bjorn from Abba except that he came from the Netherlands not Sweden. He ran through the menu: rabbit pâté, Cullen skink with local haddock, garden potatoes and onions, Canna lobster on garden lettuce, rabbit pot pie with rosemary and thyme, venison, rabbit stew with cranberries and pistachios, and rabbit casserole. I could see that the menu reflected the needs of wildlife management on the island. I chose lobster as a starter to be followed by the casserole, and ordered a bottle of Chablis. I struck up a conversation with some neighbouring yachtsmen about boats, the cleverness of fish finders and the rabbits on Canna. One of them mentioned something about dogs getting stuck in a rabbit hole. Just then Frans arrived with the lobster on a bed of lettuce from Mr McGregor's garden next door, and three homemade sauces. This was island fare at its finest. As he set things out, I asked him about the island community today.

"We have twenty here now. One is farmer from old island family. One new family is leaving."

"So few. Why don't people stay?"

"Dat is de goot question. The Trust don't want their business."

Surely, I thought, a landowner today could talk over a business plan and help find solutions, but, before I could ask, Frans had rushed back to the kitchen. He and his girlfriend were working flat-out to serve a roomful of hungry sailors. I tried the lobster. Perfection!

I turned back to the fellow sitting at the next table and asked him about the dogs and the rabbit hole. He was a doctor from Ireland who had come across the water for a few weeks' cruising in the Hebrides. With lots of interruption and many amusing asides from his crew, bit by bit the story came out. 'Toots' and 'Bramble' were his cocker spaniels. Bramble was a good-natured black bitch and the older of the two. Toots was liver and white, and the runt of her litter, yet she had tremendous zest. Just a whiff of something in the air and she was off like a hare.

The doctor continued. "We were walking in the old wood when she got onto a scent which drove her wild with excitement. She chased it so fast that she ran straight into a tree and knocked herself out. Before I could reach her she was back on her feet and off again." There was another break in the story while Frans's girlfriend, who looked even rosier cheeked than him, took their order. "One morning the two dogs went out for a run but hadn't come back by evening. I searched for them next day. Then put the word round the village and searched again the following day. There wasn't a sign of them and I began to assume the worst. Two days later, while I was having breakfast, I heard a whine at the back door. I opened it and there was Toots as thin as a rat and caked in mud. I could see right away she'd been stuck in a hole..."

Frans came back carrying the main dish – rabbit baked in a casserole with brandy, apricots and wild garlic from the woods – and set it down with a flourish. It was a chance to continue our chat about Canna.

"Why didn't the Trust help the new business?" I asked.

"They want fish farm but Trust don't want. See, on this islant is a clash of two, what you say, cultures." He hurried off to start making dessert for another table, leaving me even more curious than before. I swallowed some wine, murmured something to the great rabbit keeper in the sky and tasted the casserole. Spectacular! A few minutes later I felt a tug on my jersey. The Irish doctor was ready to continue his story of the two spaniels.

"Poor little scrap; she was in a terrible state. I picked her up and took her through to the kitchen where she drank a bowl of water and wolfed down some scraps. I called my brother over. When he arrived we took Toots outside and told her to find Bramble. She knew what we wanted all right. She was off like a shot. We followed her across the field to the old wood, where she waited for us to catch up, and then continued on through the trees to the far side, where there is an old stone wall. Under it was a big rabbit hole. A heavy stone had collapsed in the entrance leaving only a tiny gap. My brother put his head down and heard a whimper. The two of us cleared some of the wall away and then dragged the big stone out of the entrance. Bramble crawled out, so covered in mud I could hardly recognise her. She was on her last legs but she still managed to wag her tail."

"That little runt saved them both," I shook my head in admiration.

"She did that for sure. The two of them must have been trapped when the stone fell. Toots must have been stuck fast at first but after a few days she became so skinny that she managed to worm her way out." He smiled at the memory. "I love that dog."

Frans came back over to our tables to see how we were getting on. "Your casserole was fantastic," I told him. He looked genuinely happy as he cleared away the plates. "So what is this clash of cultures you spoke of?"

"That one," he moved round to my side of the table. "You see the people on this islant; they want to run a business. They want hostel. They want turbine. They want internet. They need long lease for bank. Same as on mainlant, ja? They need to be secure. They don't care so much if it is, how you say, messy. Tings lying about outsite. Satellite dish on roof. They don't notice. For the Trust, he want beautiful islant. No mess. No change. Like museum. Dat is clash." He disappeared into the kitchen with the empty plates returning a few minutes later with dessert.

"Some people from mainlant, they cannot manage islant life. They don't like to be tolt what they can and cannot do. So they leave.

267

But everyone on the islant help each other." He looked over at his girlfriend. "We love it here." He hurried back to the kitchen.

I inhaled the aroma of homemade sticky toffee pudding. Food didn't come much better than this. I took a large spoonful with ice cream. I wondered what Kyla would have said about the problems here. I thought I knew. 'It isn't easy but we have to befriend the grey in our society, or else we become oppressors ourselves.' That was how she felt about the awkward customers in communes and she had lived in plenty. But then who was being awkward here? I didn't know the whole story on Canna. As I thought it over, hot fudge sauce began to melt the ice cream. What I could see, perhaps, were two opposing dreams. The islanders wanted to develop their land and resources, they needed *security of tenure* to raise business loans and they wanted their voices to be heard. They wanted help not hindrance from the Trust. Their dream was not unlike that of the islanders on Eigg. The Trust, on the other hand, wanted to maintain a showcase island with its Hebridean landscape and seascape, wildlife, houses and archaeology. That was their purpose as an organisation which conserved Scotland's heritage; indeed, it was their duty. Unintentionally, it had become a battle of two dreams, which was leading to a kind of paralysis.

Without a bridge to unite them, John Campbell's own dream of a living, Hebridean culture, sharing its language, its traditions and its unique form of community management – a Gaelic culture that was based ultimately on kindness – was slipping away from Canna, just as the house, still much as he and Margaret Fey had left it, was fading and yellowing with neglect. What might that bridge look like? Without any other options on the table, incoming islanders are going to pursue those business opportunities which are known to be viable in the West Highlands – fish farms, tourism and energy from wind and tide. Perhaps the Trust considers these initiatives to be lacking in the communal core championed by Campbell or else likely to have negative impacts on the environment. The result was the impasse that the islanders had been telling me about. With a little imagination and some boldness of vision it is not impossible to imagine a variety of community-based ventures that are both profitable and sensitive to the environment. The Trust has the advantage of being able to plan at a larger scale. If it wishes to make John Campbell's dream a reality, if it wants to support deeply--rooted Gaelic traditions, if it seeks Smout's *positive communal response*, then it must forge an economically viable lifestyle for the islanders within these bounds, not just block their individual initiatives. It could start with the natural resources of the island and its surrounding waters and a round table gathering of Gaelic experts, island representatives, fisheries authorities and natural resource specialists.

I dipped in my spoon making sure it came up with the last dollop of fudge sauce. It was sinfully good. After a round of farewells and bon voyages, I rowed out into the harbour in a haze of fine Canna food, Islay whisky, Gaelic hospitality and gentle smirr. The second last thing I thought about before falling asleep was the little runt in the rabbit hole, digging and squeezing, digging and squeezing. What a dog. The last thing in my conscious mind was the eagle in the mist, holding its course when all was obscure.

The fog had hung on overnight, so I lazed in my bunk, reading stories of other wandering yachtsmen. At eight o'clock I went up to the cockpit to check again, and there were the hills of Rum standing out above the mist, picked out by morning sunshine. It was time to get underway. A couple of hours later I motored out of the harbour entrance in good visibility. There was a slight breeze from the southeast so I hoisted sail and drifted along the north side of Canna at about one knot. The swell was hardly noticeable, yet it heaved into a row of sea caves where it crashed like thunder. A thirty-foot Minke whale with its tell-tale hooked dorsal fin surfaced fifty yards off. It arched its back into a dive and disappeared, leaving a smooth footprint on the surface from the water pushed up by its tail. It repeated this seven more times as I drifted past, clearly enjoying rich feasting over the shallow banks. Another whale was blowing about a kilometre to the north. The wind died away completely as I watched. Reluctantly, I started the engine and steered a course of 310 degrees to take me towards Benbecula. Ten minutes later I spotted three fins. I turned off the engine and drifted closer. Two basking sharks swam lazily towards me, one following the other in a trance-like courtship. They were fully visible under the water and almost as long as *Molio*. They took up station at my stern. After a few minutes, the two mottled giants glided away and swam slowly into the distance. I started up the engine again and continued northwest. Once I was over deep water, a curtain came down on the wildlife show.

In the evening I spotted the chimneys of a power station on the southern shore of Loch Carnan, which confirmed my arrival off the south end of Benbecula. I steered *Molio* into Loch Uiskevagh, the whisky loch. Perhaps I should have been warned by its name as the Clyde Cruising Club's directions were misleading for once, nearly taking me onto the rocks. After creeping through a narrow channel amidst the skerries, I entered the inner loch, only to have my way blocked by a large fish farm which now filled the navigable sections. I squeezed round the farm and found my way into the inner sanctuary of Neavag Bay, a narrow gut on the northern side, where I anchored in two and a half fathoms.

Chapter 18

The Dark Laird

An eagle was flying over the upper end of the gut, soaring on wings as large as doors. As I watched, it came swooping down and settled on a nearby hillock. It was a sea eagle, and fully adult judging by the head and neck which were almost white. It sat there whilst I made some mid-morning coffee and then rose to its feet, took three slow strides, opened its wings and without so much as a flap lifted off. Circling, it continued to rise without effort until mobbed by a much smaller bird with a black cap to its white head, and narrow dark wings. The smaller bird had the flinging flare of a tern but was too big and dark for that. I consulted my bird book and identified it as an arctic skua. Head bent back it cried 'eee-yeow' showing off the white circle of its neck. Its mate answered the call and together they harassed the eagle until it cruised away in a wider arc.

I made up a packed lunch and rowed ashore to explore. At the eagle's hillock I found some large white pellets made of lambs' wool and bone fragments. About two miles to the west lay Rueval, the tallest hill on Benbecula although still hardly four hundred feet high. I set off across the bogs, which were as dry as those on Canna, navigating round the lily-filled lochans. Viewed from the top Benbecula spread out before me like a living map. Sea lochs penetrated into its core, interlacing with fresh lochans to create a mosaic of lovat-green islands and harebell-blue waters. To the west lay the village of Balivanich; to the north, east and south there was no sign of human habitation, just a remote, watery world that shimmered in the afternoon sun. I checked my mobile: still no signal. After a while, I walked down the southeast side of the hill looking for Bonnie Prince Charlie's Cave. It turned out to be a shallow recess under an overhanging crag with a floor of short green grass.

The cave, if we may call it that, might have offered some shelter from a shower on a windless day, but was fully exposed to the prevailing sou'westerlies, not to mention the fearsome West Highland midges. No wonder Bonnie Prince Charlie was heard to utter 'hideous cries and complaints' as he lay there for two days after his defeat at Culloden, hiding from government forces that were intent on hunting him down. I stretched out on the grass and looked over the Minch to the distant mountains of Skye. He had been saved from capture by Flora Macdonald of the clan Macdonald of Clanranald, by all accounts a wise, spirited and beautiful young woman in her twenties whose stepfather was none other than the commander of the local King's Militia. Disguised as 'Betty Burke' in a flowered linen gown with a grey-hooded cloak and woman's cap, the prince had passed as Flora's handmaiden. Under Flora's direction the odd couple made their way to a tiny inlet not far from where *Molio* was anchored. Avoiding government ships, they sneaked aboard a small skiff and were rowed by a crew of six boatmen out into the Little Minch where they picked up a breeze and sailed 'over the sea to Skye'.

It was hot in the afternoon sun and I soon fell asleep. On awaking, I watched a large eagle soaring in the blue sky above. Hunter or scavenger? What about Charles Edward Stuart – was he the bonnie prince or a 'young pretender'? He was a powerful man by all accounts, reckoned to be second to none on the hill. On the run for five months, he lived in caves and safe houses dodging a huge force of troops and facing down a thirty thousand pound reward for his capture, equivalent to four million pounds today. He traversed more than five hundred miles of rough terrain on foot, before being picked up by two French ships in Loch nan Uamh and carried back to France. In all that time not one Highlander betrayed him although many suffered in consequence.

The 1745 uprising tore our nation apart, even dividing families, as with Flora Macdonald's own family, and yet there are few Scots today whose hearts do not swell with pride in recalling the rising of the clans. As a nation we are mesmerised by our past. We glow with pride at our victories and seethe with indignation at the injustice of our defeats. I, too, am caught up in the battles but passion for our history can be as misleading as passion in daily life if it distracts from the pressing issues lying before us. It was high time on this journey to shake free of the past and turn to face the impending future. I wanted to get up close to a new pretender, one who set foot on our land at about the same time as the bonnie prince. Initially he was welcomed for his gifts and promise of greater ease and leisure time but as his power grew some warned of a threat to our freedom every bit as alarming as the ghosts of foreign troops that still haunt our small nation.

I call him the Dark Laird, the embodiment of the techno-industrial culture on whose shoulders the future of western civilisation now rests. Born at the start of the Industrial Revolution and equipped with formidable technology, the insatiable Laird first grasped hold of Britain's own natural resources and labour force and then marched forth to lay claim to those on the rest of the planet. Like any laird, he has his beneficial and unprincipled sides. Whether the tenants of planet Earth will succeed in controlling him is a question that remains unanswered.

The Dark Laird has a lot to offer. He promises solutions to human-kind's problems, such as cheap food, early detection of health issues and better traffic management. He frees urban slum-dwellers from their daily battle for survival by creating factory jobs. And that is just the start of things. He provides tools for creating completely new and fascinating commons that bring purpose and meaning to many lives: search engines, encyclopaedias and programming languages that enable the creation of digital commons of endless variety where virtual communities interact daily. This online world is already inhabited by 3.5 billion users and is increasing faster than ever.

Yet such gifts have not come without cost. In the face of unparalleled surveillance and enforcement operations, many fear that Orwell's nightmare of 1984 has finally caught up with us. They see privacy and respect, two hallmarks of civilised society, being undermined daily by the new technological powers. The boarding of *Molio* by armed customs officials was just one small example of a new philosophy that treats the entire population as potential suspects. The old partnerships between people and their chiefs, the collaborations born out of trust and mutual respect, are valued less and less. Some costs are more subtle. The Dark Laird has entered our homes and poked his nose into every corner, even arranging the hitherto private world of love and romance. Media channels are saturated with the corporate narrative of success: to be eminent or respected you need to emulate the rich, famous or good-looking. The psychology employed is hard to resist.

It can be argued that intelligent machines will free people from drudgery and danger, whilst enhancing our reach to a much wider and more relevant public. It is a partial truth. As the services enter one door, our self-reliance exits another. With it goes our self-confidence and self-respect, two hallmarks of living free. The Dark Laird then is the machine-assisted centralisation of decision-making and authority that substitutes for human judgement and independence of spirit. If the sacrifice demanded for his gifts is our personal freedom then it is indeed a Faustian bargain.

How does one counter his influence? One of the reasons I like older things – old cars, classic boats, traditional homes – is because they were designed and built with the individual user in mind. As a boy I enjoyed travelling in compartments on the older style of train carriage where I could adjust reading lights, heating, windows, screens and armrests, and go hunting for the buffet car. It was easier to tune the technology to my personal taste, assess the result, and then tweak again to obtain an even better result. In the process I grow fond of the gear. If it broke I could repair it, or find someone to help. It is worth hunting for modern technology that is easily customised. My favourite computer software allows me full control of its operations. So this tactic – about person-alising and interacting with equipment and surroundings – helps chip away at the strangling power of the Dark Laird.

When I track my position on *Molio*, I use paper charts and a variety of ancillary tools such as binoculars, compass, lead line on occasion, sketches of hills, the sound of surf, the position of stars and so on. I use a handheld GPS device in difficult conditions but I find that electronic instruments which deliver pre-cooked answers tend to cut me off from my environment. I am careful not to lean on them. Instead I look for tools that connect me to the natural world. It is a matter of personal judgement whether a particular tool is helpful in this respect. An ultrasonic detector which makes high-pitched cries of bats audible to the human ear connects the enthusiast to a nocturnal world of wonder, whereas the whirligig spinning madly on a mast top may provide an accurate wind speed but undermines habitual study of conditions on land and sea. So this is another tactic: choosing instruments that connect the user to the environment rather than those that replace the need for connection.

When I write up the day's events in *Molio*'s logbook, I use a large format notebook with plain paper. I jot down the numerical details – position, speed, wind, sea condition, twenty-four hour shipping forecast with ease. I don't need headings to tell me where to write. The open spaces on the page encourage me to add sketches and embellishments. Perhaps a thought will come to me over a mug of coffee in the cockpit or with a pint of beer in the pub which has nothing to do with sailing. Down it goes, sometimes spreading over several pages. I find the combination of plain paper and free-form writing allows my thoughts to flow naturally and creatively. By contrast formatted notebooks, prescribed forms and, worst of all, mind-numbing questionnaires with pre-cooked multiple-choices answers tend to compartmentalise my thinking and shut down my imagination. This third ploy then is about choosing materials and making decisions which enable creative expression.

Living free goes beyond the mere expression of individuality in our lifestyles. It is about enhancing our skills, deepening our connections, widening our engagement with surroundings and, most of all, cultivating an assertive participation in life that reflects who we are. It is an active process of self-development. It is a way of wresting back our independent and native human judgement from the Dark Laird.

I felt an itching in my nether regions and stripped off. A quick inspection revealed a tick embedded in a place it had no right to be – a present from Bonnie Prince Charlie. I laughed for the first time since leaving Eigg. A shallow laugh for, despite the sailing, the wonderful islands and the weaving of a story about freedom, I was numb inside and choosing not to think about Kyla. I didn't even know how to think about her. I took out the tweezers on my knife and pulled off the tick.

Chapter 19

Piloting a Craft Called Freedom

The morning's forecast was for a brisk northwesterly breeze with occasional rain later. I decided to sail north to Loch Maddy to buy some fresh supplies in the village. I motored out the gut and round the fish farm, watching the young salmon leap in their eternal quest for the open sea. Once clear of the reefs, I hoisted sail and beat up the coast, enjoying the punch of the waves. I tacked twice to work my way up Loch Maddy and used the engine to enter Charles Harbour where I picked up a free mooring. After stowing the mainsail I rowed over to the old pier with a bag of rubbish and two empty diesel cans. There were a few small creel boats moored nearby, but no sign of a fishing fleet. The warehouse next to the pier was roofless.

A fisherman in overalls was bent over a lobster pot with a border collie sitting obediently at his feet. I dropped my rubbish in a bin and walked over. He was stitching a repair in the netting.

"Lovely dog you have there," I announced, admiring the alert eyes now fastened on her master.

"Aye, my young one," he replied without pausing at his work.

"I was hoping you could tell me where to find diesel?"

He looked up now, and regarded me calmly from under bushy eyebrows. There was a glint in the eyes but great furrows across the brow, as if the eagle inside had puzzled too long on life's ambiguities. "Just along at the shop." He pointed the way with his net needle. "You'll be off one of the yachts?"

"That green ketch," I glanced over at *Molio*. "I'm just stopping for some provisions."

"Ach well, I saw you tacking in just now. I was going out for some crabs myself, but I thought it too risky."

"You have an open boat?" I asked.

"That's mine." He pointed at a blue creel boat with a tiny wheelhouse at the front, just large enough for two men. Aft of the cuddy was space for stacking creels and operating a power winch to haul up the pots. "In the big boats we would go out in anything but on my own in that wee thing... Well, it's all right provided nothing goes wrong; but if your gear gets fouled, it can get serious quickly."

"Where are the big boats now?" I asked.

"You could walk across this harbour on herring drifters when I was a boy. This pier was humming – net makers, chandlers, tradesmen, engineers. Ach, they all left after the herring disappeared. That was back in the sixties. We still had a few trawlers mind, but they were decommissioned by the EU," he spat on the pier barely hiding his disgust. "What you see is all we have."

I shook my head. It seemed to be the same everywhere. As I went to pick up my cans, the fisherman stopped me.

"You'll be wanting a lift?"

"Uh, thanks but I'll be fine."

"It won't take long and it will save you humping the cans." The collie looked up at me expectantly.

"That would be grand, then."

We walked over to his van and the three of us got in front with the collie in the middle. I filled up with diesel and then went over to the shop to begin on the supplies. The woman behind the counter was chatting to the fisherman.

"Just a wee bit fierce this morning, John, to be going out?"

"Not at all! It's a fine day for fishing but I've just got one or two things to be doing to the boat."

"Ah but really it is the volcanic ash that will be holding you back now John, we know it." The shopkeeper was looking for a rise. It wasn't so long since volcanic ash from Iceland had been grounding aircraft. She wasn't going to get one from John.

"You can't be too careful of your engine right enough." He gave me a wink.

John took me down to the pier and saw me off in the dinghy. I watched the two of them as I rowed out to *Molio*. The fisherman bent back to his work on the creels and to his bittersweet memories of an island life that could never return. The collie gazed adoringly at his master.

On board, I made up a cheese sandwich with fresh tomato and cucumber and enjoyed coffee made with island milk. In the afternoon I rowed ashore to get some exercise and ended up next to the modern ferry terminal, where there was a visitor centre. It contained a shop, museum, gallery and café and looked as new and thriving as the fishing harbour was old and decaying. I sat down for a cappuccino and muffin, aware that a few centuries earlier I would have been sitting inside a storage house that contained the salt used to cure herring. Tourism, it seemed, had become the mainstay of the island economy. After a while I walked down to the old hotel to organise a bath and my laundry. The manager couldn't help with either; he even refused to let me use the hotel telephone. It was odd to be in a land with the most hospitable people on Earth, yet come up against an unnecessary stone wall like that.

When we were boys my mother always set an extra place at the table, just in case. She taught me the 'Gaelic Rune of Hospitality':

> *I saw a stranger yestreen:*
> *I put food in the eating place,*
> *Drink in the drinking place,*
> *Music in the listening place;*
> *And in the sacred name of the Triune*
> *He blessed myself and my house,*
> *My cattle and my dear ones.*
> *And the lark said in her song,*
> *Often, often, often*
> *Goes the Christ in the stranger's guise.*

Too many strangers today perhaps? Or were the Gaelic customs retreating before the economic imperatives of mainland life – the welcome to strangers now conditional on manna from heaven? Probably it was just someone's bad day.

Back on board I listened to the shipping forecast. Storms had been tracking across the North Atlantic to Iceland without a break bringing gale force winds to St Kilda. June was coming to an end and this was supposed to be the period with least storms. My best chance of sailing to St Kilda would be in the next week. I was poised. I just needed a window in the gales. I looked at the chart. My course would take me westwards through the Sound of Harris from the sheltered waters of the Little Minch to the untamed Atlantic Ocean.

The Sound between Harris and North Uist is a broad but shallow passage. It is a labyrinth of islets and reefs, banks and shallows, wrecks and sunken rocks, with twisting channels and swift treacherous crosscurrents that would bewilder the most experienced of seafarers. It presented an almost insurmountable challenge to any vessel determined to pass through to the Atlantic side. Except that today, as *Molio*'s pilot, I am not alone. A thousand seafarers have gone before and marked out the navigable channels. I studied the sailing directions carefully. To reach the island of Berneray I would enter the sound by the Cope Passage. The channel was narrow with little tolerance for error, and at two positions I needed to turn at right angles to follow smaller branch channels. Turning at the wrong point would put me on the rocks. Navigation was feasible only because there were seventeen buoys marking the route. With the spring tide running at five knots in places, it would be imperative not to let my attention wander. Standing off the outer Fairway Buoy, I studied the sailing directions one more time. They mentioned a 'half tide rock'. I consulted the large scale Admiralty chart; a small black cross, hardly noticed before, lit up red in my mind. For this task I wanted every aid I could lay my hands on. I switched on the handheld GPS and placed it next to the chart. Binoculars were hanging on the cabin door, a hand-bearing compass slung around my neck.

Molio began to roll as the gusts blew her back from the sheltered waters of the Sound. It was time to go. I engaged forward gear and motored towards the first navigation mark, a green conical buoy, which I left to starboard. A minute later, I was surrounded by skerries and searching for a buoy that marked the turn onto a subsidiary channel. Just at that moment, a ferry from Harris cut across in front of me. I turned hard to port and entered an even narrower channel behind it. There was no room to turn *Molio* round if I lost my way; I was committed. The ferry soon left me behind, and I slowed to follow the waving line of beacons and buoys, checking off each on the chart as we passed. Whichever direction I looked, the expanse of sea was broken by rocky islets butting out from the water and by naked rocks awash and all but invisible. *Molio* bucked in the squalls.

It would have been impossible to pass without the many navigational aids. I looked around at the shoals and mentally saluted those who had made it possible. It was a collaboration that had stretched over the better part of a century: yachtsmen working with their sailing clubs had prepared the sketch charts, transit bearings and instructions; local fishermen set up perches and located safe passages; the Northern Lights Authority, Crown Estate and local Council placed buoys and lights; the Admiralty prepared detailed charts marking depths; and the international community developed the GPS technology. The outcome was a network of safe passages to harbours and anchorages in Harris and North Uist and an open gateway to the Atlantic.

The water by now was alarmingly shallow. I located the half-tide rock. It was awash, which meant there should be enough water to pass over the shallows of the next section, always assuming that the notorious shifting sands had not accumulated there in recent months. I turned hard to starboard and held my breath. *Molio* glided over the sandy bottom. I made for the next mark, a red can buoy, which I left to port. From there I lined up to pass Drowning Rock on the starboard side, before making a final turn into Bays Loch on the eastern flank of Berneray where I picked up a mooring.

In the evening, I took a glass of wine up to the cockpit and looked around at the unfamiliar world. Soon I would be making my way through the reefs and out to the Atlantic Ocean. It seemed incredible that this shallow sea, packed with shoals and skerries, could be traversed in comparative safety from any direction. It brought it home to me that the Sound of Harris was itself a great common, one dedicated to navigation and recreation. Over the generations the number of navigable sections had steadily increased. There were no restrictions applied on who could use the Sound, no prohibitions, no legislation or unnecessary regulation to interfere with people's passage across it, and no charges levied so far. The result was a navigable passageway of great value to many people. This kind of long-term collaboration amongst users and experts surely represents the ideal way to create and develop any resource, whether on land, at sea, or online.

The inner seas of the West of Scotland provide a sense of limitless freedom in great abundance. It is why my father loved to sail here. He craved to get away from the relentless pressures of the surgery to a place where he could be himself. At the heart of the Hebridean Seas, which make up the greatest natural common in Britain that remains open to the public, are three things: the freedom to be yourself, a resource to use and enjoy, and a community in which to belong. It has taken generations to build; what a waste if it were undermined now by over-privatisation and unnecessary regulation.

Standing in the cockpit next morning I watched as gusty squalls raced each other across the sunlit bay in strips of dark blue. *Molio* began dancing, jigging and swinging as one of them rushed past. Berneray basked in the unexpected sunshine, a few miles beyond lay the dark hills of Harris. I went below to make breakfast. It took two hours but it didn't seem to matter. I wasn't sure what day of week it was. That didn't matter either. The bilge pump came on twice; that mattered, but I was learning to live with it. I rowed over to the little harbour and walked to the top of Borve Hill, where I found a weak signal on my mobile. It gave me enough reception to ring some friends living on Harris and we arranged to meet up that evening. There were some messages from other friends and family. I walked down the hill and made my way across the Hebridean machair, a meadow of summer flowers and bumblebees, to the Atlantic coast. Up on the dunes I looked over a stretch of coral sand to a scene that glowed with the luminosity of a Dutch masterpiece: glazed jade in the clear waters of the shore, sea-green beyond dappled by the master's hand with silver splashes of sun. A scattering of dark islands added theatrical depth. Somewhere over the far horizon lay St Kilda. I wished Kyla was standing beside me. She would have loved this soft green island with its wildflowers and smiling folk. I shook my head, annoyed at my sentimentality, and headed back across the island.

On board *Molio*, I made a mug of tea and set it down on the saloon table next to the charts. I studied my route across the Sound one more time while waiting for the tide to rise sufficiently for a safe passage over the sandbank to the ferry channel. As the hour approached, I went up to the cockpit and took a deep breath of pure Hebridean air. I needed to focus now. The latest storm had been tracking across from Rockall to the Faeroes and in its wake it looked as if there might be a lull coming. The forecast for the next twenty-four hours was for north or northwest-erly winds of force five or six, perhaps seven at times, backing west or southwest and decreasing later with moderate or good visibility. The only anchorage at St Kilda was in Village Bay, which was exposed to the east and south. Southwest was fine but should the wind back further round it would be essential to clear out. My plan was to move to Leverburgh on the southern shore of Harris that afternoon, and to be ready to depart the next morning if conditions improved as expected. At four o'clock I motored over the sandbank, timing my progress to swing in behind the afternoon ferry from Berneray to Leverburgh. The cloud base was lower and the wind was gusting more heavily, but with my route marked by the ferry's passing I had no difficulty passing through the skerries and following the buoys to South Harris. I anchored on the west side of the pier in four fathoms, putting out twelve fathoms of chain.

Shortly before 6 p.m. I heard a shout. Looking through the porthole I spotted a tall figure at the end of the pier waving. It was Alastair. I quickly grabbed my bag of laundry and rowed over to the slip. We hadn't seen each other for twenty years, but, close up, I recognised at once the slightly stooped figure which had something of the heron about it, a clever heron that had a generous smile around the bill. There was a difference in him though, which took me a while to pin-point. Twenty years earlier he had been balanced on the edge of two worlds, the Oxford cloisters of linguistics and the windswept self-sufficiency of the western isles. As he took the dinghy's painter I could see from the assurance in his manner that he was an islander now. I clambered out and grasped the proffered hand.

"Welcome to the land of the free," he grinned.

"Tracked you down at last, Alastair."

"Come on, we'll carry the dinghy to the top."

He chucked my bag of laundry in the boot and drove us the short distance to their house which was tucked in between the towering crags of South Harris and the wild Sound below. Aileen greeted me at the doorstep with a warm smile and a hug. She fitted the Gaelic mould more closely than her husband, having the darker, almost Mediterranean features of the Pict. If Alastair was the heron of the family, then she was the delicate petrel, surviving the Atlantic storms by nesting deep inside its burrow. But then, again, my imagination was clearly running away from me. I'd been at sea too long.

She took my laundry and began organising the men. "Drop your stuff in the corner and come by the fire," she suggested to me. "Alastair, fix the man a drink while I see to the dinner." There was so much space and warmth in their home compared to my little cabin.

I followed Alastair upstairs to his eyrie, which had been built from a single fallen Douglas Fir. It commanded a view across the Sound to Uist and westward to the open sea. I looked out at the view while Alastair fixed drinks. That would be my next passage, out there beyond Pabbay and Shillay. It would take me into the vast Atlantic Ocean which, at that moment, seemed dark, moody and heaving with primordial power. It was a realm of dreams and drownings.

"Sherry?" Alastair asked.

"Thanks, this is mighty civilised." I took the proffered glass. "Did you happen to hear the forecast today? I'm thinking about sailing to

Hirta tomorrow morning."

"Let's take a look." He sat down at the console and pulled up a series of isobar charts that displayed the predicted pressure patterns for the next 4 days in twelve hour leaps. More depressions would be tracking their way across the Atlantic, passing between Iceland and the north of Scotland, right over St Kilda. At the same time high pressure was building to the south, which was slowing down their arrival. "The isobars are looking slack for the next thirty-six hours. You should be fine."

"Could you print that for me?"

"Sure, why not take your shower and I'll sort it out?"

I knocked back the sherry and went in search of the bathroom where I relished the unusual sensation of hot water and soap. Dinner was waiting for me when I emerged in my last clean shirt. I looked over the fine table with its crystal glass and silver cutlery. An hors d'oeuvres of fresh kipper pâté on toast was already out and waiting. I remembered that Aileen had been head chef at the Lochview Hotel on the mainland; Alastair had been in charge of wines. When they acquired the hotel it was a derelict ruin, with sheep sheltering in the dining room. Somehow they'd managed to turn it into an elegant hotel. Well, if tomorrow was to be my last day, then at least I would dine well tonight. I sat down to a most amazing meal: Alastair served a crisp white wine with the hors d'oeuvres, followed by something herbal and delicious in mushrooms, then there was slow-cooked beef casserole with new potatoes and garden cabbage accompanied by claret. This was followed in turn by plum crumble and cream, and finished off with Clava brie and Isle of Mull cheddar on oatcakes. Throughout it all, I was regaled with stories of island life and accounts of the natural history of the Sound of Harris with its beds of seagrass, seal nurseries and seabird colonies. Aileen told me that the waters of the Sound are so rich that scallops grow to harvesting size in three months, not the usual two years. A diver friend handpicked them. She and Alastair found they were firmer, yet more tender and better tasting, than those scraped off the seabed by Stornoway dredgers. She thought it was because of stress in the dredged shellfish which spoilt the tender flesh.

The Sound of Harris can surely be celebrated for its wildlife and wild food. But Alastair told me that the first fish farm had already been given the go ahead to be moored just opposite Leverburgh, between an island where the grey seals haul out to pup, and another with a colony of cormorants. It was an invitation to conflict between farmers and wildlife. The locals of course knew the difference: for their own kitchens they wouldn't touch the farmed fish.

Sometime later, Alastair dropped me at the pier. I rowed back to *Molio* conscious of the need to sober up and make a decision. I poured myself a large glass of water and took it up to the cockpit. A solo passage to St Kilda was not something to undertake lightly. I recognised the risks. An unexpected lurch, a careless slip on a wet surface, a sudden squall or a rogue wave were all it took to spell trouble. But the freedom I was looking for came not from avoiding danger, but from mastering the skills to overcome it. Safe sailors, like safe climbers, know their capabilities and select their gear with care. They may stretch and extend those abilities through experience, but they never lose sight of what is and isn't reasonable. When to go, which route to take, at what point to rope up or reduce sail, and when to turn back. These are judgement calls. Above all a good sailor is one who develops good judgement.

Chapter 20

Flight of The Fulmar

Something was thumping in the night as *Molio* rocked on the occasional wave finding its way round the skerries and into the anchorage; it was a heavy thump, which could be felt as much as heard. I got up to see if the spare anchor in the fo'c'sle was banging against the side of the hull, but it was fine. On deck, the rigging and spars were secure. The thumping stopped and I went back to sleep. Now it had woken me again. I lay in bed trying to figure it out. The electric bilge pump chose just that moment to switch on. I put two and two together. It must be *Molio*'s lead keel. It was knocking from side to side and pumping water up into the bilges at the same time. Perhaps the grounding on Eigg had weakened the keel bolts. I'd heard stories of such things – keel bolts corroding through, lead keels dropping off in mid ocean, yachts turning turtle in the night with the loss of all hands. If I was right it would be madness to continue. My solo passage to St Kilda was off. Instead I would have to find somewhere to lift *Molio* from the water; somewhere close by that I could reach before the keel dropped off. Then there would be the repairs. The problem was that I didn't have that kind of money. I wrestled with the worry for a minute then sprang out of bed and climbed up the ladder to the cockpit. The thumping continued but it was louder. A movement caught my eye. I looked at the tiller. Some strange combination of tide and waves was pushing the rudder back and forth, causing the solid iron tiller to bash against the horse – a heavy iron rail that carries the mainsheet across the boat from one side to the other. I lashed the tiller in place. The noise stopped and my dark thoughts dispersed like mist under a rising sun. And looking around the anchorage with relief I saw that the sun was indeed rising, bringing life and colour to the Sound. A steady wind was blowing from the north, ideal for a westward sea passage. I went below and put the kettle on.

As I was dressing a text message came through from Kyla:

Take care if you go to St Kilda.

I frowned and tapped the barometer. It fell two points reminding me of the sailor's rhyme:

> *Long foretold, long last;*
> *Short warning – soon past.*

If something was brewing it would be here soon. With a roar the twin diesels on *Sea Dog II* came to life. She was a patrol boat that did day trips over to St Kilda. Alastair had told me she could carry a dozen passengers at over twenty knots. Dropping her mooring she puttered over to the pier for refuelling. On impulse I jumped into the Avon dinghy to follow her. I wanted one last piece of weather information. Up on the pier I found a second smaller patrol boat already moored along the far side. The skipper had an undercut hair style and the hunted look of a prisoner on the run.

"Do you take parties out to St Kilda?" I asked.

"Aye we do."

The large skipper of *Sea Dog II* climbed onto the pier and muscled in: "So *you* are the one taking cruises to St Kilda now?"

"I said 'we'," apologised the undercut skipper. Evidently he was the newcomer to the business.

"Are you the guys who saw the killer whales the other day?" Again I directed my enquiry at the undercut skipper.

"Yes, that was us." This time he managed a smile.

It was too much for the large skipper: "So *you* are the one who found the whales," he butted in with dripping sarcasm.

"Well, I did see them," replied the lesser skipper trying to hold on to some dignity.

"We sent them to you," replied the big skipper with a proud smirk.

I concealed a laugh with difficulty, but it was too much for the undercut skipper who headed for the sanctity of his boat. I turned to the big chap: "Did you get the forecast this morning?"

"Nothing to worry about," he answered carelessly.

"They were talking about force 4 to 6, possibly 7 at first."

"They always add a point on," he replied with a shrug.

I nodded. Sometimes the forecasters did err on the high side. And this guy was at sea most days of the week; he would know. As I rowed back to *Molio* I noticed the lesser skipper climbing into a 4WD on the pier; it set off taking the road leading north. Scrambling on board, I hauled up the dinghy deflated it halfway and lashed it securely to the deck rails. I didn't want to lose it on the crossing if the wind got up. I put on a harness that would take a safety line, then slipped on a deflated life jacket and checked that the ripcord was free. Anticipating spray if not rain, I climbed into Barry's heavy-weather sailing trousers and pulled on a pair of sailing boots.

Molio appeared to be edging slowly towards the pier. I started the engine and hauled in the Rocna anchor which had snared a large ball of kelp. I wondered if this was a weakness in the new design of anchor. Part of the problem with anchoring in the Hebrides is the amount of seaweed, that and the presence of dodgy old moorings in the few weed-free locations. I cleared the kelp ball and secured the anchor firmly on deck. This was easier said than done as *Molio* was being pushed by wind and tide; it meant rushing back and forth from anchor to engine controls so as to adjust her position in the tight confines of the harbour. Once ready, I hauled up the mainsail and steered *Molio* round the red buoy at the entrance from where I followed the Leverburgh Channel to the northwest. Passing through the outer channel that lies between the isles of Stromay and Ensay, I put her onto a more westerly course and let fly the yankee, keeping five turns furled. As we cleared the sheltering arm of Harris the gusts grew stronger: there was no need to raise the mizzen as *Molio* had plenty of sail up. With the engine off she surged forward at over six knots, passing little gatherings of guillemots and razorbills. Gulls, kittiwakes and terns flew overhead as we took the passage between Shillay and Pabbay. I wondered what lay ahead. Would St Kilda prove an anti-climax to my ventures in *Molio*, just one more Hebridean isle on my journey, or might my hunch that it harboured the answer, a sailor's wind to carry me out of the midlife doldrums, prove right after all. I looked westward across the lonely sea. Beyond this gateway, there were another forty-three nautical miles to go. With luck, I would be on a close reach all the way.

It was time to set up the self-steering gear. I hooked the two ropes coming from the servo rudder on to the tiller and adjusted the wind vane. After a bit of fiddling I was satisfied that *Molio* was maintaining a good average direction. I looked around again. The horizon was featureless, just a smudged pencil line to mark the transition between air and water but, provided the visibility held up, I should see St Kilda appearing above the horizon in three or four hours' time.

Strangely there was no Saint Kilda and the origin of the archipelago's name is uncertain. Centuries ago, it was known as Hirta which today is the name given to the largest island. The origin of that name is also ambiguous. Some think it comes from the Norse word for shepherd, *Hirt*, indicating a long history of sheep on the island or from the word for stags, *Hirtir*, because of its antlered shape. In ancient Gaelic *irt* signified death, whilst *h-iar-tìr* meant land of the west. Hirta might also have been known as the abode of ancestors, which would accord with the Celtic myth of an island of spirits beyond the western horizon. That felt in tune with the mood of the sea.

The sun gave way to cloud which thickened as the wind strengthened. Soon *Molio* was tearing along, bounding over the wave tops, swooping into the troughs, charging across the seas at seven knots. The rigging hummed, the waves roared and I shouted fragments of half-remembered sea shanties into the wind. A fulmar flew up to *Molio* from astern, gliding low over the waves, turning in close with wings in a vertical plane just clearing the surface. It swooped under the crest of a wave and zipped upwards in turbulence to almost stall, only to fall into a glide on the far side. Others came past, some performing a half circle before flying off. Occasionally one would perform a complete circle. I shouted with pleasure at each new trick by these pocket-sized albatrosses. One approached in a daring and beautiful low level glide. I let out a great whoop of appreciation. It swerved over the crest of an advancing wave, and I whooped again. It lifted up sharply to avoid the next wave, and at each mad stunt I shouted again with pleasure. The fulmar appeared to appreciate my joining in because it stayed for some time. For a few moments it felt as if we were on the same wavelength out there in the Atlantic, as if we were playing a game together and enjoying each other's company. With a final graceful flypast, she turned, waggled her tail and flew off south. Later Aileen told me that the small fishing boats threw fulmars the odd scrap. So much so that Alastair thought their population had increased. Maybe my fulmar was only after fish, but it felt that we'd been dancing together over the waves. Dancing our joy, dancing our freedom, dancing a shared life on the untamed ocean.

No land was visible now, nor any boats. The sun was well hidden by clouds, leaving me without any visual means of checking my position. I used the compass to keep course. The pocket GPS showed our position as a dot off the northwest coast of Scotland. I looked again at the Admiralty chart. The rocky islet of Haskeir should be visible now. I searched to the south across the grey backs of Atlantic waves that were tossing *Molio* lightly aside before trundling on to the far beaches of the Hebrides. Eventually I spotted it, a tiny dark grey speck in a huge grey sea. I knew from the description by a bird survey team that it had a promontory at the northeast end which rose to over sixty feet, and that this was separated by flat rocks from a hill of one hundred and twenty feet at the southwest end. In the central part there was a natural rock bridge with two sea arches and a collapsed cavern. It was a favourite haunt of the Atlantic grey seal, the larger cousin of the common seal that had befriended Kyla. The big greys love the rocky fastnesses of these remote Atlantic skerries. Islanders down the ages had loved them too, but mainly for the chance to fill up their jars and bottles with oils rendered from seal blubber.

One of the most famous places for sealing was a sprinkling of skerries half a mile to the southwest of Haskeir, known locally as Cousamul. Boats used to come from crofting townships near the Butt of Lewis for the annual seal raid which took place just after calving. A raid in the early eighteenth century was brought to life by the author and explorer Martin Martin.

'When this crew is quietly landed, they surround the passes, and then the signal for the general attack is given from the boat, and so they beat them down with big staves. The seals at this onset make towards the sea with all speed, and often force their passage over the necks of the stoutest assailants who aim always at the forehead of the seals, giving many blows before they be killed, and if they be not hit exactly, on the front, they contract a lump on their forehead, which makes them look very fierce; and if they get hold of the staff with their teeth, they carry it along to sea with them. The natives told me, that several of the biggest seals lose their lives by endeavouring to save their young ones, whom they tumble before them towards the sea. I was told also that 320 seals, young and old, have been killed at one time in this place.'

The right to hunt seals on Cousamul belonged to a farmer on Uist. Protecting such rights was an old tradition going back at least as far as St Columba in the sixth century. At that time the Monastery of Iona had rights to sealing on a nearby island which enabled it to furnish the monks both with food and oil, the latter being essential for lightening the dark days of winter. In his *Life of Saint Columba*, Adamnan tells how the Saint despatched two brethren to catch a robber who had come to the island, hiding by day under his boat, which he covered in hay, and killing enough young seals by night to fill the boat. It must be one of the earliest recorded examples of a hunting reserve being raided.

I wondered if the sealing on Cousamul might have given rise to stories of the legendary selkies, who lived as seals in the waves but shed their skins to become human on land. I imagined a young fisher laddie who loved listening to the singing of seals on their rocks in the evening. One fateful day he accompanied his father on his first seal hunt. With the others, he clubbed the seals that he had loved until they stopped moving, then removed their skin and blubber with a knife. As can happen, one of the seals was merely stunned and after being flayed and flensed she recovered. Her large eyes looked up at the slayer and, tail still intact, she swam off leaving him holding onto her skin. A day like that would surely be burnt into the young man's subconscious leaving the feeling, perhaps, that he had killed a creature that was half human.

I had told my nightmarish fantasy to Kyla, who is heedful of the dark soul in man. She had come up with a more romantic explanation. We had been sitting in the lounge at home, enjoying the twilight, and telling each other strange and spooky stories. After hearing my bleak notions, she'd told me of a family, the MacCodrums of North Uist, who were known as *Sliochd nan Ròn* or the 'children of the seals' as they claimed to be descended from a union between fisherman and selkie. They had used kayaks covered in skin and wore waterproof jackets made from seal gut. Perhaps they had learnt those skills from a family of Lapps who used Haskeir as a summer camp. One group of Sea Sami was in the habit of coming by kayak from Norway to Shetland and on down to the Hebrides, bringing their boats ashore on Haskeir. Here they would have had ready access to fish, birds' eggs and seals. There was fresh water to be had in the spring, and being so far from land they were unlikely to be disturbed by islanders. This was the selkie story as Kyla related it:

'One still day in late October, a party of fishermen landed on a skerry off Uist to attack the seals lying with their young on the hill above the rocks. Young Callum was first out the boat and up to the hill, leaving the others to haul the boat above the surf. But no sooner had he left the boat than the tide took a turn and the surf started thundering into the one landing beach. The others pushed out in a panic and just made it clear of the breaking waves in time. After a few hours sitting off and trying to get in, it began to grow dark. The crew signalled to Callum that they would return next morning and set off for the main island. Callum found shelter for himself in a cleft in the rocks and wrapped himself as best he could in his coat. A few hours after the moon had risen he awoke with a start to the sound of singing, but when he looked he thought he saw not a seal singing but a woman. He approached quietly and there by the sea sat a beautiful girl covered in nothing but the long tresses of her own flaming hair which she was combing through with her fingers as she sang. Callum stared, brow knitted in puzzlement, mouth open in wonder. Draped on the rock beside the girl was a soft pelt, grey and dappled as lichen. Callum was as quick in the mind as he was nimble on his feet. He crept closer, all the time keeping out of sight, until he was close enough to stretch forward and snatch the skin away. The girl gave a sharp cry and stood up in alarm.

"Give me my skin," she implored him. "Please, I cannot live without my skin." Her voice was musical and her solemn dark eyes wept salt tears into the ocean.

But Callum had drunk deeply of love and could not give her up. "Come home with me and I will give you the finest shawl in all the land and orchids for your hair." Taking off his jacket, he laid it at her feet saying "This is yours and all my protection besides."

Realising that she must become an inhabitant of the land, the selkie saw that she must indeed place her life in this strange man's hands. She knelt and picked up the coat but would not let him touch her. "I will come with you then but on one condition." Callum nodded his readiness to accept. "You shall never hunt my folk again." She looked at him with unyielding determination.

"I swear," said Callum.

In the morning the fishermen returned and you can imagine their surprise at what they found. They rowed Callum and his selkie back to his village where soon the couple were married. As his woman, she did everything a wife should do about the house and went on to bear Callum three fine sons to carry on the fishing. His love for her was boundless but it was coldly returned. And when Callum was away fishing and the tide was high and the surf was thundering ashore, she would go down to the rocks where sometimes a large dog seal would appear in the water before her. Years passed this way until one day, while Callum was away from home with his parents, one of her children made a discovery. Under a stack of corn was a dry seal skin covered in dust. He ran to his mother to show her his prize. She took it and held it to her heart, heaving great sobs of relief. She forgot about the hens that needed feeding and the cow that needed milking and the fire that needed tending. She forgot about her husband. She knelt and kissed her sons and up and ran to the sea as fast as the wind. And as she ran, all she could think about were her seal sisters singing and the great dog seal that she loved waiting for her. When the fisherman arrived home and saw what had happened, he too ran to the sea fearing all the time what he would find. Down at the rocks there was no sign of his wife. He called and called to her, up and down the shore, until finally he lay down on the rocks in despair. It was then that a head appeared in the sea next to him. The seal regarded him quietly and he looked back into those dark eyes that he knew so well. In the distance a second head appeared. The selkie dived and surfaced a few moments later next to the dog seal and together they swam out to sea...'

The rocks of Haskeir slipped astern of *Molio* leaving only their stories mingling with the sigh of the wind. Thinking back to that evening with Kyla, listening again to her musical voice in my ear, I felt there was something I might have missed at the time. That gentle seal woman had been trapped by young Callum. Was that what she had been trying to tell me? That you cannot force a woman to stay with you, to share your skin, without destroying her own and that which you love?

Molio leaned right over on a wave under the weight of a gust and I heard the crash of cutlery below. Water surged along the lee deck. The wind had been building steadily and *Molio* was being pressed too far. The swell, too, had been building. The short waves coming down from the north were fifteen feet high and driving into a longer and deeper swell coming in from the southwest, creating a moving seascape of hills. Looking west towards the horizon, I saw that flecks of white spume were being whipped off breaking crests all across the leaden seas. I zipped up my sailing jacket. Again *Molio* was pushed over, this time burying her lee rail in the sea. I should have taken in a reef at Leverburgh; it had been a mistake to listen to the guy on *Sea Dog II*. I checked my position on the GPS. We were making more leeway than I'd expected. I'd been heading for Boreray, the northernmost Island of St Kilda, but with this rate of drift I'd be lucky to make Hirta. I tweaked the lower rope on the self-steering gear and brought *Molio* up into the wind a little more. Her bow kicked into the waves. Spray was drenching me. A denser cloud scudded across the sea bringing even stronger winds. The shrouds thrummed. The sea was building more now and *Molio* was over-canvassed. I'd been in strong winds with my father. I needed to get two reefs in on the main.

I put on the engine to help *Molio* face into the wind, and waited for a lull before furling in two more turns on the yankee. Then I attached a line to my safety harness in preparation for reefing the main. My plan was to bring *Molio* back into the wind, using the engine at slow ahead, and then go forward to drop the sail by a few feet. I would then tie down the sail using a reef cringle in the luff edge of the sail, repeat the same at the leech edge of the sail, and then move along the boom tying off the seven reefing points in-between. I got up and lurched along the wet deck as it heaved under my feet, watching the water rushing down the lee deck. The massive boom jerked about under the flapping sail. Up at the mast I clung onto the rigging and circled round to the front. The yankee shuddered under the weight of a gust, belly swollen and sheets bar taught, pulling *Molio* right over. The decks heaved under a wave and I glanced up to see the masts arcing across torn skies. I clung on grimly as we lunged down the far side: the bowsprit ploughed into the next wave and water cascaded past my feet. Seizing a quiet moment I hooked my safety line to a mast fitting. As I did a fulmar came skimming in close to the shrouds watching. I found the mainsail halyard and eased it off; the sail rapidly came down a yard and billowed out under the pressure of wind. I made fast and moved back round the mast where I succeeded in tying down the leading edge of the sail. Unclipping my harness, I made my way back along the deck, handhold by handhold, holding onto the boom when *Molio* leaned far over in a gust, hoping all the while the mainsheet would hold. I reached the safety of the cockpit and re-clipped to the guard wire. I threaded a line through the reefing eye in the leech of the sail, getting ready to tie it down. But as I worked, *Molio* came off her heading and the wind caught the mainsail; it bellied out with a power that was beyond my ability to control. I let it go and sat down in the cockpit, bracing my feet on the opposite seat and rested for a minute. Twice more I tried to get in the reef. On the last occasion I came closest. I gunned the engine to bring *Molio* up into the wind, threaded in the rope and pulled the sail down to the boom. I almost had it secure when the boat swung a few points through the wind, and the yankee ballooned out on the reverse tack pulling *Molio's* bows with it. The mainsail filled, flogged and pulled out of my hands. I just had time to drop down into the floor of the cockpit when the boom slammed across with enough force to knock me over the side. The bow smashed into a wave and a half ton of water came crashing along the deck. I looked up and saw a yard-long rip in the mainsail. *Molio* leaned right over as the wind caught her, laid off before it and went thundering downwind. I pulled hard on the tiller to bring *Molio* back onto the wind, heaving with both hands. She fought back like a tiger. I could feel the tiredness in my arms from struggling with the mainsail. The waves were angry now with streaks of foam. I cursed the Met Office chart with its slack isobars. Where in hell had this storm come from?

The gusts grew heavier, *Molio* was coming off the big seas awkwardly and being blown hard over in the gusts. Yet she felt sluggish on the tiller. What I needed was another hand to take the helm. My arm muscles were shaking and my mind was beginning to wander. I remembered that the St Kildans had their own way of dealing with storms.

The steward of Kilda, who lives in Pabbay, is accustomed in time of storm to tie a bundle of puddings made of the fat of sea fowl to the end of his cable, and lets it fall into the sea behind the rudder; this, he says, hinders the waves from breaking, and calms the sea; but the scent of the grease attracts the whales, which put the vessel in danger.

I didn't have any pudding. The easy option would be to turn and run before the sea to the Monarchs, a group of islands some 30 nautical miles to the southeast. Martin Martin had tried just that when his boat was caught up in a storm on the way to St Kilda in 1697. They hadn't managed it but I had a more favourable wind. I'd have to watch like a hawk for the outlying reefs. I managed to reset the self-steering vane and went below to get the chart. I was brought to an abrupt halt by the sight of water above the floorboards. That was when I first felt fear. As we heaved over on a wave, the water reached up to the bunks. I had left the automatic bilge pump switched on; we must be taking on water at one hell of a rate. That bloody keel must be pumping in water just like Packie had said right at the start in Crosshaven.

I could feel my control slipping away. A gust screamed overhead, laying *Molio* flat and throwing me against the galley. I braced myself. It wouldn't do to break a rib. More items fell into the water. I stared at the swirling liquid as if hypnotised. I had read somewhere that Hebridean sailors believe the sea will always carry their body home. Where was home? East coast, west coast? I didn't know. I didn't know where my home was. I stared at this void, conscious that the ropes anchoring my life were beginning to part. I picked up the sodden chart from the water and laid it on the lee bunk. Here was rationality. There were the Monach Islands and before them the rocks to avoid. The recommended anchorage offered shelter from the prevailing wind but if it backed to the west, as forecast, it would become untenable. Alternatives? I traced down the west coast of North Uist, Benbecula and South Uist. Nothing. The only possibility was Vatersay Sound at the south end of Barra, but the entrance was full of rocks. I had a vague memory of a sailing ship being wrecked off the island. So the Monachs then. From there I could make it back to the Sea of the Hebrides once the wind eased.

Another gust shrieked in the rigging pushing *Molio* back on her side. Water filled my boots. I felt my anger rise. Turning to run meant giving up on the edge of success. I knew that my finances wouldn't stand another summer of sailing. Heading back now meant letting go of it all. This was my only chance. I clung onto the rail above the starboard bunk as a wave pushed us back over. I needed to get control of my boat. I waded back to the galley, grabbed the jar of Mars bars and wedged myself at the top of the companionway ladder. I devoured one and pushed another into the sodden pocket of my jacket. I sat there for a minute, leaning against *Molio*, feeling her strength. Alec Rose had sailed *Molio*'s sister ship, *Lively Lady*, right round the world singlehanded. He would have had no problems with this little predicament. He had coped with storms in the southern ocean and been up on deck umpteen times to reef and change sail in conditions much worse than this. If he could manage then by God so could I. First of all I had to get that sail reefed. Only then did it come to me that my reefing technique was wrong.

The wind was creating a power kite of the lower part of the main-sail, which overwhelmed me each time I tried to pull down on the reef-ing-eye. I should have had a tackle ready to help but had nothing to hand. What I could do was go back to the mast, drop the sail further, then get ropes round the loose material fast, before *Molio* slid off the wind. It should prevent the kite filling and allow me time to get the reef in. The thought of going back along the deck to the mainmast, where wind and waves were conspiring to hurl me into the sea, was not pleasant. If I slipped, or let go of a handhold at the wrong moment, the forces up there were enough to rip man from boat. I pushed the thought away, tied two spare cords round my waist, stood up, braced myself against the sides of the companionway and went out into the cockpit. I worked my way along the lurching deck, focusing on each step. For a moment I thought about Magnus being flung into the sea and then picked up by his two French companions. I had no companions. The drag of water on a fully-clothed man being towed at only a couple of knots is surprisingly powerful. I couldn't imagine what it would be like at six or seven. It would be impossible to get back on board. Maybe I would get one shot at it. I felt my way round the front of the mast. As I did I noticed the fulmar, his wing dipping in a trough as he flew close alongside *Molio*, smooth and serene, his dark eye watching. His mastery of the elements and that steady watchful eye calmed me. I dropped the mainsail halfway down the track and secured the halyard. *Molio* was already beginning to slide off the wind. I worked my way quickly round the mast and along the boom. The mainsail ballooned out sideways like a reaching spinnaker but then suddenly collapsed. As it did, I got one of the cords round it and pulled in tight. I repeated this with the second cord. The sail was tamed. It now became a simple matter to fasten down the leech end at the cockpit using the reefing eye, and then go back along the boom towards the mainmast tying down the row of reef points. As I worked, the fulmar glided in close again. It was so graceful in the storm. In the days of sail, fishermen believed that they came back in the next life as gulls. Sailors, I think, would come back as fulmars so as to keep an eye on their brethren at sea. I gathered in the last of the sail and the reef was done.

Using the engine to bring *Molio*'s bows into the wind one more time, I hoisted the sail tight. It wasn't beautiful but when the sail set it was less than half the former area. I readjusted the self-steering gear and switched off the engine. *Molio* turned once more to the west. Her angle was comfortable and she wasn't shipping much water. I looked up at the leech and examined the tear in the mainsail. It was in the panel above the top reefing point. Taking out my knife, I made a hole above the torn section choosing a spot in the outer seam that was well-protected by stitching. I laced some cord through the hole and brought it down to the top reef cringle, making several loops, and then tightened up until tension was removed from the tear. Making fast, I tidied up the ropes in the cockpit and checked that the drain holes weren't blocked. Satisfied, I went below.

The noise of the wind and breaking seas was joined below by the creaking of timbers and the sounds of water sloshing from side to side. At least the water level hadn't risen much more. Despite Packie's dire warnings, I didn't believe the leak could be that bad. Adam and Mike had been over *Molio*'s timbers with a fine-tooth comb and I trusted their work. Just at that moment, *Molio* dived into a wave and water poured down the chain pipe next to the mainmast and onto the floorboards. There should have been a cap on deck to fit over the pipe, but it had disappeared over the side and I hadn't found a replacement. As a result, she was taking bucket loads with each wave that crashed over her bows. Perhaps that was the whole problem. Except the bilge pump should have been able to keep up. I knelt down in the oily water and lifted the floorboard that was immediately above the pump. I leaned forward searching for the float switch at the bottom of the bilges. I found the plastic casing and began to feel down its side with my fingers, seeking a little toggle that flipped a float up and down. At last I felt a small knob and tried to move it. It was jammed. I bent down lower until the side of my face was just above the water in the cabin. I got my hand under the housing and began to explore the float within. There was a sharp object sticking out. I tugged and it came free. Immediately the pump kicked into life. I eased the casing back into place while keeping hold of the object and brought it up to the surface. It was a piece of broken cassette case. I put it in my jacket pocket and washed the oil from my hands. In a few minutes the water level was below the floorboards; soon it had sucked dry.

Back in the cockpit I wedged myself under the sprayhood. An hour later, I noticed two gannets flying past in the same westerly direction that we were taking. They too would be heading for St Kilda. According to Martin Martin it was the system of navigation favoured by the islanders:

They take their measures from the flight of those fowls, when the Heavens are not clear... they prefer it to the surest compass.

It was comforting to know that I could just follow the birds and they would take me to land. We were part of the same ecology now, both responding to the distinctive calls of the land and sea. To that extent at least our lives were bound together. I didn't need the GPS, I was hooked into nature. The gusts appeared less violent; the cord lacing was doing its job. I settled down to watch the far horizon as one wave followed the next in an endless grey expanse. At some point I noticed something in that moving seascape was stationery. At first it was just a smudge, then something solid but hidden by its own obscuring cloud. The sailing directions talk of these islands coming into view 'shaped like a full-rigged sailing-ship'. To me, the first island, as I came closer, was shaped more like some monstrous pliosaur with a round, serrated back, a head with jagged teeth and a pointed tail. I let out a cheer. The wind continued to abate and I celebrated by making a mug of hot tea. The closer I came, the higher the cloud rose; eventually it let *Molio* creep under its veil and into a world such as Jason might have discovered on his voyage in the Argo. It was the island of Boreray with its attendant stacks: the round, serrated back of the main island rose over twelve hundred feet above the sea; Stac Armin in the north was its head, rising six hundred feet from the ocean swell; Stac Lee was the western fin-like tail, rising over five hundred feet. Gannets thronged the sky.

The wind eased further as we sailed ever westward, and as we moved the stacks rotated, appearing to sail majestically round Boreray. Then Hirta appeared behind its own veil, larger than its sister. As *Molio* drew closer, its veil too began to lift. At that moment, I had no difficulty in understanding why it was a spiritual haven of the Gaels, the land of their ancestors. When about five miles out a puffin arrived, performing a complete circle before heading for the island. And then the birds were everywhere, gannets, shearwaters, guillemots and dainty petrels. All of us heading towards Hirta. The gannets came from above while the guillemots flew just above the water, fast, direct and full of purpose. Kyla had told me their name derived from Guille, French for William, which, in her mind, immediately led to three new words, 'guile' and 'will', both attributes of the mind, and the Old English 'helm' meaning protection as afforded perhaps by William the Conqueror's (Wilhelm's) helmet. Of the two attributes of the mind, one has to do with intention and the other with pointy-headedness. She saw our consciousness as the mist through which the guillemots flew with purpose. I could hear her voice. 'They are little heads, little wills that fly through the realm of our consciousness.' Kyla was good with names. She thought they had much to reveal because they came from a time when everything was joined up in the mind. I walked to the bows to be with the birds and let *Molio* sail on her own towards Village Bay.

The evening sun, on the longest day of the year, lightened the sky behind Hirta. The two arms of the bay enfolded us as *Molio* gratefully slipped into shelter on a dying breeze. Once over at the grey stone church, I dropped anchor in three fathoms.

Chapter 21

Abode of Ancestors

A toot from the army landing craft next morning got my immediate attention. I dropped the map of Hirta and scrambled up to the cockpit. The captain called over that he wanted me to move nearer to the pier. It was to give them a safe perimeter for refuelling. I moved reluctantly as *Molio* was over a sandy patch and the anchor well dug in. With the manoeuvre completed, I added half a fruitcake, an apple and a bottle of water to my pack before rowing ashore. The concrete steps on the west side of the pier looked lethal with the swell crashing over them, and the shelving beach next to it was not much better. Contrary to advice, I turned and headed for the sandy beach at the head of the bay to one side of the landing craft. It looked easy enough. I surfed onto the sand and stood to jump out but the next wave tipped the dinghy and me into the water. I scrambled to my feet, grabbed the dinghy and dragged it ashore. My clothes were sodden and my dignity dented but at least I was on dry land. I carried the dinghy above the high tide mark and set off across the old fields towards the west end of the village. Finding the track leading to Mullach Mor, I hiked up the first hill and then left the track to skirt round the summer shieling at the top end of Glen Bay. From there a narrow neck of land led to the Cambir – a raised plateau a few hundred yards across, which faces the Isle of Soay. Here I entered the world of seabirds. Fulmars were nesting on the cliffs or hanging almost motionless in the updraft, and guillemots were roosting in bunches on rocky ledges. All around me was the grunting of kittiwakes and the raucous mewing of gulls. In a moment of quiet I thought I heard a purring petrel in its burrow. The seabirds provided the St Kildans with a prolific harvest. Martin Martin describes one fowling party that brought home two thousand birds and twenty-nine large baskets of eggs, the smallest of which contained four hundred large eggs.

I walked to the northwest extremity of Cambir and sat on a ledge overlooking the sea-stacks. The thumb, Stac Biorach, stood tall and thin, a monumental black spire with a splash of guillemots on its summit. Part way up is an overhang, which the fowler must surmount if he is to reach the nests. It requires a technique known to rock climbers as mantling, in which the climber gains height by pushing down, usually with the palm, on a ledge, or if on ice by pushing down on the head of an ice axe. In Martin's words: *'it is reckoned no small gallantry to climb this rock, especially that part of it called the Thumb, which offers so little to hold, that of all the parts of a man's body, the thumb only can grasp it... during which time his feet have no support, nor any part of his body touch the stone, except the thumb, at which minute he must jump by the help of his thumb, and the agility of his body concurring to raise him higher at the same time, to a sharp point of the rock, which when he has got hold of, puts him above danger.'* Another technique was climbing up the corner of a rock using only heels and elbows, with the fowler's back towards the rock.

When fowling on the steepest cliffs, the St Kildans worked in pairs tied together with a long rope made of plaited cowhide or horsehair. Women, too, might work the cliffs with their husbands, and when clambering together, they assisted one another by touches and signals so slight as to be almost imperceptible. The rope was not so much to hold them in the event of a fall, but to leave the hands free to gather eggs or grab birds. With perpendicular faces, two ropes were used. The supporter and climber began their work at the top of the cliff. The supporter first fixed himself in some recess in the rock and threw his own rope down the cliff, then taking hold of the climber's rope he put it over one shoulder and under the other arm, and got ready to lower away. The climber, meanwhile, grasped the supporter's hanging rope and prepared to lower himself on that rope. They both then lowered away together so that the strength of two men could be applied to raising or holding the weight of the climber while employing the safety of two ropes. Accidents were rare. The islanders began climbing at three years of age, when playing on the walls of their houses, and started to accompany adults on fowling trips aged ten. In the process, they developed large muscular feet and ankles with powerful tendons. They became maestros of the cliff face and their exploits have inspired generations of recreational climbers in Scotland.

The greatest fowling was to be had on Boreray, and best of all on its two stacks. From my perch I could see Stac Lee, which was so white with birds and guano it might easily be mistaken for a sailing ship in the mist. It rose sheer from the ocean looking every bit as daunting as the Thumb. The islanders would choose a calm evening in August to make the four mile trip by open boat in order to harvest this fortress. If there was a breeze they hoisted a square mainsail made of woollen patches, each given by one of the families on board. It must have looked something like a patchwork quilt. On arrival, they held the boat off the rocks with poles and the first fowler waited for the right moment to leap for the rocks. If he failed, he was pulled aboard by a rope round his waist and another tried. The first to succeed found a strong hold and his rope now helped the next. The party of fowlers scaled the cliff and began to catch the birds, sometimes using a horsehair noose on the end of a fishing rod to hoick them up. They worked on till daybreak. In the morning the boat returned and the fowlers threw the birds down to the sea from the casting rock.

If the weather deteriorated, they might be trapped for several weeks on Boreray, so they developed a simple way of sending messages. It involved clearing patches of turf on the south-facing slopes which were easily visible from Hirta: a patch to the left of a certain spot was their request for a boat with provisions, a patch to the right indicated an injury and a large patch indicated that a death had occurred. On one occasion, when their boat was smashed, the fowlers lit fires, one for each person, to indicate to their womenfolk that all had survived.

I walked back along the slopes above Glen Bay, munching happily on my apple, until dive-bombed by a pair of skuas. I ended up running a good part of the way back to escape them and then descended the western cliff edge of Ruaival at a more dignified pace. On my left side

I looked towards the Hebrides, just as the islanders must have done when anticipating the steward's arrival. He brought them luxuries such as tea, whisky, tobacco, sugar, salt, oats, leather soles and bonnets. On my right side was the misty blue Atlantic. It was in this direction that the St Kildans looked for signs of stormy weather and for the arrival of birds in the spring. I stopped at a narrow stone chamber, known as a cleit, where the islanders had dried the harvested birds. Inside I found an eider sitting on a dish of down in amongst the fallen rocks. For an islander, she was a bunch of precious feathers sitting on a dozen large eggs. That's a quick snack for those who love the highly-incubated eggs even more than those newly laid.

There were umpteen uses of seabirds on St Kilda: as a delicacy for the table, a balm for wounds, fat as a relish, oil for lamps, down for beds and great bags of white feathers that were given as rent to the steward. It didn't stop there. The two ends of a plaid might be fastened with a fulmar bone or the beak of an oystercatcher. A gannet's wing served as a hearth brush, their gullets and stomachs were strung up as containers for fulmar oil, and their necks fashioned into women's slippers. According to Martin Martin, a lady's heel fitted charmingly within the yellow crown, the gullet made a snug fit for the foot and their toes were adorned with white down from the breast. The sight of a group of slippered women so impressed one learned visitor that he described them as feathered Mercuries. Whatever was left over, typically the carcass and entrails, was put on the field as fertiliser. Although the St Kildans depended on domestic animal stock and arable farming, it was the seabirds that defined their way of life. In their hearts, they were cragsmen. The greatest present a young man could give to his sweetheart was a plump gannet, as much for the risk he took in catching it as for the worth of the bird.

Jutting out from the top of the southern cliffs was a natural arch with a slab sitting across the top that I recognised as the Mistress Stone. It balanced on the edge of a two hundred and fifty foot drop to the sea below. I scrambled up to a point just beneath it. Already my stomach was queasy with vertigo and my heart racing. The top of the slab above me was about two foot wide by six foot long, and quite flat. A young man wishing to get married must demonstrate his prowess in front of his friends and sweetheart by walking out to the lip of the stone, so that the sole of his left foot extended beyond, then balancing upon the heel of the left foot, he drew the right foot across the left one, bent forward and grasped the other foot with both hands, making allowance for any wind, then held that position until his companions were satisfied. If he managed, he was considered worthy of the finest mistress in the world. Any St Kildan lass who watched a young man make those moves could hardly fail to be impressed. She would know that the he was more than a romantic lightweight, that he was in fact a cragsman, someone who could provide birds for her and a growing family. What's more this was a man who had put his life on the line for her affection. Martin was invited to try but declined not wishing 'to be robbed of both life and mistress in the same moment'.

My own head for heights was no match for that challenge. But what if my sweetheart was in the balance and a lifetime with the woman of my dreams? Would I have dared then? I had once conquered my fear of heights to climb riverine trees in Africa where I perched all day on tiny log platforms. They were seldom more than forty feet above the ground. I looked at the lover's stone and the long drop into space. I let myself dream on. Suppose I knew my balance from years of practice on the cliffs. What then? I could feel the cold sweat on my palms as I faced the ordeal above my head. If the girl was rare and brave... if it was someone like Kyla standing there in gannet slippers with flaming hair streaming in the breeze... then yes, I like to think I would have tried.

The St Kildans celebrated their love in songs but only one was ever recorded; a duet, in which the woman and her husband sang alternately.

He: *Away bent spade, away straight spade,*
       Away each goat and sheep and lamb;
       Up my rope, up my snare—
       The birds are a-coming, I hear their tune!
She: *Thou art my handsome joy, thou art my sweetheart,*
       Thou gavest me first the honied fulmar!

He: *Thou art my turtle-dove, thou art my song thrush,*
        Thou art my melodious harp in the sweet morning.
She: *Thou art my treasure, my lovely one, my cragsman,*
        Yesterday thou gavest me the gannet and the auk.
He: *I loved thee love when thou wast but a child,*
        Love that shall not wane till I go beneath the earth.
She: *Thou art my hero, thou art my basking sunfish,*
        Thou gavest me the puffin and the black-headed guillemot.

No wonder they welcomed back the seabirds each spring!

Leaving the cliffs, I started down the green meadows which ran unbroken to Dun, the island that formed a sheltering arm for Village Bay. The slopes were well drained, cropped short by wild flocks of Soay sheep and fertilised by migratory birds. On all sides the Atlantic waves rolled by. I felt the same elation that I'd found on the green meadows of northern Serengeti, mown by wild ungulates and fertilised by migratory herds, and on the upland pastures of the High Pamirs cropped close by Marco Polo sheep. I opened my arms and ran down the slope. It would be so easy to fly, to soar, to swoop, to join the birds. But instead, I turned north and worked my way further down to the village. I didn't want to leave *Molio* unattended for much longer. Coming round a curve in the hill I spied the cottages set back about two hundred yards from the shore forming a familiar crescent of stone dwellings.

A grassy pathway led me along the front of the line of cottages where old and new styles were intermingled. The early beehive blackhouses were not dissimilar to St Molio's cell on Holy Isle. I chose one of these and crawled inside under the turf doorway. The Rev. Neil Mackenzie had visited a sick parishioner living in a blackhouse on Hirta in the 1830s. The entrance had been a tunnel in the wall several feet thicker than my one.

You had to make your way in a stooping position past a hole full of dead birds and refuse, and such like abominations, till at the end of the tunnel you reached the door. You had to climb up among the cattle and be helped over the dividing wall, then make your way on hands and knees as it was only near the centre of the house that you could even sit upright. Carefully creeping along in almost total darkness, you made your way to the top of a steep slope which led down to the bed opening. Down this you went head foremost, nothing visible from above but your legs, while you spoke and prayed.

The islanders' homes were built for survival rather than for a view across the bay. Deep Atlantic depressions can bring severe weather at any time, but the equinoctial and winter storms are unimaginable. The islanders watched the birds for signs of change. If the guillemots left the island for the open sea, it was the first clue. When the wind beat down from above raising the thatch of the blackhouses, a storm was growing close. Everyone and everything headed for cover: cats, mice and crabs. Even the insects sought shelter in the cleitean. As the storm drew closer the gusts gained strength, reaching over a hundred and thirty miles per hour in the worst cases. These hurricanes screamed over the island, tearing up turf wherever they caught hold, and killing heather and grass by exposing the roots. Rolling waves of over fifty feet were driven against the shore where they reared up and carried over the shoulders on Dun several hundred feet high, sweeping in torrents down the hillside. Massive boulders were moved about like pebbles. Even in the stone houses there was no escape from the howl of the wind and the booming of breakers. The daughter of a missionary wrote that one severe storm made everyone deaf for a week.

But the storm would pass and people could come out again to continue with their daily affairs. Village life was communal, with all contributing to common labour, such as boat launching, building of cleitean and the manufacture of ropes. One of the fruits of their isolation was the development of a highly egalitarian, if male dominated, society that centred round their own assembly. The 'St Kilda Parliament' comprised all grown males on the island. It met every day except Sunday on the roof of one of the larger houses, a fitting location for cragsmen. Affairs were conducted in loud voices and everyone spoke at once. Matters for discussion included the allocation of bird cliffs and fishing rocks, use of ropes on the cliffs, and the thorny issue of annual taxes demanded by the steward. This was paid in kind:

bags of feathers, pints of bird oil, sheep, cattle, horses, fowl, fish, tweed, blankets, butter, cheese, tallow, milk and barley. Then there was the matter of the work to be done that day which could be a life and death decision, such as whether conditions were calm enough to make a successful landing on Boreray. If there were no urgent matters, the debate could continue all morning and afternoon!

Parliament ensured that no family was raised above another, that the needs of those most in want were met, and that all shared in the common wealth of the island. Its authority may have given them the strength one day to drive off the steward's men with fishing rods and knives rather than submit to a tax of sheep that they considered unfair. Visitors remarked on the unity of the islanders. On one occasion, when a party of eighteen went over to North Uist to buy seed-corn, the Uistmen were astonished to find that all eighteen would answer each question in perfect unison, or so the story goes. Martin has described how women would gather in their own assemblies, sing together as they spun and tell each other stories. Men also sang as they rowed or even when descending the cliff on a rope. On holidays the St Kildans played shinty on the beach for prizes of eggs and tobacco, and showed off in the water with swimming and diving. Young and old enjoyed dancing. 'The merest hint of a tune on a bad violin threw them into an ecstasy of joy' especially when primed with home-brewed ale. All this led Martin to conclude that the inhabitants of St Kilda were much happier than the generality of mankind, 'being almost the only people in the world who feel the sweetness of true liberty'.

Perhaps he was overstating the case. Were the islanders truly free? Some aspects of their lives might suggest so. Their skill as cragsmen and self-sufficiency as islanders is not disputed; their right to self-govern the bird cliffs, island pastures and maritime fisheries went unchallenged; they met in their own Parliament each day; their society, though firm, did not prevent a young woman from choosing her marriage partner; and each spring they welcomed home the birds. Yet many have criticised Martin for indulging in the romanticism of his age. Island life in the seventeenth century, they claim, was harsh and isolated. The hardship and discipline of island life must have weighed heavily on the St Kildans as they amassed the produce needed to pay the laird his annual tax. Storm and disease could be devastating. There were no doctors on Hirta. By comparison with the mainland, there were few opportunities in life.

So the answer perhaps is yes and no. Within the limitations of remote island life, the disciplined work of the St Kildans was rewarded by some of the benefits of community life – a sense of belonging, the support of others, and at least occasionally an overwhelming sense of joy and freedom. It was only when natural calamity struck, or when the steward or church bore down heavily, that hardship prevailed. What stands out for me is the commitment of the St Kildans to their island way of life and each other.

I crawled out of the blackhouse and continued down the row to the far end where I found one of the modern cottages that had been converted into a museum. I searched amongst the displayed information for any clue as to why the islanders had decided to emigrate en masse in 1930. In the eighteenth and early nineteenth centuries the St Kildans were notorious for seldom ever leaving their island, let alone settling on the mainland. What went so wrong in the succeeding years that they had felt compelled to abandon their island home? As I was reading one of the posters, someone walked in and came over.

"If you need any help, I'd be happy to try." He held out his hand which I took. He had the open eyes and reflective air that I associate with field biologists. I guessed he might be an archaeologist and, if living here, that he would have thought carefully about the islanders.

"Can you throw any light on what went so wrong that the St Kildans ended up wanting to leave?"

"It's a puzzle right enough. People have lived on St Kilda for thousands of years. From what we can gather, they were well-fed and healthy for much of the time. But they did have problems to deal with."

He went on to tell me about some of the theories he'd read about. It turned out that the literature on St Kilda was surprisingly large; a wonderful archive was what he called it, one that kept on expanding. "There's much talk about island hardship, whatever that means. Some blame the harshness of the Presbyterian Church and others the tyranny of the steward. But to be fair, as often as not, the laird helped the St Kildans. It's been suggested that a collapse in the price for bird oil and feathers after the First World War brought about the exodus. It also became easier at that time for islanders to find a new life on the mainland."

I was curious about a theory that had made a scientific splash not that long before. "What do you think of the studies," I asked, "showing heavy metal pollution in the soil from their use of bird carcasses as fertiliser? Could that have caused the crops to fail?"

"It may have played a part," he agreed. "But for my money the greatest problem the St Kildans faced was disease. It was more devastating than any of the others." He described some of the afflictions the islanders had endured. "Those leading to death included whooping cough, measles, scarlet fever, tuberculosis and influenza. Tetanus got onto the island and caused two-thirds of infants to die. The problem grew much worse in the eighteenth century when there was more frequent contact with the mainland. Smallpox alone claimed ninety-seven lives in 1727. Only one adult islander and the preacher survived on Hirta together with eighteen orphaned children. Fortunately, a party of three adults and eight boys escaped because they were stranded on Stac Armin all winter. Less lethal was the 'boat cold' which infected the whole island whenever visitors arrived."

I was appalled at this roll call of the dead. "I had no idea it was like that."

"Terrible," he agreed. "The natural immunity of St Kildans must have been low and it left them vulnerable to every kind of disease. I think it became an impossible struggle to maintain a self-supporting community. The irony is that there was no escape for them even when they reached the mainland. When thirty-six of the healthiest islanders emigrated to Australia in 1852, half died from measles on the way. Apparently on hearing the news, the islanders locked themselves in their homes and wept for a week."

I shook my head in disbelief. "It reminds me of the European diseases that wiped out Native Americans."

"That's exactly right," he replied. "The St Kildans could not evade

European disease. It was their curse."

Back on *Molio*, I made a cheese sandwich with lots of Branston pickle and sat down at the saloon table with a mug of coffee to read again from Martin Martin's *Voyage to St Kilda*. It was one of the first travel books to be written in the English language. Like the Hirta cragsmen, he had set a high bar for those that followed. In the evening I poured myself a glass of Ardbeg and went up to the cockpit. A mist was descending with the shadows sending a light breeze across the bay. I shivered and zipped up my fleece. The shipping forecast was south or southwest 4 or 5 veering southeast 6 later. Village Bay would soon lose its shelter. I lifted my glass and took a deep swallow, letting the fire course down my throat.

It was good to be there. I felt the contentment stealing over me. Seabirds were flying about the bay, high and gliding, low and whirring, swooping, diving, calling, squabbling, while others sat quietly on eggs. The steep flanks of Hirta gazed down. Here and there small groups of Soay sheep were grazing. A gannet circled lazily overhead. I noticed the ensign fluttering from the mizzen and realised it was past time to bring it down. I stowed it below and then lit *Molio*'s oil lamp. The cabin felt cosy in the soft light. I cleared my bunk and laid out the duvet. Just to be sure, I lit the riding lamp and took it up to the cockpit to wait for the flame to settle. I arranged a cushion on the bridge deck and sat back. Hell's teeth. I'd actually made it. My lips parted in laughter, "I'm here!" There was no response. I shouted again to the birds, "Wake up!" The guillemots needed no encouragement: they were already flying out of the bay and into the surrounding Atlantic, hunting perhaps for the elusive herring which comes to the surface at night. I took a second swallow.

In the gathering twilight Hirta was etched with lines of life, like an old person's face. Everywhere I looked were stones that had been heaved into place by the islanders: the cleitean on the high slopes for storing the birds, the folds that held their cattle and sheep, the dry stone walls of the village, the cell-like blackhouses half buried in the ground, the cottages, the church, the harbour wall; everything built in stone and everything massive to withstand storms. It could not have been done in one lifetime. Generation after generation had laboured to build this island home. A great solid communal home, hewn from hill and heart, nested in the Atlantic and protected by ancestors. The island fastness enfolded me now as I floated in the bay, like the stone walls of a cleit sheltering a wild sheep. I leaned back and took a third swallow.

I pulled the letter that my mother had sent me from the pocket at the back of the logbook. She'd written out a poem in her clear bold hand about another voyage and the voice of a far-flung mariner. I brought the riding light close. The opening lines stood out:

What seas what shores what grey rocks and what islands
What water lapping the bow...

I went below and rummaged about for my father's chanter. The ebony mouthpiece fitted comfortably against my teeth. I moistened the reed and tried my hand at Highland Cathedral using the music Rob had sketched for me in Plockton. Giving up with that, I played Dark Island which reminded me of sailing from Oban many years before. I moved on to my father's haunting version of Bonnie Galloway which he played in the slower timing of a west coast air. It brought him right into the boat. I poured another dram and imagined pointing out the varnished lockers, the great wooden mast at the head of the table and the old brass clock ticking above the chart table. He would have been enthralled by *Molio*'s voyage, the stormy passage, the great stacks circling Boreray, and this sunny unexpected day on St Kilda. His life might have been defined by duty but his real love had been sailing his own boat in the west; that and his family.

I leaned back against the cushions and relaxed feeling the immensity of the brooding hills around me. Something had changed. For a moment I was confused and then I recognised it for what it was – a feeling of contentment that kept stealing across my mind, as if I'd awoken from a nightmare of being forever lost only to find the way home lying at my feet. And with that realisation came others. My home would be in the west near to my boat. I would start anew from there. A weight seemed to melt away at the thought. I got into my bunk and fell asleep.

In my dream I was preparing to fly over Serengeti, which was empty of people as it had been when I first lived there. I was standing at the top of a grazed pasture. On one side was a line of acacias following the drainage line down a gentle slope, beyond were rising hills. I let myself become very still inside. When I was quite still, I lifted off and flew with just my arms raised.

I awoke suddenly, knowing something else had changed. *Molio* was rolling and the tiller thudding against the iron horse. I jumped out of my bunk and rushed up to the cockpit to find that *Molio* had swung to a new breeze. Now she was pointing directly out the entrance of the bay from where the sea was rolling in. Her stern faced the pier which looked surprisingly close. The anchor must be dragging on kelp again. Perhaps it was the flat profile of the new style of blade that prevented it from penetrating the thick beds of Highland kelp. It was time to go. I hurried below, pulled on my jersey and sea boots and started the engine. Using the mast winch, I raised the anchor clear of the water with a great tangle of kelp and motored over to the lee of Dun to pull off weed and make all secure for a sea voyage. I hoisted the mainsail, shaking out the reef in the process, pulled free the yankee and brought *Molio* onto a course for the Sound of Harris.

Chapter 22

Running Free

There is a magic in making landfall on a small boat, some alchemy of skill, luck and blessing, but in my case it was a fleeting moment dwarfed by relief. Through the mist the low lying form of Pabbay appeared followed soon after by its little brother Shillay. Breathing more easily I turned *Molio* into the narrow sound between them, lowering the tattered mainsail on the far side of Pabbay which gave some shelter from the swell. Heavy rain set in as I tied it to the boom. Back in the cockpit I peered into the gloom, searching for some landmark to guide us across the Sound of Harris. As if on cue *Sea Dog II* came belting round the island. She cut speed and glided up close. The big skipper slid open the window to the wheelhouse and gave me a shout, "Need any help?"

"I'm fine, thanks. I'll follow you to Leverburgh."

"Ninety-five," he shouted back. With a roar of twin diesels the bow lifted, her stern dug down, and she was off. I fired up *Molio*'s engine and gave chase, checking the compass as I followed the line of his wake. Bang on ninety-five. I consulted the chart. It would take us on to the rocks at Colasgeir. At the last minute, *Sea Dog II* changed course and disappeared behind Ensay. By then I had sight of a navigation buoy and from there it was easy. The rain lessened in Leverburgh Channel and the hills of Harris materialised once more. On impulse I decided to try a new anchorage. The tide was on the flood and should be high enough to carry *Molio* over the shallows and into a landlocked pool on the southeast corner of Harris. I rang Alastair. When he picked up I waved at the houses. "Ahoy, Alastair, I'm right outside your house!"

"Oh I can see you, Martyn. How was the sail?"

"If you and Aileen are free for a drink later, I'll tell you about the gale."

"Just a minute." There was a pause whilst he consulted with the boss. "Where are you heading?"

"Poll an Tighmhail."

"I'll pick you up at six. You'll stay for dinner." It was more a statement than a question.

"Err, can you ask Aileen if I can borrow her sewing machine?"

Half an hour later, I nosed *Molio* into Loch Rodel. A brisk south-easterly was blowing across the Minch straight into the loch, bringing in large waves. Visibility remained poor. I hesitated about entering, not liking to take *Molio* too close to a lee shore. One of the three entrances to Poll an Tighmhail, the 'Pool of the Tax House', lay straight ahead. It looked inviting but I knew how deceptive it was, having read an account of the Ettrick shepherd who was almost wrecked there in 1804. Their schooner had borne down on the entrance under full sail in conditions just like today's. Fortunately, the local inhabitants saw the danger and in the bard's words: 'joining in a general shout, tossed their bonnets up into the air'. With difficulty, the crew of three had put the vessel about on the very brink of the sunken rocks. I avoided the false entrance, letting wind and waves push *Molio* deeper into the loch. At last I spotted what might be the hidden western entrance to the pool and turned in towards the rocks. To my relief, the channel opened up and we passed safely over the shallows into perfect shelter. There was one other yacht inside sitting on a courtesy mooring. I took the next one along, made secure and switched off the engine. I checked the ship's clock: there was enough time to remove and bag the mainsail.

On the short drive over to Borrisdale, Alastair and I chatted about St Kilda. "I've been in some lonely glens in the Highlands," I told him, "but this is the first place that felt truly wild."

"Isn't that a bit odd considering there are signs of human life in every corner?"

"It is strange. It's as if the St Kildans had absorbed the freedom of the seabirds; at least that is my take on it. The wildness of the birds was in the soul of the cragsman. Wild and free; don't you think they are almost the same?" The spirit of St Kilda was in my heart just then.

"In that case how about a new branding for your epic, 'Cragsmen of the Mist' or 'Edge of the Wild'?"

He kept his face straight but I know when my leg is being pulled. "Or even 'The Saga of the Slack Isobar'," I suggested. This time I got a sheepish grin.

Later that evening, Aileen set up her sewing machine on the breakfast table. We cut out a canvas patch from a piece of old sail with large scissors and stuck it over the tear with duck tape; then Aileen stitched as I fed the sail and patch under her needle. As we worked, I told her about Kyla.

"It's puzzling," I admitted. "No matter how much we enjoy being together, it always ends in disaster."

Aileen listened closely as I described the passion and bewilderment. She stopped me from time to time to ask a question but otherwise let me carry on until the words dried up.

"Life is different on the islands," she said. "We are further from government and miss out on many of the mainland services. That doesn't make our lives any simpler, despite what the mainland dreamers may think, but it does mean we are more self-reliant. We need to be a community. It's nothing like the intimacy of your St Kildans but still we are a community and we help one another. From what you say that is the kind of life that Kyla wants. She is community-minded. She likes to stay anchored in one place. What she doesn't need is a Captain Cook in her life wanting to take her to Tahiti." Aileen stopped stitching to see if I had got the point. I nodded grimly. "She needs a man with his feet on the ground, someone who is part of the local scene, who can take the hassle off her shoulders, bring in some money and fix the dishwasher."

"Oh, she only wants me to give up on my dreams then?" I replied angrily.

"You have to work out what you want Martyn. If you want Kyla then you are going to have to give a lot more of yourself than a few days in a boat. Stop being the hero, start being her best friend." I

318

noticed Alastair looking at Aileen with his mouth hanging open. She ignored him. "You need to put down roots. Move to the west if that is where your tribe is. Change job, one that doesn't constantly take you away. Get all that in place and maybe there will be room for some dreams down the road."

As her words sank home, I realised how little I had understood Kyla. I'd just assumed she would want to tag along with me. Did I want to substitute the slow and steady life of a rural community for the sparkle of open sea where the wind filled my sails and ideas came leaping? For once, no answers came.

Aileen must have noticed how quiet I'd become during the rest of the evening. As I was leaving she handed me some fresh rolls and milk. "You love sailing Martyn but Kyla may not. Do you know what Samuel Johnson said about sailing in the Hebrides?" I shook my head. "He likened it to being in a jail with the chance of being drowned."

I laughed at that. Alastair, another keen sailor, laughed too as he drove me back to Poll an Tighmhail. I was still grinning when I climbed on board *Molio*.

Sunshine found its way into *Molio*'s cabin to wake me next morning. The heaviness in my heart had lifted and I lay there smiling, thinking over my evening with Alastair and Aileen. I rowed ashore and climbed the small hill above the harbour. From up there I looked out across the pool of the taxman to the whitecaps on Loch Rodel and the southeastern wedge of Harris beyond. *Molio* sat patiently on her mooring like a hunting dog, content to lay by the hearth but eager to take to the hill at a nod from its master. We had achieved some kind of harmony on this voyage.

It had been difficult to get away from my consultancy, to hoist sail and let go of the contracts that kept me secure, but that passage from one life to another was just a beginning. When we set out, I was happy to drop the hassles and habits that had filled my days – the commitments, deadlines and stale routines – like a merman shedding a tired skin. My idea was to use that time away from the rat race to reconcile the different parts of my life. I was sure that the greatest freedom of all must be to live the life you believed in. I was the hunter, tracking down that life, casting about for a glossy new skin. It was an escape, as Kyla had seen, but an escape with a purpose.

All freedom begins with the flight from tyranny, the escape from the dictator's iron fist, or the laird's crushing tax. Escape is a beginning but to live freely, to soar above the waves like the fulmar, requires something more. It requires inner freedom, and inner freedom has its own locked door. When I stripped away the complexities of my life with all its convoluted decision-making, and peered underneath, there lay fear. Hidden but potent, it had guided my life. My own particular brand was the fear of losing my reputation. It might seem precious-minded but I'd worked hard for my professional credentials in the world of conservation and science. I'd mastered one set of skills for research in ecology and another for managing biodiversity. With those I'd built a modest reputation which I had no intention of jeopardising on some spiritual notion about nature, especially one that I had no real understanding of, even if I suspected it was a fundamental part of existence. Fear held me prisoner for all those years.

The voyage on *Molio* has been a journey with many companions. Amongst those accompanying me from the past were the St Kildans with their fierce commitment to an island way of life, and the dispossessed from Ulva and Canna torn from their homeland. Both had revealed the strength of communal life in the West Highlands. Many others that I met had offered practical help or simply shared their friendship. They were part of the wider boating community. We can't all live on Hebridean islands or dwell in mushroom-housed eco-villages, nor do we have to. A community is any group of like-minded people with a shared passion for the same kind of self-expression. It can be a gang of bikers, a club of hikers, a choir of choristers, a street of skateboarders, a gathering of second lifers in a virtual world, or a network of ocean-going yachtsmen and women spread across the real world. It may become your tribe. What makes a tribe out of a bunch of self-interested individuals is when they come together to support each other and their shared self-expression. Working together, they keep an eye on their creative spaces and essential freedoms. Like the islanders on Eigg, when that space is threatened they can fight and win.

Was Kyla in my tribe? I couldn't put it off any longer. I pulled out my mobile and sent a text:

Molio and I resting in Hebridean pool after voyage to St Kilda

A short while later I received a reply:

Well done Molio and you! I've been on a voyage too – working things out with Ellie's help.

It felt warm even though there was no real clue about her feelings. I returned to Molio and set about preparing for a passage. The first job was to bend on the repaired mainsail. I fed the travellers into the tracks and hoisted it up. The silver duck tape that we'd sewn into the mend made it look even more of a patchwork quilt, but it was as good a sail now as when I'd set off. Satisfied, I dropped it down to the boom and furled it up. I whiled away the day on other small jobs – fitting longer screws to the door of the switch panel to prevent it swinging open and sealing a new leak that had appeared over the chart table. In the evening I listened to the shipping forecast. The wind next day would be ideal for a passage to the Small Isles – northwesterly 3 or 4, backing west or southwest and strengthening later. If I left early in the morning I could make Canna before dark and sail on to Eigg the next day. I looked at the chart. The anchorage on Eigg was exposed to the southwest. I should try to reach it before the wind strengthened, then run east to find shelter in Arisaig. I rowed ashore and climbed the hill where I found a flat rock surrounded by a mass of yellow bird's foot trefoil. I sat down and keyed in a message to Kyla.

Will arrive off the boat slip by the café on Thursday. ETA 1100h. Hope to see you. If you are on the pier, I will pick you up.

The gatekeeper to my heart raised an eyebrow. I hesitated with my finger hovering above 'Send'. A light breeze kept the midges away. I sat slowly back and began to take in my surroundings. A pair of terns was squabbling over the pool. A heron flapped over to the islet on the far side and took up a fishing stance. After half an hour it moved to a new position. Sometime later a jingle alerted me to another incoming message.

> I've been sketching a tortoise for Molio's sail. Not right so far. Can it ever be right for us?

It was past time for plain speaking. I let myself think about Kyla as honestly as I could. It wasn't difficult to imagine her on Eigg, striding about the Manse in tight jumper and jeans, impish grin beneath laughing eyes and a tangle of hair cascading down her shoulders. The kids would be following her wherever she went. Out in the grounds, she would know each of the trees by now and most of the plants. She'd be happy helping Rob and Ellie with their green agenda. All she ever wanted was a quiet communal life in the country. I on the other hand wanted to explore narrow footpaths and cross unknown seas. We might share the same interests in nature but we hailed from different tribes. What she needed to complete her life was a warmhearted guy with a gentle nature. With the right man in the right place, she'd kick off her tiredness and flourish. Whereas I needed someone who would be happy as my companion wherever the journey took us, someone who shared the same underlying passions. Instead of helping each other's dreams to come true, Kyla and I had become bound together in a confusing co-dependency. I was the fisherman from Uist who had captured a selkie's skin, and like young Callum I'd become mesmerised by my seal-woman. She was the maiden who stayed for his protection, unable to return to the sea. We had become caught in the same enchantment. It was why I needed to shake free now and stand up for both of our futures. I put the phone in my pocket and scrambled down the hill to the dinghy. The heron flew past as I rowed across to *Molio*, its raucous call echoing off the cliffs.

Shortly after sunrise next morning I hoisted the mainsail. It flapped gently against the mast. I slipped the mooring, pulled in the mainsheet and sailed quietly across to the eastern entrance of the pool. Once over the shallows I gybed round on to a southerly bearing, let fly the yankee and adjusted the self-steering gear. *Molio* idled along at four knots. I couldn't see any other boats, just a wide expanse of blue ocean fringed on the one side by Harris and North Uist and on the other by the mist-covered mountains of Skye. I made some tea, buttered a roll, and took a cushion up to the cockpit. For a few minutes I watched the compass to make sure *Molio* was holding course for the Sea of the Hebrides. Leaning back I listened to the sounds of the boat – the water gurgling past, the odd slap from the yankee and the occasional creak from rigging in a gust. All sails were pulling now, we were running free.

Notes and Sources

Chapter 1: Wild Boat Chase

• The freedom of the London '60s scene is captured by Paul Gorman in his biography of Tommy Roberts, *Mr Freedom - Tommy Roberts: British Design*. Hero, Adelita Ltd., (2012).

Chapter 5: In The Wake of Saints

• Quotation about Arran taken from a lay of the Irish warrior minstrel Caeilte. *The Colloquy with the Ancients*, translated by Standish Hayes O'Grady. Parentheses Publications, Cambridge, Ontario, 1999. Reproduced with kind permission.

Chapter 7: The Sea Gypsy

• Elinor Ostrom's Nobel Prize in Economics was awarded for her work on community governance of the commons. She and her colleagues describe how community institutions can be strengthened to provide sustainable harvesting. The following references provide a starting point into this body of work: Dietz, T., Ostrom, E. & Stern, P.C (2003) *The struggle to govern the commons*. Science, 302, 1907-1912. 54. Ostrom, E. (1990) *Governing the Commons*. Cambridge University Press, Cambridge, UK.

• *Seeker Reaper* was written by George Campbell Hay in 1947 about a 1930s motorised skiff *Sireadh* (Gaelic for 'seeking'). © The estate of George Campbell Hay, 2000, 2003. Reproduced with permission of Edinburgh University Press Limited via PLSClear.

Chapter 8: Molio's Cave

• The nature writer, Denys Watkins-Pitchford, wrote under the name of BB. Two of his books written for children, *The Little Grey Men* and *Down the Bright Stream*, tell the story of the last four gnomes of Warwickshire.

• Rafiki means 'friend' in Swahili. I am most grateful to Dr Anthony Collins for his hospitality during my visit to Gombe.

• The case for King Arthur in Scotland is made in Carroll, D.F. (1996). *Arturius – A Quest for Camelot*. JC Books, Cottingham, UK.

• St Molio's early life is mentioned in Barrett, M. 1919. *A calendar of Scottish saints*, 2nd ed. Abbey Press, Fort Augustus.

• Cunningham, J. 2008. *In search of St Molaise*. In: *Fermanagh Miscellany 2*. Edited by Seamas MacAnnaidh, pp 17-22. Fermanagh Authors' Association, Enniskillen, Co Fermanagh, Ireland.

• Balfour, F.A. (1909). *The ecclesiastical remains on the Holy Island, Arran*. Proceedings of the Society of Antiquaries of Scotland 43: 151-6.

• Catholic Encyclopedia, http://www.newadvent.org/cathen/08637a.htm.

• It is worth remembering that most of the Celtic inscribed stones were very colourfully painted, and the early churches used to be rather gaudy too probably more like the Buddhist boulders on the Holy Island than what we're left with now!

Chapter 10: Fiddler's Green

• David Bollier has written an excellent article about loss and restoration of commons in the US: Bollier, D. (2002). *Reclaiming the commons*. Boston Review 27, Nos. 3-4. Downloaded (31 July 2013) from: http://new.bostonreview.net/BR27.3/bollier.html.

• Gunn, N.M. 1941. *The Silver Darlings*. Faber and Faber. © Neil Gunn Literary Estate. Reproduced with kind permission.

• Ownership of wildfowling rights by the Crown Estate applies to England, Wales and Northern Ireland but not to Scotland where it is a public right with certain restrictions.

• At the time of writing, the Crown Estate owned more than 17,000 licensed moorings around the UK coasts and three marinas.

• *CCC Sailing Directions and Anchorages – West Coast of Scotland*, 1951 and 1971 editions.

• There are all kinds of enthusiast clubs in Britain which bring together groups of users who share a common interest and passion. They are a treasured national institution especially the ones open to all comers. Give them ownership of the key resource – mooring and anchoring grounds in the case of yacht clubs, rights of way in the case of English hikers and horse riders, web space in the case of internet users – and you probably have the best forms of resource management because it is looked after in the common interest.

• Under the Crown Estate Act 1961, the Commissioners have a duty to maintain and enhance the capital value of the estate and its revenue income; but at the same time to take into account the need to observe a high standard of estate management practice. In the words of the 2010 UK Parliament Treasury Committee report, the degree to which the Crown Estate Commissioners have focused on their commercial duties has, in some contexts, acted against wider public interests. The Commissioners have shown commendable zeal in the first duty to raise revenue but lamentably poor stewardship in the second duty to serve the public interest (House of Commons Treasury Committee (March 2010). *The management of the Crown Estate.* Eighth Report of Session 2009-10, Vol. 1.).

Chapter 14: Cup and Ring

• The Hebrides lie in the middle of a wealth of fishing banks that once held enormous stocks of cod, whiting, haddock, monkfish, sole and skate. In the 1920s and '30s great fleets of herring drifters plied the seas bringing the threat of overfishing, but before too much damage was done the fishing banks were forcibly rested during the war years (1940 to 1945), when many boats were requisitioned. Fishing was still relatively light from 1946 to 1956 so that fish stocks fully recovered in coastal waters, including those of the Minches and Firth of Clyde.

Any opportunity for creating a new and sustainable fishing industry in the post-war years was shattered by the European Common Fisheries Policy, which opened up British waters to European fleets in 1970. The fishing effort steadily increased, peaking in the 1980s when fish landings in the region exceeded a quarter of a million tons thanks to the Russian factory ships. To make matters worse, Brussels introduced a system of harvesting quotas for single species of fish which led to enforced dumping at sea of hundreds of thousands of tons of fish. Another nail in the coffin of sustainability was the Inshore Fishing (Scotland) Act of 1984. This repealed the three nautical mile limit on trawling and scallop-dredging, which had protected inshore fish, spawning beds and shellfish stocks. As a consequence, the islanders and coastal fishing communities saw their local fish stocks depleted year on year, but were powerless to intervene. Small wonder, then, that so many in the Hebrides have now turned to fish farming. Today, the waters of the north-eastern Atlantic are the most overfished in the world.

What is so unfathomable is that we know the solution to this problem yet it still persists. Study after study has shown that sustainable fisheries are generaed when local communities are granted long-term secure tenure of their own resources. The government in Scotland is well aware of the dependency of local communities on fishing. It knows what it ought to do, but it has been shackled by the wider politics. Our fisheries require wholesale reform. It cannot happen unless management decisions are moved from Europe to the Scottish Government. With that step taken, it is then open to government to give back the fish banks exclusively to the local fishing communities. They will need to grant communities security of tenure and help them develop capacity to process and transport fish (as Frank Fraser Darling pointed out in his West Highland Survey, it is necessary to have relatively large quantities of landed fish to overcome the higher transport costs in the Outer Hebrides). They will also need to support their management institutions as the governance of common resources requires exceptional skill and patience to resolve disputes and maintain efficiency. What an historic moment it would be if the West Highlanders as a people were finally to win control of their own maritime resource.

Chapter 15: Wolf Island

• Favourite lines of my parents are taken from the poem *Pippa Passes* by Robert Browning.

• A clachan is a small traditional settlement in Scotland somewhat akin to a hamlet.

• Clark's new plan for Ulva was being implemented by other landowners, and it also fitted in with the government's emerging policy (Robert Graham's letters of 1837). By 1840, a majority of Highland landlords accepted the necessity of emigration. Thus the stage was already prepared for the infamous clearances.

• An account of Clark having the roof of a sick woman pulled down can be found in: *Report of the Commission of Inquiry into the Condition of the Crofters and Cottars in the Highlands and Islands of Scotland* (PP 1884 XXXII, Lord Napier Chairman), Evidence, iii 2254-5.

• Sir John Sinclair (1795). General view of the agriculture of the northern counties and islands of Scotland; including the counties of Cromarty, Ross, Sutherland, and Caithness, and the islands of Orkney and Shetland. With observations on the means of their improvement. C. Macrae, London.

• The seventeenth century protest chant was against English enclosure of common land. It may have originated as an English folk poem in a different age but the Scot's are keenly aware of similar injustices today.

Chapter 16: Isle of The Great Women

• The purchase of Eigg in 1997 led to wider reforms of land tenure and a greater role for communities. In 2001 the Land Reform (Scotland) Act put the community right to buy into the statute book. The community on Gigha soon followed suit and many others besides. A thoughtful account of community land ownership in Scotland which puts such community buyouts in a wider context is provided by Andy Wightman, Robin Callander and Graham Boyd (2003) *Common land in Scotland: A brief overview.* IIED Securing the Commons Series, No 8.

Chapter 17: Battle of Dreams

• If spared persecution as vermin, the natural predators should achieve some kind of balance with the rabbits, especially if woodland recovery is encou aged to provide raptors and owls with nesting habitat and perches. If the situation is critical, polecats would surely provide a quicker solution given their propensity for rabbits. It would be necessary to monitor the response as polecats will have some negative impact on ground nesting birds (and the Canna mice).

• The importance of secure user rights to sustainable management of the commons is reviewed by Elinor Ostrom and colleagues in the article *Revisiting the Commons: Local Lessons, Global Challenges.* Science 284:278-282 (1999).

• Hebrides may originally have meant the place protected by the pre-Christian fire goddess Brigid or Bride.

• The negotiation between Crown and Highland elite suggests that the latter were shifting away from their traditional function of clan chiefs and accepting new political, economic and legal realities. They probably had little choice other than to accept the real politik of their day given that the alternative was to be forced from their land. Some chiefs were even imprisoned in Edinburgh as part of the negotiation process. Alison Cathcart 2010. *The Statutes of Iona: The Archipelagic Context.* The Journal of British Studies 49: 4-27.

• The Dress Act of 1746 outlawed all items of Highland dress. The penalty was imprisonment or transportation to penal colonies. The ban was lifted in 1782.

• To its great credit, the Scottish Government recently provided legislative support for communities wishing to buy their resources jointly. A useful review of such measures is provided by Andy Wightman, Robin Callander and Graham Boyd (2003) *Common land in Scotland: A brief overview.* IIED Securing the Commons Series, No 8.

• According to the Northern Lighthouse Board, the last Scottish fog horn was switched off on 4 October 2005 at Skerryvore lighthouse.

• The early Christian sites include Sanda Island, Holy Isle and Little Cumbrae in the Firth of Clyde; Cara, Loch Caolisport, Loch Sween, Oronsay, Garvellachs and Lismore in the approaches to Glen More; and Iona, Inch Kenneth and Canna between Mull and Skye.

• One of the charms of Canna House at the time of visiting was to find its rooms much as John Campbell and Margaret Fey had left them. As with Charles and Emma Darwin's Down House, the conservation of some creative working rooms just as they were when in use would provide a unique connection for the visitor to their lives and their dreams.

• TC Smout (1969). *A History of the Scottish People* 1560-1830. Harper Collins.

• The 2005 edition of the *Clyde Cruising Club Sailing Directions*, part 4, provides a leading line of 264 degrees to a white house. Only the roof of this house is in fact visible and it is not white. There is however an old white cottage with a chimney on either end that is visible on the south side of the loch at Uiskevagh itself. If this is taken as the leading mark it will of course lead the unwary into danger. No mention is made of the fish farm filling the inner loch. It can be passed by circling either in a clockwise or anticlockwise direction with care.

Chapter 18: The Dark Laird

• At the Battle of Culloden the Jacobite army of Charles Edward Stuart was defeated by the loyalist army of the House of Hanover consisting largely of English forces but also Presbyterian clans. Charles' subsequent flight has become a legend in its own right. Insights into the conditions faced by Bonnie Prince Charlie while on the run can be found in: Ewing, Gregor (2013). *Charlie, Meg and Me.* Luath Press, Edinburgh.

• George Orwell wrote *Nineteen Eighty-Four* in the Hebrides whilst living in a remote house on the Isle of Jura in 1947.

Chapter 19: Piloting a Craft Called Freedom

• You have to go back to the seventeenth century to find Loch Maddy at its peak; at that time it hosted four hundred fishing vessels and was famous for the quantity of herring caught within the bay itself: Martin Martin (1716) *A description of the Western Islands of Scotland* (Second Edition). Facsimile.James Thin, Edinburgh.

• The importance of harvesting method on stress in shellfish and its influence on the quality of food on the table is rarely discussed. But it is well known that intensive rearing of fish and livestock are associated with stress, disease susceptibility and lower quality food products.

Chapter 20: Flight of the Fulmar

• Martin Martin (1716). *A description of the Western Islands of Scotland* (Second Edition). Facsimile. James Thin, Edinburgh.

• Adomnán, Ninth Abbot of Iona (c. 700). *Life of Saint Columba, Founder of Hy.* Edmonston and Douglas, Edinburgh (published 1874).

• The traditional story of the Selkie is published as *The Mermaid Wife in: Folk-Lore and Legends, Scotland* (1889). W.W. Gibbings, London. A charming version is recounted in: Johnson, A. (1989). *Islands in the Sound: Wildlife in the Hebrides.* Victor Gollancz, London.

• Martin Martin (1698) *A Late Voyage to St Kilda: The Remotest of All the Hebrides, or Western Isles of Scotland.* Printed for D. Brown and T. Goodwin, London.

Chapter 21: Abode of Ancestors

• It is hard to imagine that harvests of the magnitude described by Martin would be sustainable. Excessive harvests at the time of his visit might have been driven by the demands for high rents by the steward (or tacksman). There is some suggestion of a drastic seabird decline thirty years later. See notes by Alexander Buchan (1727) on eggs gathered, reported in: Harman, Mary (1997) *An Isle called Hirte: History and Culture of the St Kildans to 1930*. Maclean Press, Isle of Skye.

• Climbing the thumb stack is described in Martin Martin (1698) *A Late Voyage to St Kilda*. Mary Harman (ibid) suggests that Martin Martin's Stack Donn is in fact Stac Biorach rather than the smaller and more conical Stac Dona that also lies between Hirta and Soay.

• The climbing methods on the cliff are beautifully described by George Clayton Atkinson, in: Quine, D.A. (ed.) (2001). *Expeditions to the Hebrides by George Clayton Atkinson in 1831 and 1833*. Maclean Press, Isle of Skye.

• Mary Holman (ibid) provides an account of eleven mortalities in sixty years due to falling from rock but only some while engaged in fowling.

• This fragment of a song (slightly revised) is taken from a piece collected by the folklorist Alexander Carmichael from Effie MacCrimmon on his visit to St Kilda in 1865. The Carmichael Watson Project, Edinburgh University Library.

• An excellent broadsheet of photographs, maps and historical information on St Kilda is provided by the Royal Commission on the Ancient and Historical Monuments of Scotland (1998). *St Kilda: Settlement and Structures on Hirta*. RCAHMS broadsheet 4, Edinburgh.

• The poem by T.S. Eliot is *Marina*. The name has the meaning coast or shore and is also the name of the daughter of Pericles in Shakespeare's comedy Pericles, Prince of Tyre. The poem is about Pericles' thoughts on the brink of his journey home after long travels overseas.

Glossary of Nautical Terms

Aft	Near the stern of a boat.
Aground	Resting on or touching the bottom.
Ahead	In the direction of the bows.
Awash	Just under, or washed over by water.
Backstay	Wire from the stern to the mast head.
Beam	The width of a vessel at the widest point.
Bend, to	To fasten or attach as with a sail.
Bilge pump	Pump for removing water from the bottom of the boat. In *Molio*, the main hand pump is operated from the cockpit. An automatic electric pump is situated under the floorboards in the cabin operated by a float switch.
Boathook	A pole with a hook at one end used for picking up a mooring buoy or other floating objects.
Bobstay	A chain or wire leading up from the stem of the boat up to the end of the bowsprit to support it against the upward pressure of the jib or yankee.
Bottlescrew	A device for adjusting tension in stays and shrouds.
Bow	The front of a boat.
Bowsprit	A sturdy spar projecting forward of the bow on which the jib or yankee is set.
Caulk, to	To fill and seal a seam between planks with caulking compound.
Caulking	Material that is driven into the seams between planks to stop leaks.

Cockpit	The well near the stern from which the vessel is steered and which provides some protection for the crew.
Companionway	The entry from cockpit to the cabin.
Fender	An air or foam filled bumper to keep boats from banging against marina pontoons, harbour walls or each other.
Fo'c'sle or Forecastle	That part of the cabin which is beneath the foredeck usually with bunks and lockers.
Forestay	Wire rope reaching from the bow to a point below the masthead.
Galley	A sea-going kitchen.
Garboard planks	The planks immediately each side of the keel. The planks of the boat are its outer skin and the garboard planks are the bottom part of it.
GPS receiver	Portable radio device that obtains satellite bearings to fix the location of the boat.
Gunwale	The upper edge of a boat's side.
Gybe, to	When running before the wind, to bring the wind from one quarter to the other so that that the boom swings across.
Halyard	A rope used for hoisting a sail or flag up the mast.
Heads	The toilet compartment of a boat – home of Baby Blake!
Headsail	A triangular sail set forward of the mainmast (jib).
Heel	To lean under the influence of wind on sails.
Jetty	A landing stage or small pier at which boats can dock or be moored, often used on the west coast of Scotland for dinghies carrying passengers ashore from boats at anchor or on moorings.
Jib	A triangular sail set forward of the mainmast (headsail).
Jibstay	A stay running from the front of the bowsprit to the masthead. In *Molio*'s case, the luff wire of the yankee acts as the jibstay.

Keel   The fore and aft structural member of a ship to which all the frames, stem and sternpost are fastened. The lead keel on *Molio* attaches beneath to provide lateral stability.

Ketch   A two-masted, fore-and-aft-rigged vessel with the mizzen mast stepped forward of the rudder post.

Knot   Unit of speed equal to one nautical mile per hour.

Leech   The aft or trailing edge of the sail.

Luff   The forward or leading part of a sail.

Mainsail   The principal sail set on the mainmast.

Mainsheet   The line which controls the angle of the mainsail. It attaches to the boom at one end and to a traveller or horse at the other (aft of the cockpit on *Molio*) which improves the trim of the sail.

Mizzen   A small sail often carried at the stern of a boat on the mizzen mast.

Nautical mile   Equivalent to 1.852 km or 1.151 miles, the nautical mile is in fact the length of one minute of arc found by dividing the circumference of the Earth by the 21,600 minutes of arc making up the great circle of a sphere.

Quarters   The point on each side of the boat, midway between her stern and mid-section.

Painter   The rope attached to a dinghy's bow by which she is secured.

Pontoon   Floating structure that serves as a dock or jetty for boats in marinas.

Port   The left side of the boat; towards the left-hand side of the boat when facing forward.

Reef, to   To reduce the area of a sail by tying or rolling down part of it.

Reef cringle   And eyelet sewn into the seam of a sail (at luff and leech) at the level of the reefing points. By fastening a line to the cringle, the sail can be tied down as part of the reefing process.

Reefing points   Row of short lines sewn into the sail some distance up from its foot which can be used to reduce sail in heavy weather.

Riding Light   A lantern hung in the rigging of the fore part of a vessel at anchor which is visible in all directions.

Rudder   A blade attached under the hull's stern used for steering

Run, to   To sail downwind.

Sheet   A rope used to trim a sail, secured either to the foot of the sail or its boom.

Sloop   A sailing vessel carrying a single mast bearing a mainsail and a single headsail.

Starboard   The right side of the boat; towards the right-hand side of the boat when facing forward.

Stay   Wire rope giving fore and aft support to a mast.

Staysail   A headsail set on the forestay.

Stern   The rear part of a boat.

Tack, to   Turning across the eye of the wind in order to fill the sails on the opposite side. Frequent tacking is required when making towards an upwind destination within a narrow passage.

Tiller   A wood or metal lever used for steering, attached to the top of the rudder.

VHF radio   Very High Frequency radio used for ship-to-shore or ship-to-ship communication.

Warp   A strong rope used for moving a vessel into or out of a dock and for securing her alongside.

Yankee   A large triangular headsail used in light or moderate winds and set on the jibstay. It has a high profile and is set in combination with the working staysail.